GARDENING ENCYCLOPAEDIA

GARDENING ENCYCLOPAEDIA

BY
WILLIAM H. STEER

CLASSIC EDITIONS

This edition digitally re-mastered and
published by JM Classic Editions © 2007
Original text © William H Steer 1943

ISBN 978-1-905217-33-5

All rights reserved. No part of this book subject
to copyright may be reproduced in any form or
by any means without prior permission in writing
from the publisher.

INTRODUCTION

THERE'LL always be a garden, and always has been, for were not mankind's first steps taken in a Garden where "Adam delved"? It has been so all down the ages. Babylon had hanging gardens five thousand years ago: the Roman Emperor Diocletian, A.D. 284, boasted to his friends, "Could you but see the vegetables I have raised"; and, much later, a Bishop of the Middle Ages spoke of the "brave flowers" in his West of England Cathedral Close . . . and ever since, whether as a livelihood, a hobby or a pleasant embellishment to his dwelling-place, the average man, particularly in these Isles, has practised gardening, though, to quote, it is "full of heartbreaks, but no mysteries; merely common sense, with deep digging, sweat and manure."

It is to be questioned that there are no mysteries; there certainly is a multitude of perplexities only to be solved by one's actual long experience, or more quickly and more satisfyingly by taking the advice of others who have been through the mill of trial and error, and so arrived at an understanding of those methods by which alone can success be achieved in the many activities included in gardening.

The reason for this book is to afford help of that character and is the result of upwards of forty years of gardening in London and the country, by a writer who, for more than half that time edited dozens of works on the subject, including the books of such experts as C. H. Middleton, H. H. Thomas, etc.

It needs no emphasis, therefore, that the author knows what he is writing about and can explain in clear-cut language all those practical operations which contribute to success, whether of old-time or modern methods; whether of town or country gardening; whether of flowers or vegetables.

The plan of the book is to open each entry with concise information as to class, height, colour and flowering period, and then the cultural directions and hints for propagation, protection and perfecting. Cross references are given throughout where a plant has a popular name as well as its horticultural one. All the operations to transform virgin ground into fertile plots and to keep it in condition are included, particular attention being given to growing vegetables.

A useful feature of the Encyclopaedia is the inclusion, at appropriate places, of a couple of hundred or so of practical hints and usages gathered from records and conversations with professional gardeners and enthusiastic amateurs all over the country. Altogether there are nine hundred entries, and eighty practical diagrams. In short, here is A to Z in Garden or Allotment, alphabetically arranged, and therefore available for information or guidance with ease and certainty.

ILLUSTRATIONS

	PAGE
HOME-MADE RUSTIC ARCH	25
CUTTING ASPARAGUS	27
ASPARAGUS KNIFE	27
SUPPORT FOR PEAS AND DWARF BEANS	33
PLANNING THE PLOT	34
MARKING OUT CIRCULAR BED	35
BUDDING OPERATIONS	43
DEPTHS TO PLANT BULBS	45
BULB PLANTING IN ROUGH GRASS	46
BULB PLANTER	47
DISBUDDING CHRYSANTHEMUMS	63
TYPES OF CLOCHE	67
CLOCHE USAGE FOR YEAR	68
CUCUMBER, FEMALE BLOSSOM	75
SINGLE SPIT DIGGING	85
BASTARD TRENCHING	87
THREE SPIT END-ON SECTION	87
BORDER CHANNELING	94
PLANTING FRUIT TREE	113
GLADIOLI STAKING	122
GRAFTING OPERATIONS	125
THINNING GRAPES	126
STAKING HERBACEOUS PLANTS	134
TYPES OF HOE	137
HOW TO MAKE A HOTBED	139
HYDROPONIC TANK: WATER CULTURE	142
LAWN LEVELLING PROCEDURE	153
PATCHING WORN TURF	155
LAYERING	155
PLANTING LEEKS	156
LOGANBERRIES: LAYERING AND TRIMMING	163

	PAGE
Increasing Montbretia	171
Mushroom Ridge Bed	179
Bending-over Onions	185
Trimming Pansies for True-to-type Stock	190
Path Making: Getting the Camber	192
Camber Board	192
Dividing Polyanthus	202
Portable Light: Structure Diagrams	204
Storing Seed Potatoes	205
Potato Fork	206
Pot Plants: Average Filling	208
Potting On	208
Pruning Operations	211
Rockery Pockets	218
Pruning Standard Roses	220
Pruning Bush Roses	220
Planting Rose Cuttings	221
Rotation Plan	223
Pruning Buddleia and Deutzia	233
Seedling Guard for Sweet Peas	246
Wire-supporting Frame for Sweet Peas	246
Tomatoes in Greenhouse: Grown on Staging	253
Adjustable Flexible Rake	255
Cultivator	255
Ploughshare Cultivator	255
Combined Hoe and Cultivator	255
Planting Seedlings	256
Root-watering through Sunk Pots	271

SCHEDULES

Cropping Plan	76
Flowering Calendar	104
Month by Month in Garden and Allotment	172
All-in Vegetable Schedule	263

Abbreviations

A. Annual.
B. Biennial.
F.S. Flowering Shrub.

H. Hardy.
H.H. Half-Hardy.
P. Perennial.

A

AARON'S BEARD. P.; 18 in.; yellow; July.

Known also as Rose of Sharon. Its class is Hypericum (*which see*), commonly called St. John's Wort. Also known as Mother of Thousands, the horticultural name of which is *Saxifraga sarmentosa* (*which see*). *Moserianium* is 36 in. high and evergreen. *Tutsan* grows best in the shade. It is a hardy, attractive plant, growing freely in sandy soil, suitable for rock gardens or for bordering on slopes. The *reptant* variety flowers in July and is of trailing habit; easily cultivated and full flowered. They are perennial and increased by division, or cuttings started in a frame.

AARON'S ROD. H.B.; 5 ft.; yellow; summer.

A hardy biennial, blooming second year, with yellow flowers of varying shades. Gardeners know it as the yellow variety of the *Verbascum Thapsus*. It is tall, will flower all the summer, grow in any soil. Sow seed in boxes covered with glass till second leaf shows. Does well in herbaceous border. There is a newer pink variety and one flowering mauve; *see* VERBASCUM.

ABELIA. F.S.; 4–5 ft.; pink, purple, white; May–September.

Free flowering, suited to trellis or by wall. In the South grow in sheltered sunny spot, but in North preferably in greenhouse. The Mexican variety, *florabunda*, flowers in mid-summer and has masses of hanging blossom. A hybrid, *grandiflora*, is more hardy, is semi-evergreen, and pinky-white flowers. *Triflora*, the Himalayan species, is the grandest in appearance and fullness of flowering. It runs to 10 ft. in height, a mass of bloom and of grateful fragrance during the summer.

Planted in March or October, the abelia grows best in sandy loam and peat in sunny position, with plenty of root space and spread for foliage. Take cuttings in September under glass, prune lightly, remove blossom as it fades.

ABIES. *See* SPRUCE FIR.

ABOBRA. P.; climber; green flowers, scarlet berries; July.

Fragrant, good pergola plant in warm situation in fibrous loam and road grit. Propagate seed in heat, April.

ABRONIA UMBELLATA (Sand Verbena). H.H.A.; 10 in.; trailing; yellow, pink, white; August onwards.

Likes sun and light soil. Often classed as perennial, but better treated as annual. Good in rockery. Has a delicate perfume and small star-like flowers. Makes a suitable edging and also looks well massed in the rockery. Start seed in pots covered with glass in May and plant out in light soil. Can also sow seed, autumn, in frame.

ABRUS.

Named Rosary Pea, because seeds so used. Climber, purple, with red and black seeds. Hothouse plant, likes coarse sand and loam. Propagate by cuttings or seed in heat.

ABUTILON (Indian Mallow). F.S.; 3 ft.; climbing habit; scarlet and yellow (*Thompsonii*), white and mauve (*vitifolium*); summer flowering.

Useful in greenhouse or in warm situation against fence or wall. *Thompsonii* has variegated leaves; *vitifolium* can grow to 15 ft. Protect from frost, give sandy soil and free watering, including top sprinkling. Take cuttings of young wood in autumn, or sow under glass, February to March, transplanting when an inch high and setting well into earth.

ACACIA. P.; 4 ft. and upwards; yellow; summer in open. December–March in greenhouse.

The familiar mimosa of the florists is *Acacia dealbata* (Silver Wattle) and some of the rosy-flowered species are used for bedding-out for the backs of borders, or the tall-growing sorts, which run to 10–16 ft., are good for covering arches. They flower in summer, are planted out from pots and like a light, rich loam with sand added. The graceful, feathery foliage, of distinctive grey-green colour, shows well, even if a cold snap prevents the golden blossom perfecting. Strike cuttings, the tips and few inches of the shoots, in a hotbed in July or August or sow the seed when ripe. Re-pot in September after blooming. The plants should be placed in a sheltered position in the open in summer and benefit by periodical syringing as well as frequent watering. After flowering, cut back the straggling shoots. Other varieties, greenhouse pot specimens, are *armata*, *hastata* and *pulchella*, which can be brought into the open in the height of summer.

ACAENA. P.; foliage plant.

Rapidly spreading horizontally and grown in rockeries for its leaves, though it has crimson burrs as flowers. A grey-green variety is *Buchanani*, and that with bronze foliage is *microphylla*. Ordinary soil suits. Increases by division in spring.

ACANTHUS. P.; 4 ft.; white or pink; summer.

A fairly hardy herbaceous plant, remarkable for the beauty of its foliage. Thrives well in shade, but requires sun and rich soil to produce good flowers. *Montanus* has very long spikes of white blossom. May be raised from seed, but is more easily increased by division of roots.

ACER. S.; 10–12 ft.

This is the Japanese maple, and though most are trees, certain varieties are classified as shrubs, their attraction lying in the beauty of their variegated leaves. *Palmatum atropurpurem* has bronze-green foliage; *dissectum-atropurpurem* has crimson foliage; *japonicum aureum* has golden foliage turning in autumn to a bronze tint; *septemlobum* and *septemlobum-Osakazuki* both are green in summer, the first turning bronze-crimson and the other a decided crimson in the autumn. All should be planted in loam, well-drained and sheltered from cold winds.

ACHILLEA. H.P.; 2 ft.; profuse white or yellow; June.

Also known as the Milfoil and Sweet Maudlin. It produces, all the summer, plentiful sprays of white or yellow flowers, and will thrive in any plot that is not sunless, but prefers a heavy soil with a little sand worked in. The dwarf sorts are 6 in. high, and a giant yellow variety, *filipendulina*, attains 4 ft. The *millefoliums* (Yarrow) are 2 ft. high. *Clauennae* flowers white in spring. Being perennial they are increased by division. Fresh stock is by seed sown in open, in spring.

ACHIMENES. P.; 6–18 in.; various colours; summer.

A warm greenhouse plant which is tuberous rooted, and grown in sandy loam reinforced with manure, and liking plenty of water. Start the tubers in March, and when an inch high transfer to pots, putting three in a five-inch pot or hanging basket. They multiply from the tubers.

ACONITE (Eranthis). P.; dwarf; yellow; January–February.

Even before the first spring flowers appear winter aconite gladdens us with its bright-yellow blossoms, and its beautiful shining foliage is in itself an ornament. It flourishes best on a warm, chalky soil, in a half-wild state on banks, or under trees and, to gain its full effect, it should be planted in large bold patches. Though the surface of the soil should be renewed every other year, the aconite should not be disturbed too often. Lift a large patch when transplanting the tuberous roots in order to make sure you have enough "eyes" for propagation. This is a plant which should not be grown where there are children, for both yellow and blue aconites are poisonous.

ACONITUM. H.P.; 4 ft.; blue.

Popularly known as Monkshood, and its rural name Wolfsbane denotes its poisonous nature, yet the almost black-blue blossom has its place in the herbaceous border, with cool position and average, not light, soil. *Anthora* (2 ft.) and *sycoctonum* are yellow. Increase by spring division.

ACROCLINUM. *See* EVERLASTINGS.

ADIANTIFOLIUM THALICTRUM.

Known as the hardy perennial Maidenhair, of which *capillus-veneris* and *pedatum* grow best in open, in sand and peat, and increase in size and beauty each year. It has elegant fern-like foliage, and when cut and placed in water is more lasting than fern fronds: excellent foliage for decorative effect with cut flowers. Start by buying roots, then divide up each season.

ADONIS (Pheasant's Eye). H.P.; 18 in.; yellow; spring.

This useful rock plant thrives in a shady position if sown in March and planted out in a mixture of loam, peat and leaf-mould. It has feathery foliage and *autumnalis* has crimson flowers, averaging 12 in. in height.

AETHIONEMA (Burnt Candytuft). P.; 12 in.; rose tints; June.

The variety *grandiflorum* suits the rockery. A red variety (*buxbaumi*) is only 6 in. in height, flowers in June, and is often treated as an annual. Propagation by seed. An average soil is suitable.

AFRICAN MARIGOLD. H.A.; 18 in.; orange, lemon; August.

Sow April in boxes, plant June, 18 in. apart in good, well-drained, not heavy soil. The variety *Legion of Honour* has brown tips; *signata pumila* is a dwarf and its leaves give out fragrance.

AGAPANTHUS (African Lily). H.H.P.; 3 ft.; blue; August.

A bulbous-rooted plant with graceful foliage and large heads of blossom. The blue variety is the most successful in this country but a white variety can be got. The bulbs should be stored in winter and planted out in early spring to flower in August; they are mostly grown in pots or tubs, in loam mixed with a little sand and well manured. Water abundantly in summer with weak liquid manure.

AGAVE. H.H.P.; 10 ft.; greenish-yellow; seldom.

This is the American aloe, mostly a conservatory denizen but in mild districts can be grown in large tubs and wintered inside. They do not flower freely or often, are slow growing and have fleshy leaves with spines. Give a rich mixture of half loam, and the rest cow manure, leaf-mould and sand. Detach suckers and pot in warmth to increase.

AGERATUM. H.H.A.; 9 in.; purple, blue, white, pink; June–September.

Mexicanum grows to 14 in. Favourite for edges of borders. Very small seed; sow in pans, hardly covering with soil, and start under glass. Likes well-composted soil; transplant gently when sun not strong to 4 in. apart.

AGROSTEMMA. H.A.; 18 in.; strong pink; July.

The perennial variety of this branch of the lychnis family is familiarly known as the Rose Campion and the annual as the Flower of Love, or Rose of Heaven. The annual is pink and the perennial crimson, with grey, hairy foliage and grows to about 2 ft. Both thrive in any soil and are raised from seed sown in position in spring. Self-sown seed increases the supply year by year.

ALKANET. *See* ANCHUSA.

ALLIUM. P.; 1 ft.; yellow; June.

Will grow in any average soil, is hardy, and a good rockery plant. The favourite variety is *Moby*. A white variety is *Neapolitanum*; and a newer species, which has blue flowers, is *Beesianum*—as hardy as the others, but preferring a sunny position.

ALLOTMENT.

Where the secretary of an allotment association is unknown, application should be made to the local municipal offices. An allotment garden is usually on a yearly holding and 10 rods in extent, or say 30 ft. by 90 ft., ample space for supplying the vegetable needs of an average family. Particulars of the most economical planting lay-out of the area are issued by the Ministry of Agriculture, Whitehall, London, S.W.1, who also send free leaflets advising on the culture of allotments, seed quantities and directions for growing the most useful vegetables.

The most profitable crops are potato, carrot, beetroot, celery, onion, runner bean, broad bean, parsnip, turnip, spinach, leek, peas, cabbage and winter greens. Lettuce, spinach and radish can be grown as catch crops between the rows of other vegetables. New allotments on ground that has become rough and weedy should first have the coarse grass and weeds taken off and composted before the ground is trenched. Lime the ground after trenching (*see* Lime). If the turf is good it should be dug in or composted. Land broken, *i.e.* rough dug, in the autumn will be in first-rate condition for sowing and planting in spring if the surface is left rough or ridged up to expose it fully to wind, rain and frost.

Legal Points.—,,Allotment garden" means an allotment under 40 poles wholly or mainly cultivated by the occupier for vegetable or fruit crops for himself or his family. Subject to special local agreements, the tenant is entitled to at least 12 months' notice of termination of his tenancy, to expire outside the cropping season, *i. e.* on or after September 29th or on or before April 6th. At whatever season the notice expires, he is entitled to compensation for crops growing on the land and for manure applied, and, where provision is made in the agreement for re-entry at not less than 3 months' notice for urgent purposes, 12 months' rent for disturbance is payable in addition.

Those having an allotment are expected to keep it in good cultivation, and particularly, for the common good, to keep it free from weeds and rotting leaves which foster insect pests.

Throughout this book are ample directions for every cultural activity and for growing vegetables of every kind, as well as directions for destroying insects and combating plant diseases.

Quick Reference Allotment Guide.—In the entry " Month by Month in Garden and Allotment " is given a schedule of operations for the whole year. Here is a condensed guide to sowings for vegetables and roots which will be handy for quick reference. The first and second early potatoes, which provide tubers from July until Christmas, can be lifted in July and August, thus allowing the land to be re-cropped. Spinach, sow in February for spring use and perpetual spinach in April and July for autumn and winter. A succession of peas in summer is assured by sowing early and mid-season varieties in March and April. Broad beans are sown in February and March, dwarf and haricot beans in April and runner beans in May. Of the root crops parsnips are sown in February and March for winter supplies, short-rooted carrot, sown in March and June for summer and autumn, and long-rooted carrot, sown in April for winter produce. Globe beetroot from a March sowing is ready for use in summer, and long beetroot sown in May provides for winter. Onion and leek, sow out of doors in March or under glass earlier in the year. Jerusalem artichoke, plant in February. Winter greens, as well as cauliflower, autumn cabbage and colewort are sown in spring. Celery and tomato plants can be planted in June, or they may be raised by sowing seed under glass in February.

The vegetable plot can be made to yield full measure by clearing spent crops and filling the sites again by fresh sowings and plantings. As soon as the first row of peas has been cleared, turnips should be sown; the ground prepared for the peas by trenching and manuring will suit them perfectly. Alternative sowings are of small-rooted carrot and lettuce. Runner beans can be grown without the use of tall sticks or special supports, in which case the ends of the shoots must be pinched off frequently to make the plants form well-branched bushes. Leeks planted in July will furnish useful winter produce.

It may also be handy to group here for quick reference some of the sowing depths: for brassica (cabbage, savoy, broccoli, cauliflower, etc.), carrots, celery, leeks, onions, turnips—1 in., not more. For lettuce—$\frac{1}{2}$ in. For beet, parsnips, spinach—$1\frac{1}{2}$ in. For peas and dwarf beans—2 in. For runner beans and broad beans—3 in. If soil is light a slightly greater depth is advised.

ALLOTMENT LAYOUT, *see* CROPPING PLAN; PLANTING AND MATURING TABLE, *see* VEGETABLES.

ALLOTMENT, YEAR'S WORK. *See* MONTH BY MONTH IN GARDEN AND ALLOTMENT.

ALMOND.

The tree is a picturesque addition to any garden where space allows, its pink blossom coming so early, before the leaves unfold, as to give welcome colour in March or in cool districts in April. Its planting and culture follows in general that of Fruit Trees (*which see*). It is the *Amygdalus* section of the prunus family. A dwarf variety, *nana*, is 30 in. high, and a rather warmer pink in colour. It has no fads about soil, and will grow anywhere so long as it is not given an arid situation. Almond blossom is single petalled; the clusters of double bloom are those of the Japanese cherry, *Hisakura*, variety of prunus.

ALOES. *See* AGAVE.

ALONSOA (Mask Flower). H.H.A.; 18 in.; scarlet, creamy pink; May.

Sow in August under glass in warm house, prick out into sunny position in May, set in sandy loam. They do better as a greenhouse plant, and there stop back a few to secure winter flowering. *Warscewiczii* is a compact variety, 12 in., scarlet.

ALOYSIA. *See* LIPPIA; *also* VERBENA.

ALPINES.

An Alpine section is a novel attraction to the garden. It should face south or west and can take the form of a rockery (*which see*, for construction), or it can be a level stretch of silver sand, gravel and grit over a prepared bed, with a foundation of small stones and filled in with soil suited to the particular species of Alpines favoured. The moraine bed gently rises and falls like a tiny valley slope, and some ambitious enthusiasts build the foundation so that water can percolate through underneath the surface at only sufficient depth to irrigate the roots. If this is tried, some means must be provided for turning off the flow, as it is not always needed. Suitable plants, apart from special sorts that seedsmen would recommend according to locality, conditions of climate, etc., are anemone, rock jasmine, aubretia, acaena, dwarf columbine, thrift, sandwort, draba, dryas, cyclamen, gypsophilla, dwarf linaria, primulas, sedum, thyme, dwarf veronica and the maidenhair plant. Put in your selection in spring or autumn, watering the pockets first, and spreading the roots well down with firmness. Add a little compost to each pocket, well packed in above the roots. The compost should include sand, loam and well-matured

Alstromeria 17 Alyssum

and broken-up top spit. In winter give protection by renewing the top-dressing of grit and well-broken-up stone chips, after scarifying the surface a few weeks earlier. Seeing that the list of "favourite, beautiful alpines" of a well-known firm numbers some one hundred and fifty, the selection must be left to the individual, but it may be indicated that for shady corners, those which will do well are sedums (yellow, pink), drodia (fern), comecons (white), hepatica (blue, white), tiarellas (white), phlox (various dwarfs in differing colours), anemone apennina (various colours), corydalis (purple, yellow), epimedium (red), epimedium maracanthum (blue and white). Where there is a little sun, but still on the shady side, such plants can be raised with success as anemones, columbine, forget-me-not, gentians, amerias, linaria, which will provide a pleasing range of colour. Alpines are admirably suited to be grown in a cool (not hot) greenhouse, either in pots on the stages, or with the stages slate covered as illustrated under "Tomatoes," and made up with ash and soil into which the pots can be plunged, giving a more natural effect. Generally, cultivation is as for the open, the seed being sown thinly and the pots covered with paper till germination has started. With special varieties it is well to take the advice of the florist from whom they are obtained.

ALSTROMERIA (Peruvian Lily). P.; 24 in.; various; July.

Excellent for cut flowers and grand border plants of very easy culture. Will increase and last for many seasons and are propagated by division. Colourings: rose, crimson, salmon, orange, yellow and pink, often spotted, splashed or edged with contrasting colours. They must be given a well-drained, sandy soil to which some lime should be added, planted in a warm and sheltered position, kept well watered, and treated to periodical mulching.

ALTHAEA ROSEA. *See* HOLLYHOCK.

ALUM ROOT. *See* HEUCHERA.

ALYSSUM. H.A.; 6 in.; white; June–August.

The varieties, sweet alyssum and compactum, are invaluable as edging plants, their white blossom being prolific and on short stems. There is also a lilac variety. Sow in March in open, in ordinary soil. The perennial sorts, *saxatile*, grow to 9 in. and quickly spread. They throw up sprays of orange or pale yellow blossom in April and May. Sunshine and a loose, friable soil are best, and they should not be disturbed.

AMARANTHUS (Love-lies-bleeding, Prince's Feather). H.H.A.; 24 in.; variegated foliage plant; late summer.

Easily raised from seed sown in March in gentle heat. Love-lies-bleeding is a fine variety, 2 ft., going up to 4 ft. when cultivated in rich soil. Prince's Feather is mostly grown as a pot plant. The leaves of each are richly variegated. Sow seed under glass or on a hotbed. Plant out in sandy loam and give plenty of water.

AMARYLLIS. H.P.; 10 in.; rose-pink; August.

The most robust is the Belladonna Lily, the bulb of which should be planted 9 in. down in June, being given a rich soil with a percentage of sand. It must be given a warm position—against a wall is an advantage—and kept well watered. Among horticulturists this plant is known as *Hippaestrum*, and the *lutea* species as *Sternbergia*.

AMELANCHIER (Snowy Mespilus). F.S.; 8 to 15 ft.; white.

The varieties *loevis, canadensis* and *germanica* (the medlar) may be classified as trees, as they grow to 30 ft. and more. Of the shrubs suited in height to the average garden, *alnifolia asiatica* (gracefully slender) and *rotundifolia* (of European origin) are recommended, the last showing large white flowers profusely into May, whereas the other varieties are over toward the end of April. They like rich loam mixed with lighter soil, and in open prefer a sheltered corner. Propagate by seed, cuttings or layers in July under a cloche.

AMERICAN BLIGHT or WOOLLY APHIS.

The apple and the oak are most subject to this pest. It is more correctly known as the woolly aphis, a woolly-looking substance of insect growth, infesting the bark of the tree, piercing the sap vessels, and ultimately destroying the branch it attacks. It lies dormant at the foot of the tree during winter, but in the spring it renews its ravages and will spread throughout the tree if its progress be not stopped. The blight leads to canker. The best remedy, after a good hosing with water, is the free use of paraffin, rubbed into the crevices of the bark with a hog-hair paint-brush on to the insects; and in the winter, to prevent a recurrence of the trouble, a spray of soft soap and paraffin, with a little soda, may be applied.

AMERICAN COWSLIP. *See* DODECATHEON.

AMMOBIUM GRANDIFLORIUM. H.H.B.; 2 ft.; white, yellow centre; summer.

One of the "everlasting" group. Sow in July in a sandy soil and a sunny position for flowering next year, planting out in May.

AMPELOPSIS (Virginian Creeper).

A vigorous climber clinging by its own tendrils and quickly covering walls. Useful as a background to herbaceous borders, and its red autumnal colouring is picturesque. Preference is given to *vitis inconstans*. Will grow anywhere in any soil. Strike cuttings in greenhouse in September.

ANAGALLIS. H.A.; 6 in.; blue, scarlet; April.

This is the cultivated Pimpernel; it blooms freely. Raise from seed in greenhouse in spring, pot up, and when developing transplant to sunny spot in loam, leaf-mould and sand. *Linofolia* (blue) is a good greenhouse variety. Another popular variety is *Breweri*.

ANCHUSA (Bugloss or Alkanet). H.P.; 4 ft.; blues; June–July.

Average soil, sunny position. Quick and lush growth. Propagate by root division in sand in frame. Annual variety, 18 in., same treatment; quite hardy.

ANDROMEDA. F.S.; 3–6 ft.; white; March–June.

Bell-like flowers, not unlike outsize Lily of the Valley. There are three popular varieties: *Pieris japonica*, *Pieris floribunda* (the Fetter bush) and *Pieris mariana* (the Stagger bush). The first has graceful drooping spikes of blossom; the second, flowering in March, has erect spikes, more profuse blossom against dark foliage, and the third is also free flowering. These all flower in March and April. Another variety, *Pieris formosa*, equally beautiful, flowers in May, and its fresh foliage is warm ruby in colour, while the old remains dark green. A dwarf variety, *polifolia*, is pink, is 12 in. in height and blossoms in June. They all require damp peat and rich loam to flourish, and prefer shade. Propagate by cuttings, division or seed.

ANDROSACE (Rock Jasmine). H.P.; 3 in.; pink; May–June.

An easily grown rockery or moraine plant, doing well in loam, leaf-mould, sand and a small proportion of lime, if placed among stones. Increased by division in spring.

ANEMONE (Windflower). H.P.; 8 in.; many colours; early summer and autumn.

Slow germination, sow February for autumn flowering, or April to May for following spring. Can also be raised from corms. Better sown where wanted, open position, do not coddle, but thrives in good soil and increases steadily. The *fulgens* class is a distinctive brick red. The popular *St. Brigid* is in the *coronia* class. Seed should be covered very lightly with soil, as germination is slow, and the plants should be thinned out so as to stand 5 or 6 in. apart and, when 1 in. high, pressed lower into soil at roots. The blossom is in many colours.

ANGELICA. Culinary Herb.

The seeds are used for flavouring, but the best-known use is the stalks, which are treated for candying purposes. Sow seed in open, either in spring or September, in drills on friable soil in warm situation, thinning to 12 in. in between each plant.

ANNUALS.

Flowers which only last the one season are annuals. They are in two classes. Those of which the seed can be sown in the open in the spring, as early as mid-March, and will grow lustily, are labelled hardy, and expressed in the alphabetic lists of this book as H.A. The other group is labelled throughout as H.H.A., *i.e.* half-hardy annuals, because they require gentler treatment, either being sown in the open in May if the weather has broken into warm days, or more successfully in April under glass—a frame or greenhouse, or the useful cloche.

Hardy Annuals.—Sow sparsely where they are to bloom, thin out first when ground is moist, then again a fortnight later, leaving the sturdiest seedlings with at least 6 in. between each for the less bushy and anything up to a foot for those of more spreading habit and height. Good effect is achieved by putting one plant at each corner of a 6 in. or larger triangle, according to size. Support early and sufficiently with stakes not higher than ultimate height.

The plot should be deeply dug, allowing free root run, adding lime if not naturally present (6 lb. to the square rod), but hardy annuals do not need bolstering by rich manuring unless the ground is definitely poor, then let a fortnight elapse between liming and manuring. Superphosphate is good, a thumbpotful to the square yard. Rake ground to a fine tilth and do not sow on a cold damp day. If sowings are made in September and protected from winter frosts by twigs and grass cuttings an early spring show can be secured; remember to water the seed-bed well a day before sowing.

Use artistic discretion in selecting annuals according to colour and height as given in each case, and so produce "harmony." Generally let strong colours be central, grading to lighter shades at sides of borders or plots.

Half-Hardy Annuals.—Mix sand (half and half) with sowing soil. Keep from cold air till seedlings are 3 in. high, but do not coddle or they will damp off. Give air during sunshine and gradually harden by bringing into open in warm daylight, taking back at night, for about a week. Then plant in border where to flower. It is more trouble, but prevents "checks," to sow in pots rather than boxes, as the seedlings can be transplanted without root damage. Once in the border the H.H.A. has same treatment as H.A. In both classes pick off faded blossoms and seed-pods. Keep soil free by hoeing and water well only when wanted rather than sprinkle daily. For most half-hardy annuals the best compost is a mixture of two parts of fibrous loam and one of prepared peat and sand. Watering should be unnecessary till the seedlings show through the soil, and the water should never be cold. As with all seedlings, it is important to keep them as near the light as possible or they will be drawn. Avoid over-heating; a temperature of 53 degrees in greenhouse or frame should not be exceeded. They need as much air as possible, but not draughts. When large enough to handle they should be transferred to boxes 4 in. deep, at 3 in. apart. At no stage should asters or any half-hardy plants be checked in growth, and it is not always easy to decide when they should be transferred to a cold frame to harden off. In case of doubt it is wise to wait till mid-May. When large enough, the plants can be put into their flowering positions. Between seasons in the greenhouse a few annuals in pots make a good show of colour; *see* GREENHOUSE.

ANTENNARIA. H.P.; dwarf and 2 ft.; pink; July–November.

The taller variety belongs to the Everlastings, the variety being *margar itacea*, and does well in average soil. The dwarf has silvery foliage and is of creeping habit, the variety *tormentosa* looking conspicuous in the rockery. Increase by division.

ANTHEMIS. *See* CAMOMILE.

ANTHERICUM. H.P.; 18 in.; white; June.

The class includes St. Bruno's Lily (*liliastrum*) and St. Bernard's Lily (*liliago*) grown successfully in rich, deep soil, well drained. Plant in autumn and increase by root division in late July.

ANTIRRHINUM (Snapdragon). H.P.; usually cultivated as annual; 20 in.; wide range of colours; free flowering, June till frost.

Sow February to March under glass in compost for same year. June in open warm border, barely covering minute seed, for next year. Can multiply by cuttings, July. Likes heavy soil with chalk in, warm border and average water. Own seed seldom true to type. Flower spikes rather brittle. There is a dwarf variety, 6 in.

ANTS.

If the nests appear in the turf, boiling water should be poured in. When ants attack wall fruit, lay a broad band of tar, mixed with a little sugar, on the bottom of the wall and around the stems of the trees. Bands drawn in white chalk will have the same effect. They do no particular harm on their own account, but as aphides come after them they are best eradicated.

APHIDES. *See* PLANT LICE.

APHIS (Green and Black Fly).

A good handful of guano to a two-gallon can and watered over the affected plants will clear green fly away in quick time.

Where liquid cannot reach them, nothing is better than tweezers made from a pair of soft brushes joined together with a cane bow, so that by pressure of the hand they are brought in contact and the bud between them is cleared. *See also* INSECTS ON PLANTS, to destroy. *Note* that Aphides are different; they are PLANT LICE, (*which see*).

APPLES.

The apple tree requires good soil—a rich, sandy loam is the best —and as the tendency of its root growth is to run just below the surface it does not usually require root pruning, but a good depth of soil is desirable. Trees can be grown as standards, bushes, espaliers, cordons and fanwise, and each will yield well under proper treatment. The most suitable setting is a moderately heavy, well-drained soil, and where virgin ground is being turned, grow a crop of vegetables for the first season. For planting refer to the entry " Fruit Trees." Cordons, etc., are usually grown in northern or bleak districts for the protection the wall provides, but in warmer regions semi-standards or standards are the rule. Autumn planting is safest, and pruning in March. In September, grease band to keep pests at bay, and when the blossom is in the pink-bud stage the ravages of pests and diseases can be combated by spraying with nicotine, derris or lime sulphur respectively. Apple scab, the commonest fungus disease, is controlled by spraying with lime sulphur. In pruning, reduce branches of standards and bushes to two-thirds; only slightly shorten cordon espaliers and fans, cutting back spurs to three buds and last year's growth half-way. For manuring, mulch in May, and give liquid manure to established trees in autumn. Pull off all fruit for first year; thin out next season and then use judgment according to robustness. Slight summer pruning to thin out, in July; in December, cut back side shoots to form buds. See general instructions on pruning and adjust to needs of particular varieties. Differing districts find this or that variety most suitable and growers can supply those most appropriate from among the most reliable kinds, which are: *Dessert:* Worcester Pearmain, James Grieve, Ellison's Orange, Lord Lambourne and Laxton's Superb. Others, less certain in cropping, but of the finest flavour are, Cox's Orange, Ribston Pippin and American Mother. Some of the most prolific cooking apples are Early Victoria, Cellini, Lane's Prince Albert, Arthur Turner and Bramley's Seedling.

When storing, lay the fruit on the floor or shelf so that they do not touch one another. They should be frequently examined, and any that show signs of decay should be removed. Rough-skinned apples such as russets keep best. If space is limited, wrap each apple in oiled paper and they can be boxed without danger of infection. Should a bruised apple get in, the paper will keep the rot from spreading to others.

APRICOTS.

See " Fruit Trees " for general cultural practice in planting, etc. Remember that the apricot does best on a south wall, with top protection when blooming, even if it be only netting, to form a frost and wind-break and deter birds. They are also better trained to fan shape. Blossom precedes leaves in February or March. They do well on chalky soil or well-drained loam with a sprinkling of lime but no heavy manuring. Plant young trees, usually three-year-olds when bought, in autumn after cutting back robust roots to within a foot of the base. Fasten the branches permanently in position in the spring, after cutting back young shoots to about half length. Fruit should be thinned when it swells and the foliage given periodical syringing. Keep well watered and give a mulch of decayed compost when the warm weather comes. A good, reliable variety is *Helmskirk* which ripens in August.

APRIL GARDENING. *See* MONTH BY MONTH IN GARDEN AND ALLOTMENT.

AQUILEGIA. *See* COLUMBINE.

ARABIS (Rock Cress). H.P.; 6 in.; white, pink; spring flowering but will bloom in winter if mild.

Any soil. The pink variety is *aubrietioides*. Sow outdoors May for flowering following year. An excellent rockery plant. A fine double variety is *flore pleno*. Strike cuttings in sandy soil in shady spot.

ARALIA. *See* FATSIA.

ARBOR VITAE. *See* THUYA.

ARBUTUS (Strawberry Tree). F.S.; 10 ft.; cream, tinged pink; July–October.

The strawberry-like fruits show a year later than the flowers in both varieties: *Unedo* (October flowering) and *Menziesii* (July flowering). Grow in pots in spring from seed till large enough to place in selected warm position (they dislike transplanting). Only prune slightly by shortening long shoots, in April, to maintain shapeliness.

ARCHES.

It is generally considered that an arch breaks the long line of a path, and can carry a rambler rose or other flowering climber to artistic effect. Metal arches are easy to erect, though standardized in size and not so graceful as one of the rustic variety. A home-made one is easily constructed to any exact size required. Fix the posts and transverse top first; then interlace curved branches, tying or wiring where required rather than nailing. A length of old covered insulating wire is excellent for the purpose.

To construct a pergola extend the length to that needed, using interlacing-branches idea, say every 8 ft.

ARCTOTIS. H.H.A.; 18 in.; white, blue centre; also red, orange, wine, white, contrasted centres; early summer.

Start seed under glass, plant out after frost, in average soil, and sunny situation. Allow room for bushing. *Grandis* is the annual and most grown, but there are perennial varieties.

ARENARIA. H.P.; 3 in.; trailing; white; summer.

Good rockery or alpine, using *montana* variety. Sow in shady but warm position and plant in any soil in cool situation.

ARGEMONE. H.A.; 2 ft.; white; July.

Flowers like a poppy and has golden anthers. Sow in spring, plant in average soil, in sunny position.

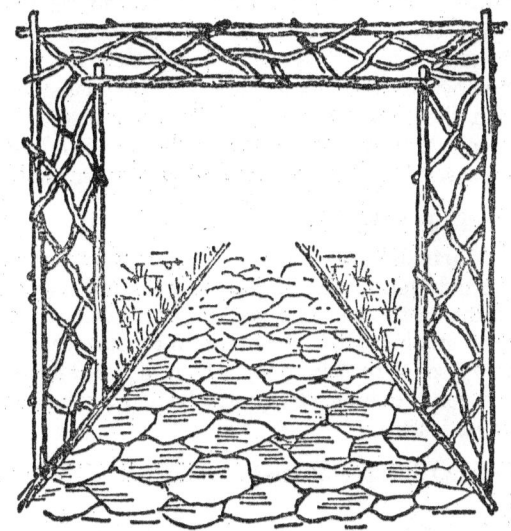

Rustic Arch
of interlaced branches.

ARMERIA (Thrift). H.P.; 6 in.; pink: June–July.

Grow the ordinary variety, a strong growth *armeria maritima*, in average friable soil. Propagate by division. The Giant Thrift, 18 in., has same treatment.

ARTEMISIA. H.H.P.; 4 ft.; cream and yellow; August.

Start in the frame or under cloche in April and give a place in warm border, and keep some in pots in greenhouse. The variety *lactifolia* has the cream blossom; *abrotanum*, popularly known as Southernwood, has a delicious fragrance; and *stelleriana* is yellow, has silvery foliage, and is 1 ft. high. Increase by division. Tarragon belongs to this class.

ARTICHOKES, GLOBE.

The globe variety gives larger heads and more fleshy edible parts than the oval. They can be grown from seed sown in spring. Plant the young shoots in ground that has been well worked and manured. Place in rows about 5 ft. apart and 2 ft. between the plants and give plenty of water. Trim the tops and roots before planting. They do not mature till the next season. Plant a row or two each year to secure a succession of crops from June to October. Bring to a large head by cutting off the side suckers when about as large as an egg. Gather when the scales open and before the flowers appear at the centre. Break down the stems close to the ground after gathering. Stock is increased by suckers, which detach when rooted.

ARTICHOKES, JERUSALEM.

A row of artichokes set about 18 in. apart makes an excellent screen for an ugly fence. They will grow in almost any soil so readily that it is difficult to clear the ground of them again. Propagation is by setts or cuttings of the roots as for potatoes. Plant them in light, ordinary soil 4 or 5 in. deep, 18 in. apart, allowing about 2 ft. distance between the rows. They may be had for the table throughout the autumn and winter.

ARTIFICIAL (Artificial Manures). *See* FERTILIZERS.

ARUM. *See* LILY.

ARUNDODONAX. Grass; August.

An ornamental grass flowering in August and growing to a height of over 6 ft. It is a perennial not unlike Pampas grass. At first the plumes are red but on maturing turn white. It requires a moist soil in a cool position. Increase by division in spring.

ASHES.

The fertilizing value of the ash from burnt wood or heavy garden refuse is well known for the yield of potash. By heavy garden refuse is meant cabbage and other stalks, prunings, fibrous material not readily reduced to compost by decomposition, and coarse weeds, which survive if put on the rubbish pit, and so should always be burned. The ash from household fires—coal and peat—also has a value in protecting from frost. A good layer on which pots can be stood or into which they can be plunged enables plants to withstand frosts, allows freer drainage, and prevents insects getting at the plants. They have, however, no nutritive value and on light soils will make it too porous, though on heavy clay they improve drainage and aeration.

ASPARAGUS.

Sow seed in April 1 ft. apart; grow in a light, easily worked soil and in a situation open to the sun. The following year, in spring, divide off into beds 4 or 5 ft. wide and leave a 2 ft. path between each bed. Dig in plenty of rotted manure before planting matured roots in March of the following year. Always keep beds free from weeds.

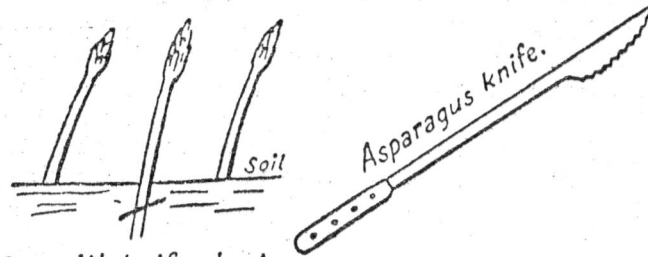

Cut with knife about one inch below soil surface

Cutting Asparagus.

Give fertilizers in spring. In a small garden asparagus is hardly suitable for reasons of space, but if room allows, remember it likes a deeply-dug, well-drained, friable loam, a warm situation, and the addition of humus in good quantity. If buying already matured plants, see they are three-year-olds and do not cut the first year. Heads are cut in May, some may be ready a month earlier, when the heads are about 3–6 in. above ground, and they should be cut at least 1 in. below the ground, using for preference an asparagus knife, and taking care not to sever any heads still below ground. All asparagus for use should be cut by mid-June.

ASPARAGUS PLUMOSA. P.; 5 ft.

Grown for its graceful fern-like foliage. Plant in warm situation in rich soil with sand and leaf-mould, or in greenhouse. Increase by division in March or April. Smilax is similar, being the horticulturist's *Asparagus medeoloides;* its foliage is rather more open and benefits from periodical syringing. It grows best in the greenhouse and should be cut hard back each year.

ASPERULA (Woodruff). H.A.; 1 ft.; pale blue; June–July.

A fragrant variety is *azurea setosa*, of which an autumn sowing gives April blossom lasting into the late summer. The perennial variety is *odorata*, which flowers white in July, is scented and thrives best in the shade. A shorter variety which gives masses of white blossom also in July is *hoita*. There is no difficulty in growing any of these from seed in the open.

ASPHODEL. H.P.; white; spring and autumn.

The giant asphodel runs up sometimes to 6 ft., and is more generally classed as *Eremurus (which see)*. A variety, *ramosus*, likes the shade, blooms in May or June and runs up to 4 ft. In the *asphodeline* section is *lutea*, with large spikes of fragrant yellow blossom and there is a double white. A dwarf variety, *acaulis*, flowers pink. Plant in autumn, give ordinary soil and treatment, but some shelter.

ASPIDISTRAS. P.; 3 ft.; foliage pot or tub plant.

If they flag, remove some of the soil and sprinkle a little bone meal on the roots as a food. Keep well watered. The best sorts are *variegata* and *lurida*. Any soil will do, but a little silver sand placed in the pot will greatly improve the plants. Keep leaves clean by washing in lukewarm water.

ASPLENIUM. *See* SPLEENWORT.

ASTER. H.H.A.; 18 in.; many colours; single and double; late summer and autumn.

This is a large family, including the Michaelmas Daisy (which is a perennial and is entered under its own name), and deserves a place in every garden. They put forth their beauty in autumn. They are of varied colours, white, blue, crimson, pink, etc. To secure a succession of bloom there should be several sowings, and the first in March will need artificial heat. The best results are often obtained by growing asters entirely in the open, in which case the sowing should be made in April on a well-prepared bed of rich soil lightened with wood ashes. The seedlings should be thinned out so as to give each plenty of room to grow into a sturdy plant before being transferred to its final quarters, toward the end of June. Here again the soil should be dressed in readiness with well-rotted manure, while the plants should be assisted with weak liquid manure until they begin to flower. They are often troubled by black fly, which must be brushed off as soon as seen, otherwise the plants will be spoiled. Another trouble is stem-rot, for which, wash with Cheshunt Compound. Asters can do with a good lot of water. China asters (*callistephus hortensis, chinensis*), are popular, run close by Victoria, Ostrich Plume and the chrysanthemum flowering. Giant Ray, yielding profuse and large bloom, will stand a wet season and grows to 2 ft. high. The peony-flowered aster has incurved petals and large blossom.

ASTILBE. H.P.; 3 ft.; white; May–August.

Excellent for growing in average soil in a shady situation, where the soil is moist, and they need frequent watering. Treat as the *spiraeas*, which its foliage and bloom resemble. Division in autumn or spring. For red flowering choose *Granat;* for purple, *Davidii*. The whites are *Thunbergi* (2 ft.), *Astilboides* (3 ft.), *rivularis* (4 ft.). A dwarf form, 9 in., is *simplicifolia,* white and rose, and needing less moisture can be grown in the rockery.

ASTRANTIA. H.P.; 9 and 18 in.; white and striped; June.

Easily grown in friable soil, well drained, but in shade. The white variety, *carniolica*, is the dwarf, and the taller, which is striped pink, is *major* and does better in a somewhat moist situation. Give annual top-dressing of leaf-mould. Increase by spring division.

ATRIPLEX HORTENSIS. H.A.; 4–5 ft.

Grow for red foliage, in open, April, warm position, do not let get dry. Some people like the leaves cooked in the same way as spinach.

AUBERGINES (Egg Plant).

The fruit is edible, being prepared as a vegetable entrée. It is raised in a sun-swept greenhouse, from seed in February, then potted on as soon as it can be handled, and when the roots fill them, transferred to 5 inch pots, and again as the plants develop to 7-inch pots to mature. As the popular name suggests, the white fruits are egg-shaped. Use good, rich compost—that from a spent hotbed is admirable—keep watered and give enough air to keep from damping off, especially when young.

AUBRIETIA. H.P.; dwarf and trailing; blues and reds; spring flowering.

Sow seed May, plant out when in fourth leaf. Excellent for walls, rock gardens and sloping banks; easily grown from cuttings, or by division, or raised from seed; indeed, the seed will sow itself in the earthy chinks of a wall in autumn and bloom in the following February. After flowering put in sprigs of a dozen together here and there, to take root for next spring's flowering.

AUCUBA. F.S.; 8–12 ft.

This is the well-known variegated laurel, which has inconspicuous flowers with red berries following. Its value is its free foliation in bold leaves, glossy and substantial, some spotted cream. It bears male and female in separate shrubs and needs pollination if increased by seed, but more generally by cuttings, which strike easily.

AUGUST GARDENING. See MONTH BY MONTH IN GARDEN AND ALLOTMENT.

AURICULA. H.P.; 6 in.; wide range rich colours, edged; April–June.

Any position, any soil, but keep well watered. Increase by dividing roots in February or March, or sow early spring in pans in frame (sandy soil), and transplant singly while still small into pots, for later planting in border.

AZALEA. F.S.; 3–10 ft. and over; spring.

Wide range of delicate hues, and many varieties multi-coloured, in vivid contrast to dark green foliage. The azalea is classified with the rhododendron, though generically it has affinity with the honeysuckle; it flowers in May and June, and a group is a spectacle of gorgeous colour, exhaling a delicious perfume. The Flame Flower, *calendulaceum*, runs to 8 ft. in height and blossoms a vivid scarlet and orange, with others gold, flame and cream, all the more striking because flowering is before the leaves are fully out. *Nudiflorum* has clusters of pink-scented blossom before the leaves have developed, and a deliciously-scented white variety is *viscosum* which blossoms in June. Of hybrids, the Ghent class is most sought after, as the soil and conditions there are ideal for developing fine and sturdy specimens. There are at least a hundred different varieties of azalea, from which choice to suit climate, soil, locality and colour preference can be made. They require a sandy soil with a good proportion of leaf-mould, and must not be grown where chalk or lime is present. Propagation is by seed or cuttings of half-ripened shoots struck in warm situation or under glass in July. In choosing plants, note that Chinese varieties must be treated as greenhouse plants, but the American varieties, being hardier, will grow in the open if planted in a sheltered position.

AZALEODENDRON. See RHODODENDRON.

AZARA. F.S.; 10 ft.; yellow; April.

The *microphylla* variety is mostly grown in this country, the name referring to the smallness of the leaves, almost as fragile in appearance as maidenhair fern, on gracefully drooping spray-like branches, and the tiny clusters of flowers springing from under the leaves. Against a wall or over a veranda the azara is at its best, though it looks artistic grown as an independent bush. It flowers in April, and should be sheltered from north or east winds. Plant in dry, light loam. Take cuttings of ripened wood and strike in gentle heat.

B

BABIANA. P.; 12 in.; scarlet, white and blue in stripes; spring.

These bulbs are suited to the border if placed in a warm spot in well-drained, light soil. They do well, also, in the greenhouse. Plant bulbs in October; increase by division. A good blue and white variety is *stricta;* *ringens* is scarlet.

BACHELOR'S BUTTON. See RANUNCULUS.

BALM. See HERBS.

BALSAM. H.H.A.; 18 in.; white, rose, mauve, scarlet; summer.

Mostly grown in pots, but can be grown in warm border, in sandy loam and leaf-mould and given plenty of water, but watch for overdoing it; test by tapping pots. Sow in spring in heat and transplant to 6-inch pots. It belongs to the *Impatiens* family (*which see*).

BAPTISIA AUSTRALIS. H.P.; 4 ft.; blue; June.

Sow in a sunny spot in good friable soil, preferably a mixture of one-third peat, two-thirds loam and a proportion of sand. The flowers tend to purple and have traces of truer blue. Give plenty of room. Increase by division.

BARBERRY. *See* BERBERIS.

BARTONIA AUREA. H.A.; 18 in.; yellow; June–August.

Sow in spring in ordinary soil, thin out to a foot apart. Best effect is secured by grouping.

BASIC SLAG.

When soil lacks lime, basic slag may usefully be applied in winter, and because it contains phosphates.

BASIL.

One of the flavouring herbs, raised from seed under glass and transferred to the herb plot in June. *See* HERBS.

BEAN, ORNAMENTAL. Climber; H.A.; 10 ft.

Pods are cream, strongly-marked scarlet. Sow in May where wanted in average soil and no particular treatment beyond that for annuals.

BEANS, BROAD.

If first crop is wanted early sow " Windsor " in November, choose a dry soil in a warm situation and protect against frosts and birds. Put the seed in 2 in. deep and in double-staggered rows, allowing 1 ft. between the lines and 6 in. between plants. Sow again (*Seville Long Pod*) late in January, but the main crop need not be got in until March. Pinch out the tops when the bloom shows or earlier if black fly appears. Put a layer of compost in before sowing. Reject seed with holes in. For Black Fly, dust with nicotine.

BEANS, FRENCH DWARF.

Make sowings in pots in January and February for early crops and keep in a temperature of about 60 degrees; give protection when planting out, a covering of moss litter is adequate; for main crop, sow end of April and keep up successive sowings till the end of June. Sow in a sunny position in light, rich soil in rows 18 in. to 2 ft. apart, leaving a space of 6 in. between each seed. The plot should have been autumn dug, and manured well below the surface. Put in supporting short pea sticks as soon as seedlings show. Gather the pods when young and brittle, allowing no old pods to remain on the plant. Water freely. Two good sorts are *Canadian Wonder* and *Masterpiece*.

BEANS, HARICOT.

As soon as weather is fair at end of April sow in drills 2 in. deep, 1 ft. apart and 18 in. between the rows, following the same cultural methods as for Dwarf Beans both as to preparation of soil beforehand

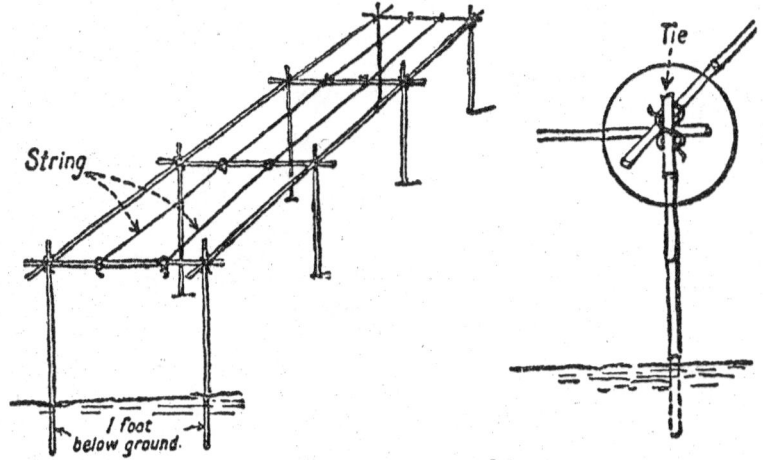

Support for Peas or Dwarf Beans

and the care of the growing crop. These are grown for the beans rather than for cooking when pods are tender, so leave till pods turn brown, pull up and bundle to dry and ripen in an airy shed till pods shrivel and beans are thoroughly dried, then store in boxes till wanted. Haricots are not always a success in bleak districts.

BEANS, SCARLET RUNNERS.

Prepare ground by deeply digging in in March a plentiful layer of manure well matured and moistened, and a sprinkling of lime added if wire worm is present. Let this settle, and in May sow in drills, each seed 2 in. deep and 1 ft. apart, with 2 ft. between each drill. From time first seedlings appear the plants must never want for water, and the stakes must go in at once, 8 ft. high, and firmly fixed. In exposed or windy sites support with transverse stays. Train the young stem round stake; the tendrils will then grip as the height increases. If staking is difficult, by pinching off the top shoots the beans can be grown satisfactorily as dwarfs. As flower appears, feed with liquid manure. A good dusting with soot will keep off slugs. Keep beans well picked to prolong production. Do not grow on same ground as last year. Use nicotine wash for Black Fly.

BEANS and PEAS.

To preserve the seeds from mice soak the seeds in salad oil and then dip in powdered resin before sowing. Some soak them in a solution of bitter aloes; others roll in powdered red lead made adhesive by adding a little paraffin.

BEDDING OUT.

Much of the beauty and appearance of a garden depends on the wise disposition of plants, giving scope for artistic taste and harmony of colouring. Pay attention to height and colour when placing in plots, and do not commit the amateur's error of not allowing for spread, to avoid which the accompanying diagram, "Planning the Plot," will give some guidance. Take note, too, of flowering times (*see* FLOWERING CALENDAR) so as to secure a succession of blossom as the year proceeds. Keep herbaceous borders for the taller plants of which there are enough to make a show from early spring till winter, only right in front use smaller plants, and have them all of one sort, such as catmint (*nepeta*), the foliage of which is distinctive and the flowering profuse and lasting.

When desiring to make a circular plot, a quick and easy method is shown in the illustration here given and which needs no description.

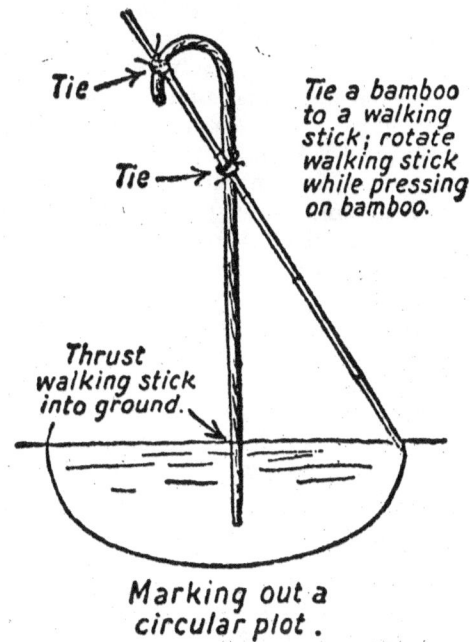

Marking out a circular plot.

BEE BALM. *See* MONARDA DIDYMA.

BEET, GLOBE and TAPER.

Sow in drills, and 1 in. deep, towards the end of April, and again in June in light, deep, rich soil, which has been well manured for a previous crop and free from recent manuring, in rows of 18 in. apart, and thin out to about 6 in. apart for globe beet and 9 in. for taper beet. The roots should be lifted, without breaking or bruising the skin, before the frost touches them and stored in dry sand. Twist off the tops, not too closely, and free from earth. Soak seed for twenty-four hours prior to sowing.

BEET, to keep. *See* STORING VEGETABLES.

BEET, SPINACH or PERPETUAL SPINACH. *See* SPINACH BEET.

BEGONIA. H.H.P.; 12 in.; various colours.

There are two varieties in general use—the tuberous, which is summer and autumn flowering, and the fibrous rooted, giving winter bloom. The tuberous variety is classed as a half-hardy perennial, and from seed sown in March good plants may be obtained early in June. Make a sowing also in May for late summer flowering, in a compost of equal parts of peat, leaf-mould and sand, well mixed and sifted and put into shallow pans half filled with small drainage crocks. Fill to within ½ in. of the rim and water with a fine rose. Sow the seed and lightly press it in, do not cover it, water again and cover the pans with glass. Place in a warm greenhouse until germinated. Prick off when ready and harden off gradually. After flowering, the tubers should be carefully lifted (the decayed stems being gently removed) and stored in sand in a cool, frostproof place. For summer bedding the tuberous Begonia produces a fine effect, the colours ranging from white to rose, pink, crimson and darkest scarlet.

The fibrous-rooted variety will flower in summer-time, but is at its best in winter, if sown in heat in early spring or raised in greenhouse from cuttings taken in January. The flowers are smaller than those of the tuberous class. For the greenhouse are *Gloire de Lorraine* and *Masterpiece* (pink); *alba grandiflora* and *Turnford Hall* (white); *Winter Romance* (salmon) and *Lloydii* (mixed) for the hanging basket.

BELLIS. *See* DAISY.

BERBERIS or BARBERRY. F.S.; 3–5 ft.; spring.

There are numerous varieties, twenty-four being listed, but the most frequently grown are *Mahonia* (*aquifolium*), *Darwinii*, *Thunbergi* and the *Common Barberry*. A fifth variety, *Japanese Mahonia*, is also achieving wider popularity. The *Common Barberry* (*The Holy Thorn*) is the easiest to grow and for long was a feature of rural gardens, but of late it has been officially discouraged as it favours the breeding of wheat rust. *Aquifolium* has racemes of yellow blossom set in a frame of holly-like leaves and showing dark berries in the autumn. *Darwinii* has rich orange flowers in late April which, though small, are in masses, contrasting vividly with black-green foliage. It is quite hardy and will grow in any soil, preferring to front a wall. *Thunbergii* has small leaves in crowded rifts and single flowers of no great attraction, but in the autumn it is a glory of brilliant scarlet fruit surrounded by leaves of vivid crimson. *Japonica Mahonia* has bigger leaves, very spiny, and the flowers, in March, are clustered at the branch tips and are fragrant. The fruit is long and purple. It requires much sun and shelter from wind. All Berberis varieties prefer a warm, moist loam, can be propagated from seed or cuttings of ripened wood, raised in a frame or by division.

BERGAMOT, SWEET. *See* MONARDA DIDYMA.

BETONICA. H.P.; 1 ft.; various; July.

The usual variety grown is *grandiflora* which has been developed to yield scarlet, yellow, violet, white and rose blossom; the last, *rosea*, being very attractive. One variety, *lanata*, has white furry leaves. They are not particular as to soil and can be increased by spring division. Gardeners increasingly label this plant as *Stachys*.

BIENNIALS.

Seed for these is sown in June of one year; the seedlings become established in the autumn and are transferred, say in September or October, to the plot, where they will flower the following year. Apart from these requirements their culture and treatment are as for annuals. It hardly needs mention that biennials do not survive the year of flowering.

BIGNONIA. Climber; reddish purple; summer.

Although this is a hothouse plant, the variety *capreolata* will succeed in the open in a sheltered wall position in southern counties. The flowers are orange and red, trumpet-shaped. Keep well watered and plant in well-drained rich soil of loam, leaf-mould and humus. They can be layered, or cuttings of half-ripe shoots kept in heat under glass till established.

BILBERRY. *See* VACCINIUM.

BINDWEED.

The runners flourish underground and make for future mischief if not dug up and the roots burned. The convolvulus is the most frequent variety. Do not be content to pull down the climbing tendrils. A smaller variety frequents turves and should be eradicated before laying for the lawn.

BIRD CHERRY. Tree; white; spring.

This is the *padus* variety of prunus, and once established goes on flowering in profusion spring after spring. In planting give it free root room and plenty of depth in well-drained soil in good heart, assisted by a foundation of compost and well staked at the time. Autumn planting is recommended. It is of medium height.

BIRDS.

A spring problem is the protection of seedlings and later that of soft fruit from the depredations of birds. Where the amateur has only a few rows in the back garden a run of continuous cloches is enough, but where these are not in sufficient number simpler methods, even if not so effectual, must be adopted as soon as the seedlings (flower or vegetable) show through the soil to prevent damage by birds, or the losses may be severe. Netting supported by short sticks, wire netting fastened to long strips of wood, and scares of various sorts provide alternative methods, as given for Bush Fruit (*see* FRUIT). It is only while the plants are small that they are likely to suffer damage.

BLACKBERRY.

With ordinary care wild plants can be lifted and planted in garden plots in deep soil, kept manured, and in a year or two a good supply will result without further trouble than keeping clear of weeds and periodical hoeing. Give plenty of room when planting, keep well watered, and prune old wood after fruiting in autumn and where growth is rampant; the next fruit is on the new shoots. They do not thrive well in shallow soil. To increase, either layer or divide. Where cultivated blackberries are preferred, get *Ed. Langley, Parsley-leaved, Bedford Giant* or *John Innes.*

BLADDER POD. *See* VESICARIA.

BLAZING STAR. *See* LIATRIS.

BLEEDING HEART (Dicentra). P.; 12 in.; pink; spring into summer.

A favourite under its older name Dielytra, it has a fitting place in some sheltered nook in the rock garden, where its slender stalks of blood-red flowers can more safely display their peculiar beauty. *Spectabilis* is the popular variety. Plant in leaf-mould and sand. Increased by division.

BLUEBELL.

The bluebell of the woods is a difficult proposition to uproot, because of the depth of the bulbs. The cultivated varieties are mostly

Blue Gum   39   Bordeaux Mixture

campanula *rotundifolia*, scilla *festalis* and *nutans*, and the Spanish bluebell, *hispanica*. Treat all as for scillas. They like moist, semi-shade in fertile soil, and go on multiplying each year.

BLUE GUM. *See* EUCALYPTUS.

BOCCONIA. *See* PLUME POPPY.

BOLTONIA. H.P.; 4 ft.; white, pink, violet; July–August.

Admirable for cutting the profuse blossom for room decoration. They are rather like Michaelmas Daisies but more bushy and spreading, the foliage also being attractive. Start from seed sown in a frame in spring and plant out in friable soil, giving plenty of room. Increase by division in autumn or spring, taking the outer shoots.

BORAGE. H.A.; 1 ft.; blue; summer.

This aromatic herb is grown by bee-keepers because it is liked by bees. It also has culinary use for flavouring. Raise from seed in any soil, in drills, rather sparsely and thin out to a foot apart.

BORDEAUX MIXTURE.

To be used for potato blight, celery blight or leaf spot, peach or almond, leaf-curling and generally for diseases affecting foliage of fruit trees, root crops and herbaceous plants. It is more effective when freshly prepared: hence make in small quantities at a time, using hydrated lime, instead of the old custom of quicklime, and 98 per cent. pure copper sulphate (blue-stone) in powder or grains.

For making $2\frac{1}{2}$ gallons of spray, use:

Copper sulphate	4 oz.
Hydrated lime	5 oz.
Water	$2\frac{1}{2}$ gal.

The mixture must be made in a wooden, not metal, vessel. Of the $2\frac{1}{2}$ gallons of water pour a quart into an earthenware crock, into which stir the copper sulphate, and while this is dissolving put the lime into the bulk of the water and stir briskly. Then add the sulphate, as soon as dissolved, to the lime mixture, stirring till all takes on a sky-blue colour. It is then ready for spraying on.

The following advice on spraying this or Burgundy Mixture (*which see*) is issued by the Board of Agriculture:

The sprays should be applied before a disease makes its appearance, or at least in the early stages before much spread has occurred. They are preventive, not curative.

Spraying should be done before rain, rather than after, and it is more necessary in a wet season than in a dry one.

It is often necessary to spray crops two or three times during the growing season to renew the deposit washed off by rain and to ensure that new growth is kept properly covered.

Spray on a fine day, so that the spray has an opportunity to dry before rain comes; it will then stick much more satisfactorily to the surface of the lants. Do not spray if a frost is likely to be experienced the same evening.

Spray should reach the under side of the leaves, if possible, as well as the tops. If no sprayer or syringe is available, Bordeaux or Burgundy Mixture may be applied to potatoes by sprinkling from a watering-can with a fine rose, but spraying is preferable.

If spraying roves injurious rather than beneficial in or near certain industrial towns, it is owing to acid fumes in the air. Local advice should then be sought.

BORECOLE (Kale).

Borecole and kale are the same, and are popularly known as winter greens, as they provide abundant supplies of excellent green food even during the severest winters. They require a deep, moderately rich, well-decomposed soil. For first crop sow not earlier than the beginning of March, and prick out seedlings about the end of April. These will have formed sturdy plants, and be ready for final planting toward the latter art of May, for use in early winter. A sowing should be made between the middle of May and mid-June, ricked out and planted in beds in July, to furnish a supply during winter and spring. The plants should be from 2–2½ ft. apart each way, put in firmly, carefully watered when necessary, and in cutting, the top or heart of the plant should be taken first. A good crop to follow when potatoes or peas have been lifted. A mixture of 2 arts superphosphates to 1 of sulphate of potash can be applied when transplanting.

BOUGAINVILLEA. P.; greenhouse climber; lilac-rose; summer.

Though more at home under cover they do well outside in warm position and loamy soil, well drained, with sand and leaf-mould added. After flowering keep the plants dry, but while in bloom they need plenty of water. Blooming often continues to autumn, after which prune closely. Increase by cuttings under a cloche. They are subject to thrip and mealy bug, against which early precautions should be taken.

BOUVARDIA. P.; dwarf; red, pink, white; late summer.

If treated in the same way as the warm greenhouse fuchsia, satisfaction results. They have the advantage of flowering in winter as freely as in the warm months, the sprays lasting for some time diffusing a pleasing fragrance. Strike young shoots under a cloche, in greenhouse, in spring, grow in pots in loam, sand and leaf-mould; pinch out growths to secure bushy habit; exercise care in watering with chill off. After flowering cut hard back to encourage young shoots for propagation as indicated.

BOX.

In many formal gardens, box, *buxus suffruticosa*, retains its hold as edging. When planting, best done in September, a good soil, deeply dug, is advisable as box is a gross feeder. Clipping is best done in May or June; for young plants only the tips need snipping off.

BRACHYCOME (Swan River Daisy). H.H.A.; 9 in.; blue, pink, white; June–August.

Sow in April in a warm situation and allow for spreading. The centres of the flowers have differing colours. The variety *iberidifolia* is popular.

BRASSICA.

The family name for vegetables of the cabbage variety—broccoli, savoys, sprouts, cauliflower, cabbage and such.

BRIDAL WREATH. *See* FRANCOA.

BROAD BEANS. *See* BEANS, BROAD.

BROCCOLI.

Sow thinly nearly an inch deep in April on an undisturbed plot, but not in same plot as last season, and prick out the young plants when large enough to handle. Transplant in July into rich loamy soil, in rows 2 ft. apart. Give waterings of liquid manure during hot breaks. A sprinkling of salt on the ground in autumn will be beneficial in hard weather. Lower the heads of the plants northwards before frost sets in, disturbing the soil about the roots as little as possible. A hybrid type, *Cauli-Broccoli*, produces good white heads; but it is not hardy enough to flourish in cold areas. *Calabresse (which see)* has green heads and cooks tenderly. Treat as Broccoli for culture. *Purple-sprouting Broccoli*, quite hardy, is grown in the same way, and stands the winter.

BROOM. *See* CYTISUS.

BROWNALLIA. P.; 2 ft.; blue.

Perpetual flowering greenhouse plant, easily raised and cultivated. The *elata* variety is blue, half-hardy, an annual, and grows to 18 in. Sow seed of either in April or May.

BRUSSELS SPROUTS.

Sow thinly in March and for succession in April and May, and transplant when strong enough in rows 3 ft. apart by 2 ft. into soil which has been deeply trenched and liberally manured a month earlier. Early sowings can be in a cold frame. Transplant 6 in. apart watering the plot the day before, and in May plant out permanently 2½ ft. apart, treading in each plant very firmly. In a month hoe up the soil round the stems. Although the vogue is to aim at producing sprouts of greater size than formerly, the old choice sorts with small sprouts, about 1 in. in diameter, take a lot of beating for tenderness and tastiness. Seedlings of brussels sprouts are sensitive to careless handling, for brief exposure of the roots to sun and wind results in permanent damage. When planting them they should be kept wrapped and taken out singly as needed. They should be planted firmly 18 in. apart. Do not cut off the head of the plant till the sprouts are stripped, a process which should start at the bottom, taking a few from each at a time, so as to leave the upper ones to fill out till required. In stripping, cut the sprouts rather than pull them off, damage to stalk is thus avoided.

BUCHAN'S COLD SPELLS.

These are well established as weather conditions recurring frequently at or about the periods indicated. Buchan was a Scotsman who lived about a century ago and based his conclusions upon long meteorological observations. Gardeners in South-East Scotland will do well to note when the cold spells may be expected in any year and how long they last: February 7th to 10th; April 11th to 14th; May 9th to 14th; June 29th to July 4th. Dates vary in the rest of Britain.

Buchan also noted the yearly repetition of two abnormally warm spells: the first, July 12th to 15th, and the second, August 12th to 15th.

BUDDING.

Used mainly for fruit trees and roses, and is best done in damp weather; roses at any time between mid-July and the last week of September; fruit trees in the earlier part of this period. The operation

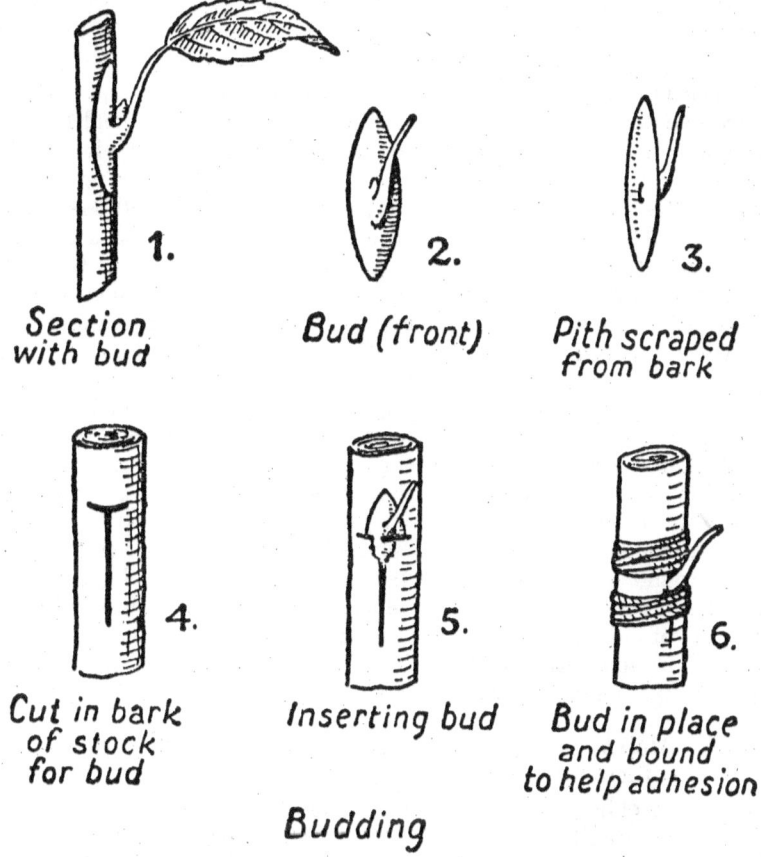

1. Section with bud
2. Bud (front)
3. Pith scraped from bark
4. Cut in bark of stock for bud
5. Inserting bud
6. Bud in place and bound to help adhesion

Budding

is to insert a bud from a tree or rose into new wood of a rooted stock. A budding knife is necessary for the work, and the excision and insertion need delicate handling. With the budding knife, make a cut half an inch above the selected bud (1) and work down to the same distance below, thus obtaining a piece of bark around the bud (2). The wood at the back of the bud must be removed by careful paring (3), but not the bark. Next make a cut in the stock nearly 2 in. long, and where the longitudinal cut starts make a slight horizontal cut for not more than ½ in., thus forming a T (4), but do not cut deeper than the bark. The next step is to lift gently with the knife the lips so formed and slip in the section bearing the bud (5), working it down inside till the bud is below the lips. Gently cut off any wood belonging to the bud that shows above the lips, and then bind together with soft string or strong raffia round the stock above and below the cut (6), so that the bud will be held firmly in place in close contact with the bark. This done, leave it alone till November, when the bud and bark may be expected to have welded and the binding can be removed; otherwise growth will be impeded. Protect from cold winds by tying a cluster of hay on a stake, so arranged as to form a pad over the budded region. For fruit trees the wood buds, which are more pointed than the fruit buds, are those to be taken for budding. For roses drier weather than for fruit trees is better, though the air should be on the cool side. Choose buds from shoots that have borne flowers, taking plump ones found nearer the joint. The budding is done on the stock of bush roses, removing some of the earth for easier working, and in standards on laterals near base of current year's growth. When the buds are taken and the wood removed from the back, the germ of the bud must be kept: if what seems to be a pin hole is seen, reject the bud and cut another; that is to say, the bud and its nucleus, and the surrounding bark is what is taken, and the adhering layer of wood behind removed, so that the nucleus is strapped against the sappy part of the stock when tied in. It is all less complicated than it sounds, and with care there is no reason for doubting success. See accompanying diagrams.

BUDDLEIA. F.S.; 5–10 ft.; mauve, pink, orange (Ball variety); June–July.

The oldest is *globosa*, flowering orange in colour and like little rough-coated balls. The generally seen variety is *variabilis* with its closely packed spikes of mauve blossom to be followed by November with reddish masses of seed pods. This variety has several subdivisions, all hardy, and all varying shades of mauve except *rosea*, which is strong pink; and *Pink Pearl* which is a pastel lilac pink with yellow centre. A dwarf of *variabilis* is *nanhoensis* showing mauve-pink flowers. They need a lot of sun, a rich loamy soil and plenty of room as they bush out quickly. Increase by seed sown in sand, or old wood cuttings with a heel in autumn. The mauve varieties repay for hard runing each year in March, the reward being a nine-foot bush laden with imposing spikes in July and onwards.

BULBOCODIUM (Spring Meadow Saffron). P.; 6 in.; purple; February.

A bulb of the lily tribe, *vernum* being the best known and one of the earliest of the spring flowers. It should have a place in every garden, in sunny position in rockery or border, and set in loam with an admixture of sand. Propagate by division in summer.

BULBS.

Directions for garden planting and culture for the bulb family are given under each respective variety, but a handy guide for planting

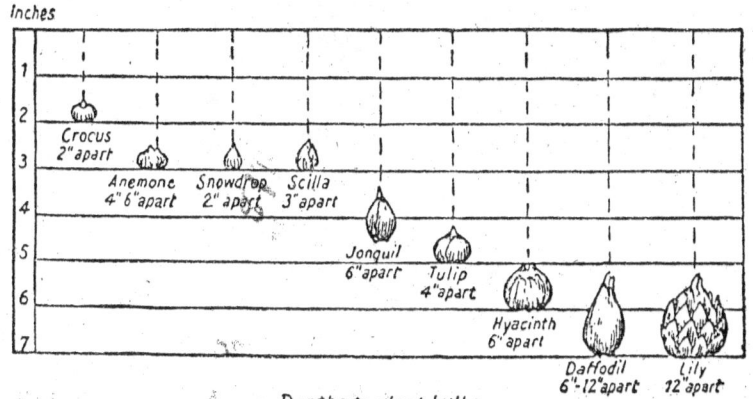

Depths to plant bulbs.

depths is given in the accompanying diagram, which will apply for bulbs of similar size. The general rules of culture may be summed up: Well till soil after removing summer bedding plants and fork over to reduce soil to workable tilth. When planting, a better effect is obtained by grouping. Keep grass from edges as shown in diagram "Edges". In each hole bed the bulb on a spoonful of sand and, generally, give a light dressing of compost. Take account in planting of height, flowering time and colours. Difficulty is experienced in locating bulbs after flowering; put in twigs, which will be inconspicuous among summer bedding plants, and in autumn the bulbs will not be injured by digging.

Lift bulbs when leaves have faded. If it is necessary to move them while the leaves are green, they must be taken up carefully, re-planted on a spare border, and left until the leaves change colour.

Many experienced growers find that finer flowers is the reward of planting in August or September rather than later in the autumn.

In Rough Grass.—For growing bulbs in rough grass *see* plan indicated in accompanying diagram. So long as couch and deep weeds are removed, success may be expected and no further trouble need be expended to assure a display year after year. When the bulbs have been put in, the turves can be reinstated, but when rolling

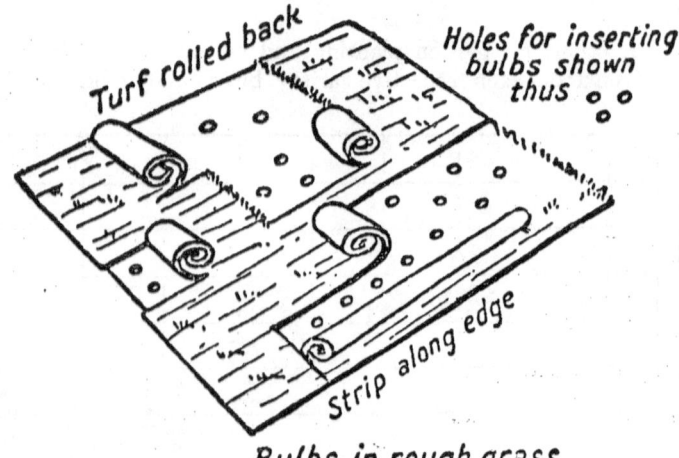

Bulbs in rough grass.

them back, thrust a twig through just over where each bulb is situated, so that, after pressing turves into place, small holes can be made with a fern trowel over each bulb, as indicated by the twigs. Another method is to use a tool known as a bulb planter, but the underlying couch grass and weed roots and runners are not eradicated. The more tedious way indicated in diagram is the best in the long run.

Bulbs in Bowls.—Select bulbs in early autumn; grow in pebbles, shell-gravel or damp moss, but the most successful medium is coconut fibre. This fibre needs to be thoroughly soaked by immersion in water, squeezed out, and enough put in each bowl for the bulbs to stand in without touching—overcrowding is a fatal mistake. The bulbs should be placed firmly, with the tips just showing, and more fibre packed round them so that the bowls are nearly full. Some small lumps of charcoal form the best drainage at the bottom of the bowls.

An alternative method of fibre planting is: the fibre compost should first be slightly damped, then place a layer of lump charcoal in the bottom of the bowl, and upon this a layer of the compost, 2 or 3 in. deep. Into this insert the bulbs, taking care not to press them down too firmly or the roots will be unable to penetrate the compost, then fill up with more compost to within 1 in. of the top and sprinkle with water until the whole is thoroughly damp, but not sodden, and the operation is complete.

Whichever method is adopted, the bowls should be placed in a cool dark room or cupboard, where the air circulates freely, but from which frost can be excluded in order to encourage root action, and during this period they should be examined periodically and watered when necessary. At the end of six or eight weeks the bulbs should be well rooted, and will probably have made an inch or more of top growth; they may then be removed to the room in which they are to flower, placing them close to the window to keep the foliage dwarf and sturdy. As they come into bloom, rather more water will be required, and the condition to be aimed at is one of uniform dampness. Do not water when fibre surface is still damp, but when watering, do it thoroughly. *See also* CROCUS and other bulbs by name.

Bulbs to Grow.—The bulb family is very large, and the varieties of many more numerous still. The amateur, however, can make his selection from the cultural directions for the majority of which, if not all, are under their respective entries:

Bulb planter.

Allium.	Crocus.
Belladonna Lily.	Cyclamen.
Bulbocodium.	Daffodil.
Camassia.	Dog's Tooth Violet.
Chionodoxa.	Freesias.
Chlorogalum.	Fritillaria.
Colchicum.	Gladioli.
Crinum.	Hyacinth.

Iris.
Ixia.
Leucojum.
Lilies.
Mariposa Lily.
Montbretia.
Muscari.
Narcissus.
Schizostylis.

Scilla.
Sisyrinchium.
Snowdrop.
Sparaxis.
Star of Bethlehem.
Tigridia.
Tritonia.
Tulip.
Winter Aconite.

BULRUSH. See TYPHA.

BUPHTHALMUM. H.P.; 2 ft.; yellow; summer.

A useful lant for the herbaceous border. Sow seed in spring and transplant when large enough to handle to permanent quarters in rich, deep soil, well drained and in a sunny spot. Increase by division in spring.

BURGUNDY MIXTURE.

Used for much the same purposes as Bordeaux and particularly for potato spraying. The difference is that ordinary washing soda is used instead of lime (as in Bordeaux), the proportions being:

Copper sulphate	4 oz.
Washing soda (fresh)	5 oz.
Water	2½ gal.

Mix in the same way as Bordeaux (*which see*.)

BURNING BUSH. See DICTAMUS.

BUSH HONEYSUCKLE. See DIERVILLA.

C

CABBAGE.

Whether spring or winter cabbages, the culture is the same, the time of sowing being: spring, August; winter, April. Sow thinly not more than 1 in. deep, keep watered and protected from birds. As soon as the plants have made from four to five leaves they should be planted out from 24 in. apart on a well-manured and deeply-trenched piece of ground prepared beforehand; a liberal supply of liquid manure is useful during the growing season. When planting, tread in the young seedlings firmly, both at roots and on surface, and if ground is dry, water a few hours earlier. Dip roots in soot when putting in. The destructive caterpillar must be picked off every evening from first noticing and put into salt and water to make sure of destruction. The pest can be checked in advance by early syringing or dustings of Derris powder on the young plants to keep off the white butterfly, which deposits the eggs or larvae, and these too should be wiped off regularly.

The custom is increasing of planting spring cabbages only 9 in. apart, but keeping the usual distance between the rows; then when they are big enough for early spring greens to pull alternate plants, thus leaving 18 in. for the maturing of those which are being grown on. Spring cabbages are often planted on the ground from which onions were lifted. The soil there is ideal for them. It should not be loosened by digging, but merely weeded and levelled with a rake.

Red Cabbage. Seed should be sown in August, following the procedure above, to be ready for picking the next July.

CACALIA COCCINEA (Tassel Flower). H.A.; 18 in.; deep orange-scarlet; June.

The favourite variety is *Emilia flammea;* it is good for cutting for house decoration. Sow in spring, ordinary soil and treatment for annuals.

CACTI.

These greenhouse perennials are a class by themselves, growing slowly, of solid texture, having spines, some varieties flowering only at long intervals, and though a general even temperature must be maintained by day and night—say 45°—they thrive if given plenty of air during periods of sunniness. The greater number are grown in pots; some of them are of small size, others of climbing habit. For growing soil, a gritty compost with some brick dust added is suitable. They require watering, using it lukewarm through a syringe, during the early summer at the time of new growth, and from autumn till March very occasionally a little water may be given to prevent a bone-dry condition. Re-potting can be done from March to May, using sizes only comfortably taking the roots. Cacti that are backward or look out of condition are best given a fresh start in new pots, after shaking out all the old compost, the composition being three-quarters fibrous loam and a quarter of brick dust and charcoal in equal proportions. Propagation can be by cutting, grafting, division or by seed. The last is less complicated, though many prefer to experiment and need not be deterred from the other ways of increasing which mostly succeed. Sow in a mixture of grit and sand, well-drained, using small pots, in the warm house in spring. If making cuttings, the length taken varies according to variety, from 1 in. to 1 ft., but all need care in adjusting watering so that there is only little moisture. Lay cuttings on a sunny shelf for an hour or two before inserting in pots, or on sunless days put them there for a couple of days to evaporate a percentage of the sap. In grafting, the spines can be used to fix in. The most useful general purpose variety is *epiphyllum*, but note it requires slightly more moisture than the more specialist kinds. For colours, *russellianus* is rose; *gartneri*, full scarlet; *truncatum*, red; and these flower in the spring. For autumn flowering use *echinocachis*, white; and for a white flowering in summer *echinopsis eyriesii*; good two-colour varieties are *oputia rafinesqui* which is red and yellow in summer, and *rhipsalis cassytha* which flowers green and white in the late summer.

CALABRESSE.

This is the Italian Green Sprouting Broccoli, which develops a head of good size, but less compact than cauliflower and of a green colour, nevertheless very palatable, while the sprouting shoots are tender and succulent when cooked. A fairly new introduction, it should be sown in the open in March, planted out when seedlings are 4 in. high, 2 ft. apart, with 3 ft. between each row. General treatment as for broccoli. The heads will be ready for cutting in August, and the sprouts ready from September onwards for continuous pulling till November or later.

CALANDRINIA. H.A.; 18 in.; rose tint; 9 in. is rich red; July.

The taller variety may be sown out-of-doors at end of April in sunny position, and the dwarf on the rockery at the same time. A still smaller variety, *umbellata*, has a magenta flower and is 6 in. high. They like a friable soil and the dwarfs will throw self-sown seed to multiply each year.

CALCEOLARIA H.H.A.; herbaceous, 24 in.; shrubby. H.A.; yellow, brown; summer.

The golden blooms of the shrubby variety are effective for bedding; the herbaceous kind are better suited for the greenhouse. Both kinds need plenty of leaf-mould in the soil and abundant watering.

Propagation of shrubby calceolarias is by cuttings made during October and kept in sand in a cold frame for the winter. For herbaceous species propagation may be by seed sown in a cool house in June, in pots or pans filled with a rich porous soil. There are also winter blooming hybrids from greenhouse flowering. Another variety, *violaceae*, is a shrub 2 ft., mauve tinted with yellow. Flowers freely in summer, but *integrifolia* is late flowering. Grows well in warm situation, particularly in the south.

CALENDAR OF FLOWERS. See FLOWERING CALENDAR.

CALENDULA. H.A.; 1 ft.; lemon, orange; July.

Sow in boxes to keep over winter and plant out 2 ft. apart in May in average soil. They self-sow freely, but the resulting seedlings are apt to revert to marigolds, which are the *officinalis* variety of calendula.

CALICO BUSH. See KALMIA.

CALIFORNIAN BLUEBELL. See NEMOPHILA.

CALIFORNIAN POPPY (Eschscholtzia). H.A.; 15 in.; yellows, mahogany; June–July.

Mass for effect in dry position in sun. Allow plenty of room and freer flowering will result. A double yellow variety is *crocea*. They like a good soil and if choicer seed is obtained sow in pans early, prick off into frames and do not plant out till May.

CALLIOPSIS (Coreopsis). H.A.; 3 ft.; yellow, brown; August.

A very general favourite. Seed should be sown early in April, in the place where intended to bloom, and by later sowings flowers may be had continuously from July to October. There are varieties 1 ft. (yellow and brown) and 9 in. (crimson and compact). The variety *tinctoria* combines the two colours. Coreopsis, strictly speaking, is the perennial sort, 2 ft., increased by division and subject to same treatment.

CALLISTEPHUS (the China Aster). See ASTER.

CALLUNA. P.; 1 ft.; red, white; August.

This is the ling or heather and suited for the wild garden in good soil with a proportion of peat, and grouped in a situation which gets the sun. The white variety is *alba;* *alportii* is red and the dwarf variety is *pygmaea.* They do not tolerate lime in the soil. Increase by cuttings put in a frame in peat and sand.

CALOCHORTUS. P.; 1 ft.; white, yellow, lilac; June–July.

The Mariposa Lily, as this is popularly named, is very attractive, is tulip-like in character and should be planted in autumn, 3 in. deep in a bed of leaf-mould and sand placed in a sunny position and built up above surrounding level to secure drainage. Weather through winter by straw covering. After flowering store till October and then re-plant. Colours: *albus,* white; *splendens,* lilac; *lutens,* yellow. Culture requires careful attention.

CALTHA. H.P.; 18 in.; yellow; May.

A plant for a moist corner, as its popular name, Marsh Marigold, implies. Given such a situation any soil will produce good results and free flowering. Increase by division in spring.

CALYCANTHUS. F.S.; 6 ft.; brown and purple; early summer.

The flowers are rather insignificant, but unusual and of decided perfume, being of the Allspice family. It mostly flowers in June and requires good peat and shelter from cold winds. Grow from seed. *See also* CHIMONANTHUS.

CAMELLIA. F.S.; 6–10 ft.; red and white.

The various sorts all flower early, February to April, and make striking contrast against the sombre foliage. *Japonica* is the tallest, 10 ft. and more, and has single and double blossom, white and red. *Alba* is a single white; *chandleri elegans,* a bright double pink and *imbricata rubra plena,* a double deep carmine. All sorts are hardy and can be grown in the open in sheltered position, set in a mixture of loam, sand, peat and charcoal. They make striking tub plants and flourish in a cold greenhouse. Poor drainage and irregular watering are to be particularly avoided, but they need no coddling.

CAMOMILE (Anthemis). H.P.; 2 ft.; yellow; summer.

May be bought as sturdy plants in pots for bedding-out. The bright green foliage is feathery and graceful, and the marguerite-like flowers are in shades of yellow, some are white. *Kelwayi* has unusually large, deep-hued yellow flowers from June until November. The perennial varieties are compact in growth and require staking.

They prefer the sun but thrive in any good soil or situation. An annual variety is 1 ft. high. Camomile has medicinal properties.

CAMPANULA (Harebell, Canterbury Bell). 2 ft.; blues; June.

The campanulas are a big family, some biennials, as the Canterbury Bell, the rest perennials, the Bell Flowers, varying from 3–6 in. in the Alpine varieties. The taller border plants run to 4 ft. and are among those perennials that can be planted with safety right up to the end of April, with care as to watering. Canterbury Bells are hardy biennials and will flower in May and June. They flower —dark and light blues and white—earliest in sunny positions. A rather light, well manured, limy soil suits the Campanulas. The root does not expand very quickly and so 1 ft. will be enough to allow each way for development for a couple of seasons. These tall species bear the flowers on upright stems that do not need to be staked. A dwarf variety, *attica*, has violet flowers; and *loreyi*, which flowers in July, is 1 ft., with blue and violet blossom. The trailing, pot or hanging basket sorts are grown from seed sown in heat in March or by division in spring.

CAMPION. *See* LYCHNIS.

CANARY CREEPER. H.A.; 10 ft.; yellow; May–July.

This *tropaeolum* is a free climber, with small yellow flowers in profusion for a long time. Sow in May for summer flowering in sunny position and average fertile soil. It is less frequently grown than formerly and is an annual. It is attractive in hanging baskets and kept to moderate length.

CANDYTUFT. H.A.; dwarf and 1 ft.; whites, lilacs and pinks; July.

The blossom is in spikes in both heights. Soil preferred is dry loam with lime in and a sunny position should be chosen. The perennial sorts, known as *Iberis*, have same treatment and are rock-garden plants, early summer flowering.

CANNA. P.; 24 in.; varied colours; June and July.

Although largely grown under cover, they can be treated as outdoor plants and make a striking display. Sow in spring in heat, after soaking the hard seed for 24 hours, gradually hardened and planted out at end of May or preferably early in June allowing 24 in between each. They are not particular as to soil, but a warm spot is preferred. For increasing treat as for dahlias.

CANTERBURY BELL. *See* CAMPANULA.

CAPE ASTER. *See* KAULFUSSIA.

CAPE JESSAMINE. *See* GARDENIA.

CAPSICUM. H.A.; 18 in.; white; August.

Sow seed in a hotbed in March or April and plant out in a sunny spot in May or early in June at a distance of 1 ft. The flowers are insignificant, but develop into rich red or yellow fruits which are distinctive. The pods are also of culinary use, being ready for storing in September.

CARNATIONS. H.P.; 18 in.; various colours; summer.

Sow seeds 1 in. apart during April or May, in pots of two parts loam and one part cow manure. A little bonemeal and old mortar rubble may also be added. Plant out 10–15 in. apart when there are five or six leaves, protecting them from frost during winter. They will be in flower the following summer in a variety of colours. Plant in a compost of two parts turfy loam and one part coarse sand. The ground should be deep dug, but heavy manuring is unnecessary. Unfortunately the newer species of carnation is more susceptible than the old sorts to fungi, which shows in rust and spots, for which spray with 1 ounce of liver of sulphur in $2\frac{1}{2}$ gallons of water. Layering can be done in July from non-flowering side shoots; the shoots, cut with a tongue which should be kept open when embedding, being pegged down in mounds of sand. If taking cuttings, do so just below a joint. After taking and splitting the cuttings, lay in water for three hours to open out the ends and then rooting will be more certain. Pot up when roots formed, which will be in about three weeks. Keep moist till rooted. If preferred, the rooted layers can be put at once into the plot. The secret of good carnations is planting in a sunny position and in a soil that is not too rich, picking blooms as they mature, and at all stages keep a sharp eye open for disease. Before the plants are put out in the garden, however, whether this is in the autumn or the spring, the soil must be well prepared. About a month before the plants are to be put in, the beds or border where the carnations are to go should be deeply dug and a little well-rotted farmyard manure should be worked into the land. This should be 6 or 7 in.

beneath the surface, but it is easy to do more harm than good by using manure too freely. After digging is completed the land should be firmly trodden down. In the case of a heavy clay soil, old mortar rubble or cinders should be added to make this more suitable to receive the plants. After planting, the soil round the base of the plants should be trodden down very firmly.

The *Perpetual Carnation* owes its value to the fact that, although it needs heat during the winter, the amount is only slight and it may be had in bloom throughout practically the whole twelve months of the year. It is also useful as a summer bedding plant. Propagation is by cuttings, which should be rooted in a house having a temperature of about 50°, if a little more bottom heat is available to encourage the formation of roots so much the better. Mostly the cuttings are rooted in sand, but successful results may be obtained with a very light loam or with a mixture of sand and loam. Shoots chosen for use as cuttings should be about 4 or 5 in. long and should be taken from plants which are both vigorous and healthy. If taken from plants which are even slightly diseased the whole of the work will be wasted. The cuttings should be firmly inserted in the rooting medium. They should not be allowed to get dry, but at this stage they require comparatively little water. As soon as roots have formed, however, water may be given more freely. Malmaisons are treated in the same way, and Picotees and Pinks require similar cultural treatment.

Of late years specialists have developed the carnation amazingly, and books have been written dealing solely with them; a multitude of new names and colour-mixtures are given in catalogues.

By lifting and potting with care not to disturb roots, carnations after summer flowering can be put into the greenhouse, where they will continue to bloom till Christmas.

CARPENTERIA CALIFORNICA. F.S.; 6 ft.; white; June.

Plant in sheltered situation as it is half-hardy, preferably against a wall. Any ordinary garden mixture will do and it can be increased by cuttings struck in gentle heat.

CARROT.

The carrot requires light soil, a good fresh loam, which has been trenched to double spit depth, and reinforced with thoroughly decayed manure the previous autumn. If natural manure is scarce, use fertilizer when sowing the seed when, too, a top-dressing of sand and lime will help to prevent maggot. Early in March, work out the stones and leave to settle for a week or two, then choose a fine day of first fortnight in April, after rain, to sow. If seeds are covered with burnt refuse before filling in drills, there is less danger of maggot. Seed is small; mix with sand and cover only lightly, but press down. An allotmenteer of long experience says, "A sprinkling of ordinary table mustard and wood ash in the drills when sowing carrot seed, and a dressing of the seedlings with soot once a week, will work wonders."

Sow thinly ¼ in. deep in drills 9 in. apart; and when the plants are about 3 in. high, thin out to 2 in. apart; after a few weeks to 6 in. apart. Thin once more after a few weeks to 1 ft. apart. Early crops can be secured by growing under glass in January. For the open ground sowings finer specimens result if when sowing the dibber is used to make holes, each of which fill lightly with fine sand and loam and bury two seeds just below the surface, thinning out the weaker of the two when they show—a long job but worth it. Keep down weeds, keep soil loose, keep watered. Make fortnightly sowings for succession till mid-July. A good, sweet, intermediate variety for maincrop is *supreme*, needing less thinning than most. Sown thinly in April an 8in. breadth of it will be packed with the rather straight roots by July. An old plan and specially useful where space is limited is to mix radish and carrot seeds, the first grows quickly and may be pulled before the carrots need all the space. In thinning carrots, if the roots left in the soil are exposed they fall prey to the carrot fly. Therefore firm in along the row as the thinning proceeds.

CARROTS, to keep. *See* VEGETABLES, STORAGE OF.

CATANANCHE. H.P.; 3 ft.; white and blue; June–August.

Has distinctive blossom for using in vases, as the clusters are on stiff stems and bicoloured (*bicolor*), the variety *caerulea* being all blue. They also last for some time with decorative effect if dried. Any soil of good texture suits them. Sow the seed in spring in flowering place.

CATCH CROPS. *See* CROPPING PLAN.

CATCHFLY. *See* SILENE.

CATMINT. *See* NEPETA.

CAULIFLOWER.
Sow in mid-August in an open situation on plots deep dug and well manured previously. The drills should be about 9 in. apart; plant out in November in beds, or in frames with about 3 in. between each plant, or in a very warm border. They will be ready for use in May. Another sowing may be made in heat in February and a third in March for use from June to September. Transplant in 8 weeks from seeding. The rows should be 2 ft. and the plants 1½ ft. apart in permanent quarters. Keep well watered and plant in very firmly. Mulches are beneficial in the hot season. When the white heads start forming, tie leaves across to foster bleaching and keep compact. If buying cauliflower seedlings choose the smaller, sturdy ones. The heavy heads of cauliflowers call for firm planting, and the plants should be put in right up to their leaves so that they sit on the soil, as it were. Where space is available it makes stronger plants if, rather than the spacing above, 2 ft. between the plants and 3 ft. between the rows can be allowed.

CEANOTHUS (Mountain Sweet). F.S.; 10 ft.; blue; July.
The seven evergreen varieties flower in spring and summer, *azureus* being the favourite because of the profusion of its spiraea-like clusters of exquisite light-blue flowers. There are also eight summer and autumn varieties. Most of them are of bushy habit, hardy, easily propagated and thrive in any situation so long as the soil does not contain much clay. The foliage is bright green, with a velvety paleness on the under sides and make an artistic foil to the flowers, which are at their best in July and August. *Veitchianus* flowers in May, with a profusion of flowers of deeper blue and smaller and darker leaves. *Thyrsiflorus* inclines to be grey-blue in blossom and flowers freely in thick spires. *Americanus*, called the *New Jersey Tee*, has white clusters in summer and autumn, and has long leaves. It is deciduous. *Gloire de Versailles* is summer and autumn flowering, the blossom tending to lavender tint, and is as beautiful and popular as *azureus*. They are best grown against a south wall and are increased by cuttings raised in gentle heat in August.

CELASTRUS SCANDENS. H.P.; climber; white; July.
These do well against a wall and in ordinary soil, particularly in a cool position with some shade. Although the flowers are attractive, their outstanding charm is the late autumn show of orange-gold berries. Prune shoot tips in February and propagate by layers in October.

CELERIAC.

Follow directions as for celery for raising from seed. Plant out in shallow drills 18 in. apart with 1 ft. between each plant, in well-dug and previously-manured ground, preferably using humus. Remove side shoots when they show, and keep thoroughly watered in hot weather. Lift in November, but lift as needed for use during October. Storage is as for carrots.

CELERY.

A well-trenched, heavily-manured soil is required for celery. For early use sow on a mild hotbed in the beginning of February, and for the general crop first week in March. Prick out when sufficiently large and harden off. Choose suitable weather in May, June or even July for planting out, and water freely should the weather prove dry. Dressings of liquid manure will improve the quality and produce of the crop. When earthing up, choose a dry day and carefully close the stalks to keep out the soil. The process can begin when plants are 15 in. high and need not be more than slight, but the two subsequent earthings, at three-week intervals, must cover more fully but not above base of leaves, while the fourth and last earthing has to cover all the stems, from which the soil should slope at a regular angle. Celery trenches should be 8 in. deep and 1 ft. wide allowing 10 in. between each plant: or if two plants abreast 18 in. wide, earth up for blanching gradually till October. For winter protection cover with straw or bracken. To control the leaf-mining grub use an infusion of elder and yew leaves, which is claimed to be more effective and less expensive than nicotine spraying.

CELOSIA (Cockscomb). H.H.A.; 24 in.; red, orange; summer.

Largely grown in the greenhouse, in warm districts they make a good show out of doors, their feathery plumes giving variety to the border. Sow under glass in winter, pot off singly and plant out in June, in leaf-mould and sand. Keep moist and give weak liquid manure occasionally. A dwarf variety grows to 12 in.

CELSIA CRETICA. H.H.B.; 5 ft.; yellow; June–August.

A good back of border specimen which can be started from seed sown in warmth under glass and given plenty of room in soil of average fertility. The blossom has a brightness which makes it distinctive. A variety, *arcturus*, is 4 ft. and blooms in August. Increase by cuttings struck in the greenhouse and taken from young wood.

CENTAUREA. *See* CORNFLOWER and SWEET SULTAN.

CENTRANTHUS (Valerian). H.P.; 24 in.; red and white; summer.

The foliage is grey and bushy. Flowers will be borne throughout summer if seed heads are removed promptly. This also prevents self-sowing, which is profuse. It likes a light, limy soil and sunshine, and if the need arises does not suffer from transplanting at any time. A red variety, *macrosiphon*, and a white, *albus*, are annual. The popular perennial sort is *rubra*, which also makes a striking wall plant.

CERASTIUM. H.A.; dwarf; white.

These edging and rockery plants prefer a light soil, and seed should be started in a frame. It spreads quickly and so must be kept under.

CHARLOCK.

This weed is worth developing by cultivation in a spare plot as it is used for bird-seed. It is prolific in seeding, so be sure to gather seed before quite ripe; it can be sun dried.

CHEIRANTHUS. H.B.; 1 ft.; orange; May.

The Siberian wallflower, as amateurs know it, produces richly coloured flowers, continuing till early autumn. Flowers quickest in sunny positions, on rather sandy light soils; but will flourish almost anywhere. Treat as for Wallflower. A long-flowering variety, often treated as an annual, is *allionii*, and is in fullest bloom in July. Sow seed in May in open, transplant when 2 in. high to growing bed, well spaced and with tops pinched, and to final quarters in autumn for spring flowering.

CHELONE. H.P.; 3 ft.; scarlet; July–August.

Rather like pentstemon, all making handsome plants for July flowering. Easy of culture, of free growth in average soil, and may be raised from seed or increased by division. *C. barbata*, bearing long racemes of bright scarlet, grows to 3 ft., while *obliqua* is purple and 4 ft., and flowers in August.

CHERRY (Flowering). Tree; white; May.

This species of the prunus, known as the Japanese cherry, variety *serrulata*, is a mass of flowers in the late spring and rightly esteemed for its beauty. Once established in spacious ground of depth and average fertility it needs no attention save keeping in shape and removing old wood.

CHERRY (Fruit).

First decide on the kind which best suits local conditions, while at the same time consulting personal preferences. Then, in preparing the ground, bear in mind two things: it must be thoroughly well drained, and whatever the character of the soil, lime rubble must be added, except in chalky districts, which are ideal for cherry growing. Even then make sure the chalk is present in the particular ground chosen. A medium texture of soil is best and where clay is the chief constituent add wood ash and crumbled brick, as well as the lime, and fork well to get even mixing. Do any planting in October or November, placing bushes or pyramids 10 ft. apart; standards 15–20 ft. apart, and on walls, fan-trained or espalier, 15 ft. apart, giving plenty of root space, trimming off damaged roots, firming and staking securely, and noting the general instructions under Fruit Trees. When established, trim up the general contour to secure a shapely tree, but apart from this do no pruning the first year. Subsequently the cherry requires little pruning; do some shortening of the side shoots of the sweet varieties to four buds in mid-July. Any pruning found necessary should be done as soon as the fruiting is over but be chary of pruning in winter as it often causes gumming, which the summer pruning does not. Because of this gumming propensity avoid any branches rubbing against each other by cutting away to eliminate the trouble. There is no cure for gumming, but its occurrence can be lessened by a mulch of sulphate of iron, $\frac{1}{4}$ ounce to the square yard, strewn over the area, covered by the spread of the branches and also a good liming to the roots. Pruning instruction is given under Fruit Trees, and also under Pruning.

If the garden is restricted and only one tree is possible, select *May Duke*, which pollinates itself, as other sweet cherries are not self fertile and more must be grown to be a success. It is a good plan to pair up when planting. Thus in the Bigarreau class put a *Napoleon* next to a *Bedford Prolific*, the former a red and yellow fruit ready in August and the latter a dark red ripe in July; or a *Frogmore* (July, red and yellow) with a black fruiting *Early Rivers* (June). To secure late fruit plant *Emperor Francis*. The *Morello* is self-fertilizing and a champion kind for cooking; it thrives best, fan or espalier trained, on a wall with a northern aspect. Old wood can be pruned from Morellos as fruiting is on the new shoots, which should be fan-trained three in. apart. All wall cherries need adequate watering at all times and liquid manure after the ordinary watering is beneficial.

Among the troubles of the cherry is the slugworm, known also as the cherry sawfly, which devours the soft tissue of the leaves, of which only the fibres are left. As soon as noticed apply Nicotine Insecticide (*which see*). This mixture can also be used where black fly is noticed. Sometimes leaf scorch causes the foliage to hang limp late in the year, to prevent which use Bordeaux Mixture (*which see*) just before the buds break; another spraying is recommended when the petals drop. The fungoid disease named Silver Leaf is recognized by leaves showing a silvery sheen. Any wood from which such leaves stalk should be cut out and burned, but it may do no good as the disease is too deep-seated to be diagnosed at the start. If its scaly purple fungus appears in overlapping growths the whole branch must be cut out and burned, and if the trouble continues the tree itself must go and thereafter no stone fruit grown on the ground. All tools used in removing branch or tree must be sterilized afterwards. A good liming when a tree seems ailing without specific cause often works wonders. *See also* PESTS.

CHERRY PIE. *See* HELIOTROPIUM.

CHILEAN FIRE BUSH (Embothrium Coccineum). F.S.; 4 ft.; crimson; May.

A little-known but beautiful shrub, all ablaze with honeysuckle-shaped flowers on a background of dark foliage. It is half-hardy and so is more suited to the south, or a warm situation sheltered from cold winds. It flourishes in peat and loam with grit worked in, but free from lime. Propagation is from spring-sown seed or cuttings struck under glass.

CHIMONANTHUS. F.S.; 5 ft.; yellow; winter.

The *praecox* variety of calycanthus. It is grown against a wall, making a striking splash of colour in mid-winter if planted in a south-west position. Plant in spring in ordinary soil and after flowering cut hard back, leaving any young shoots for next season's flowering. Increase by layering in sand in summer as with carnations, leaving it for a year before severing. There is a red variety, but the yellow is mostly grown for its large blossoms and its fragrance.

CHIONODOXA. H.P.; bulb; 6 in.; white and blue; February.

They bloom as early as the snowdrop and massed make a fine show. Plant bulbs a couple of inches deep in early autumn in average soil and only when crowded divide up. A gentian blue variety is *sardensis* which flowers in March.

CHIVES.

Divide the roots in the spring or autumn, leaving a few small roots together in each slip, and plant at intervals at about 6 in. If raising from seed, put ¼ in. deep in drills 1 ft. apart and thin out to 4 in. between each. They multiply quickly from offsets, thrive in any soil and come up year after year. The taper leaves are used in salad, being of a mild onion flavour.

CHOISYA TERNATA. H.H.P.; climber; white; early summer.

In colder districts this remains a shrub 6 ft. in height, but in mild regions, planted against a sunny wall with partial shade, in moist soil, three parts loam, it will climb to a considerable height and spread well, its profusion of stellate blossom making a striking picture. Slight pruning is beneficial in April. Increase by layering, or cuttings under glass, both in August. The popular name is *Mexican Orange Blossom*.

CHRISTMAS ROSE. *See* **HELLEBORUS.**

CHRYSANTHEMUM. P.; 3 ft.; various; October and November.

These favourites, which flower so freely in the autumn, require a rich light soil and abundant moisture. Propagation is by root division in early spring, cuttings in March, or in sand under glass in February, and layers in July and August. Those grown by layers may, if transplanted, flower the same year if the autumn is mild. They grow freely in the open and also in the cool greenhouse, the latter producing bigger and purer flowers if kept supplied with liquid manure and grown in extra large pots. Of recent years the strain has been improved both in range of colours and variety of petals. The singles remain popular, though the doubles have greater range of colour and are, perhaps, more widely grown, particularly the Japanese, the newer Cactus-petalled varieties and the Incurves. To get larger blooms the number of buds must be reduced, *see* diagram. Budding is expert work, but soon learned. In the spring, when about 1 ft. high, take off the top of the plant; then three shoots will grow from the top; pinch out any other shoots, and when the crown buds form nip off the leaves around them. These three buds will give fine blooms within three months if all the other buds are removed. Where a large display of flowers is wanted, remove fewer buds; the blooms will, of course, be smaller. The stalks of all chrysanthemums, even when thick, are brittle, and so all plants must be securely staked. Varieties are too many to list here.

The *Annual Variety* averages 18 in., is in many colours, and

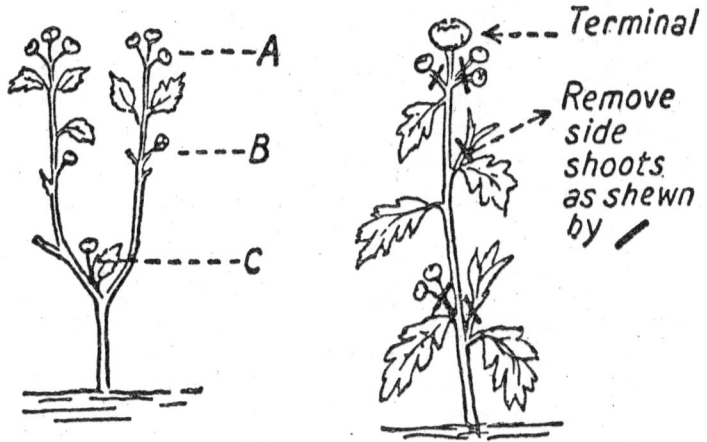

A. *Terminal buds*
B. *Crown buds.*
C. *First break*

For Exhibition display keep the best shaped Terminal Bud.

Chrysanthemum Buds & Breaks.

flowers June and July. It is hardy and free flowering, thrives in any garden from seed sown in the open in spring. One variety, *Bridal Robe*, is only 9 in. high and white. The *Coronarium* class include some 36 in. high and there are whites and golds 24 in. high. All chrysanthemums do best in the open during the warm months. Bring out greenhouse varieties in May and take them back in October, but water well; in hot dry weather they need watering twice a day and the stems should be securely tied, as well as the pots secured from being overturned in boisterous winds. Watch for green or black fly and syringe with liquid derris.

CIMICIFUGA. H.P.; 3 ft.; cream; August.

A useful specimen for the herbaceous border as their feathery spikes of blossom show up well. The three favoured varieties are *racemosa* and *foetida* (both flowering August) and *cordifolia* (July). Other good varieties are *simplex* and *japonica*. Give them a heavy, humid soil; otherwise plant them in the shade. Increase by spring division.

CINERARIAS. P.; 18 in.; various colours; winter.

These should be cultivated in greenhouse as pot plants, for they are in profuse flower, blue, red, purple, from December to May. Grow in ordinary light soil and keep just moist. The cactus-petalled variety is popular and not difficult to grow. Propagate by root division, cuttings or seed sown in June. The variety *maritima* has silver leaves, can be grown in open as bedding plants.

CISTUS (Rock Rose). F.S.; 4 ft.; white with yellow eye; June.

As well as those of shrub height, there are others, and perhaps better known, more suited for slopes and rockeries, averaging 18 in. in height and of bushy habit, varied and profuse blossom, making fine masses of colour, though closing in the evenings and being of short-flowering life, which is compensated by a close succession of blooming. Of these *purpureus* and *crispus* have purple flowers spotted crimson; *albidus* has large white flowers, and *obtusifolia* grows close to the ground. The taller varieties are *lusitanicus*, white and yellow; *loretii*, white blotched crimson; *hirsuti*, a hardy, white flower; *laurifolius*, white laurel-like foliage and a favourite shrub, and *Sunset*, rose blossom.

All respond to ordinary treatment, though not all are hardy, and flourish more freely in a warm situation on the dry side in light soil. Give protection of leaves in winter and do not transplant at any time. Increased by cuttings in heat.

CLARKIA. H.A.; 18 in.; pink and white, double; June; and 2 ft. salmon, rose, white, crimson, double; which flower in July.

It is easy of culture and flowers for a long time in delightful pastel colours on 30-in. spikes. A good sandy loam is best and a warm position desirable. It makes an excellent winter plant for the greenhouse and for table decoration if sown in autumn in a cool house.

For growing in open, sow in April and thin out to 1 ft. The variety *elegans* is graceful and full flowering; *pulchella* is also a good strain.

CLEANING THE GROUND.
This applies to virgin ground or a neglected plot, and means preparing it for cultivation by skimming off the grass, clearing off the surface weeds, digging out and burning the roots of the deeper weeds, removing and burning every possible runner of couch grass, collecting stones, etc., and in this way getting it ready for rough digging over and a thorough liming (8 oz. to sq. yard). Do all this in the autumn if possible so as to get the help of the winter frosts and rains in maturing the ground by breaking up clods, killing off insects and generally purifying the ground preparatory to the work of hoeing off fresh weeds, re-digging in the early spring and raking to a suitable tilth for sowing. A first crop on cleared ground is often potatoes. Where the need for use is not urgent for food crops, and the plot poor, it can be sown with lupins from own seed, of which there is usually a big surplus, and the plants dug in in the autumn to nourish the ground, as they are rich in nitrogen. The potatoes can then follow. Young weeds will not survive a watering of well-diluted pink solution of permanganate of potash for uncultivated ground.

CLEMATIS. P.; climber; blue, white, claret; July–September.
A profusely flowering climber, much improved of late from the deep blue and always favourite *Jackmanii*, by expert grafting and hybridization. The *Montana* is early flowering and white, and can be increased by cuttings after blooming: the *coccinea* varieties, pinks and reds and crimsons, flower in July: the *Florida* classes, greys and whites, are best for the greenhouse, and the *patens* group, ideal for pillars and pergolas, are in various colours. *Jackmanii* can be had in white, red and claret, as well as the old rich blue, and thrives best if planted early and cut back to within a foot of the ground. The old white Virgin's Bower is *Flammula*. The whole species do not thrive on heavy soil but otherwise give no difficulty if planted in sunny positions. They repay manuring. The branches are brittle and when being tied as they climb require care in handling. In earliest spring they often seem quite dead, but the first sun soon brings life into the buds. When planting, note that this is an exception to rule; when doing so keep roots compact; do not spread.

CLETHRA. *See* LILY OF THE VALLEY TREE.

CLIANTHUS PUNICEUS (New Zealand Glory Pea). Climber; scarlet; June.

Though usually regarded as a greenhouse plant, this handsome shrub will withstand a winter in the open if it is planted against a wall and the root well protected with litter and matting. Grow in a mixture of loam and well-rotted compost. Propagation is by cuttings and suckers. A cool house variety, *dampieri*, is used in hanging baskets and has scarlet flowers with black centres.

CLIMBING PLANTS.

The majority of plants in this class are put in to stay. Accordingly it pays to consult their individual likes and dislikes, as indicated in cultural directions under each particular name. In general also, whatever the kind, give adequate root room when planting and a good depth below the root for providing a bed of manure or half-decayed compost so that when the climber makes progress and its roots penetrate downward, there is ready a store of extra nutrition to round-off the establishing process. For light ground use pig, cow or chicken droppings with decayed beech-leaf. For heavier soil use well-matured humus, the remnants of a worked-out hotbed and a percentage of soot. When prepared, the bed should be left for a fortnight to settle before planting. Plant so that air can circulate behind the stem, and where growing on a house, for preference use a trellis rather than nailing to the wall, though with certain foliage climbers their own tendrils or suckers suffice, as in *ampelopsis veitchii*. For arches and pergolas use raffia, it looks even better than green string, and is gentler to the shoots. When fastening, first tie the raffia round a rib of the arch and then loosely make another tie round the shoot. For heavier branches a strip of webbing wrapped round and tacked on to the arch is more secure, but allow room for the increase of girth, and when the branch has made wood, the tie can be removed. Iron or wire arches, etc., may be used; they do not injure plants by scorching as some aver. Take a glance at the roof projections and gutters and plant the climber sufficiently away from the wall to avoid rain-drip: it can easily be trained nearer the wall as it climbs. Keep plants robust by a good mulch annually and prune as required; mainly for the purpose of cutting out old wood to benefit new shoots and keeping air space between the growth. Only a few climbers are annuals, and among perennials there is enough variety in the hardy kinds to satisfy average taste without adventuring among the more fragile half-hardy classes.

CLINTONIA. H.H.A.; 4 in.; blue, white; May-June.

The variety *dowingia pulchella* is a pretty blue with a white eye, and *umbellata*, which can be grown as a perennial, is 6 in., white, and increased by division; *borealis* has greenish-yellow blossom.

CLOCHES.

The true cloches are bell glasses, but a cheaper vogue is simply two sheets of glass resting at an angle to each other and supported

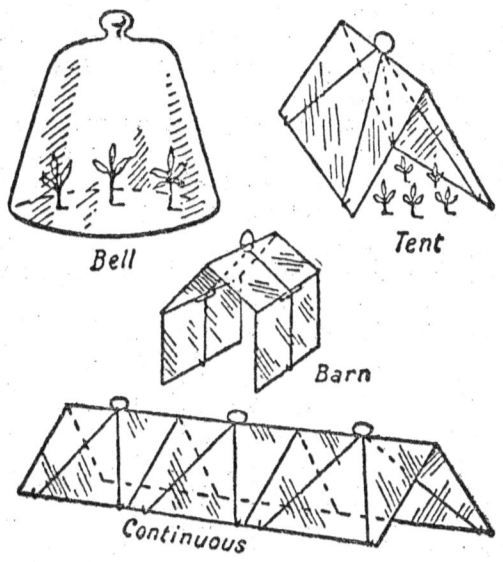

by wire. They can be moved about the garden to give protection and warmth to seeds or seedlings as and where required. More of these glasses can be added to give a continuous run. A variation is achieved by four sheets of glass to one cloche, two upright and two forming a top arch; these are aptly called barn cloches. It will be realized that each end is open, and while cold conditions rule a piece of glass or card can be placed so as to keep the interior cosy, but it must be moved for airing, as damp is far more fatal to seedlings and young growing plants than is dry cold, even a slight degree of frost. In particular this applies to vegetables and salad produce, which are hardier than flowers. It will be noticed that the ground

Cloches

inside the cloche seldom becomes frozen. When bell cloches are used, they must be raised for an hour during good weather to give an airing.

Neither sort of cloche needs removing to water what is growing under them: the natural condensation from glass is sufficient. In open situations it is good to group cloches and protect from draught and cold air by surrounding the group with screen of short bundles, or sacks stretched over stakes. Do not place the cloche-group under trees. When setting out a run of cloches put a ridge of soot all round the area to keep out slugs.

As a general rule, sowing and care is as Intensive Culture (*which see*), bearing in mind that a fortnight later for sowing and transplanting is recommended.

For sowing flower seeds, the tent cloche is invaluable, as it gives just enough protection for germination and growth without setbacks.

A leading maker of cloches has issued the following useful table showing when certain vegetables, etc., are best protected by cloches:

Cropped in	Jan.	Feb.	Mar.	Apr.	May	June	July	Aug.	Sept.	Oct.	Nov.	Dec.
Dwarf Beans					^	~					^	
Broad Beans				^	^	~		~	~	^		
Runner Beans					^	^	~	~	~	~		
Beetroot				^	^	^	~	~	~	~		
Carrots	^			^	^	^	~	~	~	~	~	~
Lettuces	^	^	^	^	~	~	~	~	~	~	^	^
Marrows						^	^	~	~	~		
Peas				^	~	~						
Potatoes				^	^ ~	~						
Radish			^	^	~	~				^	^	^
Spinach			^	^	~	~						
Turnips			^	^	^	^				~	~	
Spring Cabbage			^	^	~							
Onions								^	~			
Asparagus				^	^ ~	~	~					
Strawberries					^	~	~					

^ Grown under cloches.   ~ Grown in the open.

It is, of course, unnecessary to indicate that in the flower garden protection is secured by using cloches till frosts are over or for the first stages of hardening off seedlings removed from warm house.

Where a long run of continuous cloches is used on open ground close each end with a pane of glass as otherwise a draught-tunnel is the result to the detriment of the growing salad or flower plants. Give, however, a daily airing by removing these ends for ten minutes. *See also* **PORTABLE LIGHT**.

COBAEA (Cups and Saucers). H.H.P.; climber; purple, white; July.

A half-hardy which with a little protection will survive an ordinary winter. It is a useful plant, for in good soil and with liberal watering it will grow rapidly and flower freely during the summer, either in cool house or open. There are two varieties, *scandens*, with purple bell-shaped flowers, and *scandens alba*, with white flowers. Seed should be sown in early spring, in gentle heat, the seedlings potted off as soon as they will bear it, hardened off, and planted out in June. Often treated as an annual.

COCKSCOMB. *See* CELOSIA.

COLCHICUM (Meadow Saffron . Dwarf; white, purple; autumn.

A family of hardy bulbs, valuable because they bloom late. They are hardy and should be planted 4 in. deep, 9 in. apart. Give them a suitable position where the bloom will not be splashed with earth by the autumn rains. A sunny, well-drained spot in the rock-garden is excellent. Increased by offsets.

COLD FRAME.

Useful both for raising from seed and for bringing along seedlings. Lettuce sown in a frame in the autumn will survive the winter and provide a tender salad earlier in the spring than otherwise possible. There is not a great deal in the making and it is more than worth the trouble, especially where there is no greenhouse. Adjust the size to a couple of old window frames which can be picked up for very little. If constructing from the start, make a wooden frame 6 ft. by 8 ft., of a height of 1 ft. in front and 18 in. at the back. The depth from back to front will be 6 ft., the width being to accommodate two lights, each 4 ft. wide, which makes lifting for airing much easier than if in one piece. The sides, of course, will be made to slope to meet the height of the back. When put together get everything firm as possible. The "lights" are laid on, not fastened, as they are taken off or raised to give air when there is no frost. The trouble of making the glazed tops of the cold frame can be avoided by getting a pair second-hand, but old window frames are much cheaper.

To use, put a layer of rough earth at base, after digging out to about 1 ft., and press down. To increase space between soil and glass light, set frame on a layer of turves to about 1 ft. This allows it to be used for the taller plants. *See also* PORTABLE LIGHT.

Seed sown in the frame will germinate more surely than in the open
and the seedlings not get broken by winds; but take care to give
air for a time each day so as to avoid the danger of damping off, a
greater cause of losing seedlings than frost.

Early vegetables, though not so early as by the intensive or hotbed method, can be secured by sowing and bringing on in a cold frame,
so as to be well ahead for planting out as soon as the harder frosts go.

Over the rough earth, make a good soil bed, the seven parts of
which should be four of garden loam, one of manure from a spent
hotbed, or well rotted, one of peat moss and rather less than one
part sand. Where manure cannot be readily obtained use a half-part
of hop manure. Make this up in January and fill to depth of 6 in.
in frame, protect from wet and let settle for a fortnight; take light
off when fine.

In this bed sowings and culture of whatever is wanted can follow
same lines and for same products as Intensive Culture (*which see*).

COLEUS. H.H.A.; foliage; 18 in.

This greenhouse or bedding plant, valued for the beauty of its
variegated foliage, is best treated as an annual. Sowings should be
made in March—in pots rather than in pans, so as to have depth of
earth—in sandy loam with moist heat; water seedlings sparingly,
as they are liable to damp off. The final pots should be of moderate
size only as plants do best when pot bound. Pinch tops to make
bushy. Note that weak seedlings produce best leaf variegation.

COLLINSIA. H.A.; 9 in.; white, salmon, lilac and white; June.

Sow and culture as annuals in average soil. It grows rapidly, and
if sown in April will be in bloom in May or June. It can also be sown
in September. Many of the plants have bi-coloured blooms.

COLLOMIA. H.A.; 9 in., also 2 ft.; orange, stellate; June.

Either the dwarf or taller varieties are attractive and free flowering, the dwarf being mostly orange. Of the taller varieties *coccinea*
is red and *grandiflora* red and yellow. They thrive in ordinary garden
soil. Sow September for spring flowering, in mid-March for summer
flowers.

COLUMBINE (Aquilegia). H.P.; 3 ft.; various; May–July.

They are deservedly popular. Each flower can be divided into
parts each of which resembles a *columba* or dove, and the newer

sorts have long spurs. If protected with litter during the winter will thrive in ordinary soil. They yield finer blooms if treated as biennials. Seed sown in July in warm plot will be strong enough to stand the winter and can be planted in flowering quarters as soon as the frosts disappear. They flower freely, and the later sorts have a grand variety of delicate pastel colours, on wiry stems, with maidenhair fern-like foliage, doing well either in sunny or shady position. They are not exacting as to soil, but when once established they are impatient of removal unless in late autumn or spring. When bedding-out be most careful to leave root ball undisturbed. Water in well, and keep moist until growth has begun again, then do not let get dry. They do not divide successfully.

COLUTEA. F.S.; 6-10 ft.; yellow; June.

Known as the Bladder Senna, this gives fuller blossom than its cousin *Coronilla*. A reddish variety is *cruenta*. All varieties need cutting back in winter as they grow quickly even in poor soil, indeed they thrive better in dry, starved ground. Propagate from seed.

COMPOSTING.

In a corner of the plot, well away from the house and so situated, if possible, that the most prevalent winds do not carry aromas toward the dwelling, dig a substantial hole, and in it put all garden refuse, mowings from lawn, cabbage and other leaves, the gathered autumn leaves, particularly beech, from nearby copses, and all such vegetable material which by decaying slowly makes what is known as compost. The refuse of this autumn will not be ready as compost for at least twelve months as rotting takes time, but it can be assisted by adding salt, soda and lime at intervals as more refuse is thrown in, and a few buckets of water poured over the heap to hasten decomposition. Fork over now and again to let air and damp get in to speed up the rotting process. This mixture, when black and well rotted can be forked out, mixed with animal manure (humus) and spread over the plot at any time or used as a mulch (*which see*). In this way the organic chemicals taken out of the earth by one year's growth are ultimately returned. Compost can be used more freely on light soils than on heavy. For heavy clay soils add sand and lime.

There is method in making the compost, the refuse is not merely thrown in haphazard. Start with 6 in. of refuse, which if dry moisten, do not saturate. On this put 1 in. layer of humus, which overlay with 1 in. of ordinary earth mixed, if available, with 25 per cent. of old hotbed soil. Go on in this order till hole is filled, or if a heap, till a height of 36 in. is reached, after which start another if material available. Coal ash and cinders are not of use, and cabbage, etc., stalks are too harsh. Be very sure no rank weeds as nettles, docks, etc., are put in. These should be burned and the ash thrown in. Be thorough in making the compost bed, else decomposition fails to raise enough heat to destroy seeds if any weeds get in. Decomposition can be hastened by using chemical preparations on the market.

A method of composting evolved by Dr. Rudolf Steiner is claimed to secure better, more dependable results. There are four experimental centres in Great Britain, and also, it has long been carried on at Old Mill House, Bray, Berks, where it has been found satisfactory.

The system is outlined as follows:

The Steiner compost heap must be in shelter or covered, and can be added to at will. It should have a shallow base 3 or 4 in. deep with a clay foundation if possible. All organic substances from field, yard, garden or kitchen should be collected fresh and mixed. Where material will not rot, as in the case of prunings and hedge-trimmings, burn it and add ashes to your heap. Only log-fire ashes should be used. Put seeding weeds in the centre of any compost heap and not at the sides. At 1½–2 ft. add a proportion of lime and cover with earth. (Unslaked lime is best.) Then carry on with layers to a height of 5 or 6 ft. and by sloping you get a roof shape. Finally, cover with 1 or 2 in. of soil which can be got by digging a shallow trench round the heap. Peat moss is recommended for the covering, or bracken may serve if this is not available. A shallow trench should be made on top of the heap, and water, or water mixed with cow manure, applied to the compost heap at regular intervals.

Apart from general compost there is a *special* kind prepared without lime. It is of cow manure and compost in alternate layers and is for fruit trees.

CONVALLARIA MAJALIS. *See* **LILY-OF-THE-VALLEY.**

CONVOLVULUS. H.H.A.; climber; 8 ft.; many colours; August.

It has trumpet-shaped blossom. Sow May against south wall for grand display August to September. The scarlet variety is *Ipomoea coccinea*—a good trellis climber. *Minor* is hardy, 1 ft., flowering June, pink, white, blue.

COREOPSIS.
The perennial form of *Calliopsis*, which see for culture.

CORNFLOWER (Centaurea Cyanus). H.A.; 2 ft.; blue, pink, white; July onwards.
Profuse flowering. Dwarf variety, blue, rose. A late flowering (August) variety, 18 in., is light-blue, named *American*. Grows and seeds freely and self-sowns need to be kept down.

CORNUS (Dogwood). F.S.; 8 ft.; yellow; March.
Planted in average soil they thrive if in a moist situation. The yellow variety is *cornus Mas*, the white flowering is *sibirica variegata* which has variegated leaves, while another variety, *capitata*, white, flowers in August. Increase by summer layering or cuttings in autumn.

CORONILLA. F.S.; 6 ft.; yellow; June.
This is the *Scorpion senna*, with delicate foliage, pale yellow blossom and pods in autumn. Requires plenty of sunshine, a good soil and room to spread. Propagate from seed.

CORYDALIS (Fumitory). P.; dwarf; yellow; May–June.
Of trailing habit that needs to be kept in hand. It grows well in sandy loam, particularly suited to places where limestone is present. The variety *lutea* is best suited for the rockery, being only 6 in. high, whereas *nobilis* grows to 1 ft. A tuberous variety, *alleni*, has cream blossom with a tinge of purple. Propagate by division after flowering.

COSMEA. H.H.A.; 4 ft.; various; July–September.
Raise in warmth in February, noting that seed is slow in germinating. Gradually harden and plant out in May, giving 2 ft. between each to allow for bushing. They flower profusely and the foliage is graceful. An early flowering variety is *Rose Queen*, having lilac blossom.

COTONEASTER. F.S.; 10 ft.; white shaded pink; May–June.
The more than twenty species rely for their place in the garden on the autumn and winter displays of scarlet, dark red and orange berries, though there is a massed prettiness in the small blossom in very early spring, set among the dark foliage. Popular varieties

are *rotundifolia* and *frigida*, both profuse in flowering, and the show of rich coloured berries continues for weeks; *Vicarii*, an improved *frigida;* a short variety, 4 ft., *Harrovana* and a distinctive variety profuse in red berries, which extends its branches only just above the ground, *horizontalis*, popularly called Rockspray. There are a half-dozen dwarfs, including *humifusa*, *congesta* and *thymifolia*. All kinds are easy to grow once established in rather poor soil and in medium dry position. Prune in August. Increase by layering.

COTULA. H.H.A.; 3 in.; yellow; summer.

One of the newer introductions for rockery or edging, *barbata* being the best variety. It blooms very freely in fine clusters, button-like in formation and small. Average soil.

CRAB APPLE. *See* PYRUS.

CRANBERRY. *See* VACCINIUM.

CRANE'S-BILL. *See* ERODIUM.

CRESS. *See* MUSTARD AND CRESS.

CRINUM. Bulb; 24 in.; various colours; summer.

The bulbs should be planted 9 in. deep in autumn by a warm south wall in friable, well-drained soil. When in growth keep well supplied with water. The varieties include *moorei*, pink; *powellii*, white and rose; *longiflorum*, also white and rose but only 1 ft.; *kirkii*, red and white, flowers in September. The varieties also flourish in the greenhouse.

CROCUS. H.P.; dwarf; yellow, blue, purple; early spring.

Plant bulbs from September to November, 3 in. deep, in a rich sandy loam. Protect from birds by black cotton threadings. Take bulbs up every third year after the leaves have withered, for division and transplanting.

For pot culture grow the bulbs in well-drained, shallow boxes filled with rooted manure and leaf-mould, from which they may be separately transplanted into the ornamental pot or basket as soon as they begin to bloom, thus securing a successive display of yellow, blue and white flowers in the same stage of development in each pot. *See also* BULBS, to grow in bowls.

CROPPING PLAN.

The plan overleaf provides for the cropping of a garden or allotment to produce a steady supply of vegetables to the kitchen in every week of the year. It is issued by the Ministry of Agriculture, who recommend that any alternative crop selected should mature at the same season as the crop displaced; otherwise, too much would be ready at one period and too little at another. [*See* Plan *overleaf.*]

CUCUMBER.

Sow one pip in a thumb (smallest pot) in March and plunge in hotbed. When the plants are in early leaf, admit air and finally plant in rich turfy loam. Frame-grown plants should be on mounds from which the shoots will radiate. The ridge varieties should be sown first week of May in gentle heat or under a cloche (which remove when seedling grows against the glass), and gradually hardened off, planting out in June on ridges of manure surfaced over with about 1 ft. of good turfy loam. The top of a spent hotbed will do, but still add the loam. The secret of success depends on allowing nothing to check rapid growth. The temperature should not fall below 60° at any time.

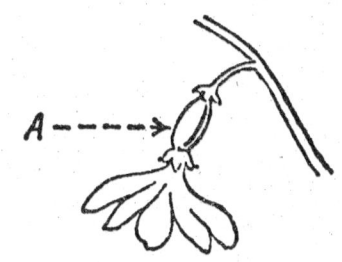

A. Female blossom showing potential cucumber or marrow.

Never allow roots to get dry, and always use water the same temperature as the house. Do not let plants run riot. Allow three stems to get 2 ft. 6 in. long, then stop by pinching. It is good to fertilize plants, as they have male and female flowers, the male having thin stem; the female one is swollen, being the potential fruit as here illustrated. In greenhouse culture prevent overcrowding by breaking out shoots as needed, and when roots show above soil add more.

CUPHEA. H.H.A.; 1 ft.; red, white tipped; June.

An unusual tubular blossom which attracts attention in the border, where it should be used as edging. The usual variety grown is *ignea;* the all-white variety is *alba.* Sow seed in winter in heat, prick off, pot up, transfer to larger pots and plant out early in May.

CROPPING PLAN FOR AVERAGE ALLOTMENT GARDEN

Plot is 30 ft. wide by 90 ft. long
Allow 6 ft. right across for Utility Space

Compost Heap Marrow	Tool Shed Radish, Parsley	Seedbed Tomatoes
	Section I — 28 ft. long — 1st year	
Dwarf Peas · · · · · 3 rows 2 ft. 6 in. apart.	Intercrop with Spinach and follow with Leeks · · · · 1 ft. apart.	· 2 rows · 4 rows
Dwarf Beans · · · · · 2 rows 2 ft. 6 in. apart.		
Onions · · · · · 8 rows 1 ft. apart.	Follow with Spring Cabbage · ·	· 4 rows
Shallots · · · · · 2 rows 1 ft. apart. Broad Beans · · 1 double row	Follow with Winter Lettuce. Intercrop with Summer Lettuce.	
Runner Beans · · · · · 1 row		
	Section II — 28 ft. long — 1st year	
Parsnips · · · · · 3 rows 15 in. apart.		
Carrot (Maincrop) · · · · · 5 rows 1 ft. apart.		
Potatoes (Early) · · · · · 3 rows 2 ft. by 1 ft.	Follow with Turnips.	
Potatoes (Others) · · · · · 6 rows 2 ft. by 1 ft. 3 in.		
Spinach Beet or Seakale Beet · 1 row		
	Section III — 28 ft. long — 1st year	
	Maincrops Cabbage (Winter) · · 2 ft. by 2 ft.	· 3 rows
Intercrop space for Savoys and Brussels Sprouts with Early Carrots, 2 rows, and Early Beet, 1 row.	Savoys · · · · 2 ft. by 2 ft. Brussels Sprouts · · 2 ft. 6 in. by 2 ft. 6 in.	· 2 rows · 2 rows
Early Dwarf Peas · · · · · 1 row	Sprouting Broccoli · 2 ft. by 2 ft. Kale · · · · 2 ft. by 2 ft. Swedes · · · 1 ft. 3 in. apart. Globe Beet · · · 1 ft. 3 in. apart.	· 2 rows · 2 rows · 2 rows · 2 rows

Refer to Rotation for 2nd and 3rd year uses of sections.

Looks well for greenhouse decoration, when keep in the same pots and do not over-water. A manured loam, in which is some sand, is the right mixture.

CUPRESSUS (Cypress). Perennial evergreen for hedges or screens.

Bought as young plants their lusty habit soon increases bushiness, and in a year or two they add feet to their height. The variety most used for hedges is *Lawsoniana*, because of its more symmetrical habit and quick growth; *erecta viridis* takes on a more pyramidal shape, while for light soil the appropriate variety is *macrocarpa*, but it dislikes transplanting. There is no difficulty in propagation, and ordinary soil suits, though a richer one quickens growth. They need and benefit by pruning according to use: if for hedge, prune tops 1 ft. every year, to extend bushiness; if for wind-screen or enclosing, prune side-shoots. Whichever variety is planted, stake very firmly till thoroughly established.

CUPS AND SAUCERS. *See* COBAEA.

CURRANT, BLACK.

Grow in fertile soil of average depth, allowing 5 ft. of space all round each bush, as they are of vigorous habit. Best time for planting is from November to March, spreading roots well, and firmly treading in. Stake when first planted, and below roots, with a few inches of soil intervening, give a layer of strong compost. Increase by cuttings 1 ft. long in September from same year's growth.

With the black currant the pruning is quite different from that of red and white currants. On the black currant the fruit comes from the young growth, the growth of the previous year, so an annual thinning out of the old wood must be made to get new fruit-bearing wood for each successive season. No spurs must be permitted, for as the fruit is produced from the wood of the second year the growth of new wood must be encouraged and the bush kept well open in the centre to light and air. The black-currant bush is a strong grower and therefore requires a good soil with heavy dressings of manure at intervals to enable it to produce fine fruit. *French Black, Boskoop Giant, Goliath* and *Baldwin* are recommended strains.

CURRANT, FLOWERING (Ribes). H.P.; F.S.; 5 ft.; scarlet; spring.

A shrub that is attractively ornamental, profusely flowering in graceful racemes and successful in any soil. Give plenty of room for bushing; prune during May. They are increased by cuttings in June, 1 ft. long, well set in ground and left till following year. Good varieties are, *King Edward VII*, red; *aureum*, yellow; *speciosum* (rather tender but prettier); *laurifolium*, yellow-green; and *sanguineum*, red. As these flowering shrubs are unisexual, choice sorts should be pollinated rather than leave it to the bees. The blossom and first leaves often appear simultaneously, especially if the spring is mild. Increase by long cuttings after flowering, or in August.

CURRANT, RED AND WHITE.

Being less bushy, the red and white currants need only 3 ft. of space between each and are less particular as to soil so long as there is a good root depth. Plant firmly and stake for first season. Keep free from suckers and do not allow buds for first 6 in. of stem. They can be grown as cordons. The fruit is borne by the old wood, and as soon as the requisite form of the bush has been attained, the pruning should consist in cutting away annually the young shoots, leaving only those which may be needed as new branches for extending the size of the bush or for retaining its proper form. The lateral shoots should be cut back to within $\frac{1}{2}$ in. of the bed, the effect of which will be to cause large clusters of spurs to be formed in due time, and from these spurs the bunches of fruit are produced. As the bush grows old the spurs may become overcrowded; thin them out and remove any old moss-grown wood as soon as it appears.

The pruning may be done at any time from November to February, but not later, and in the autumn the ground should be manured and gently forked over. In the spring, as soon as the buds begin to swell, a good dressing of soot should be given both to the bushes and ground as a preventive against caterpillars as well as being beneficial as manure. Best varieties are *Laxton's Perfectum*, *Red, Dutch* and *Fay's Prolific*.

CUTTINGS.

Taking cuttings and getting results is not so simple as it seems. All the same, with attention to little things that matter, a high percentage of striking may be expected. Some cuttings are best taken immediately under a joint; others with a heel, i.s. the shoot pulled off, not cut, so as to get the joint where it has grown from the stem or branch. Study too the best time for taking, which mostly is soon after flowering or in early autumn so that they may be well rooted before the frosts start. Striking can be promoted by covering cuttings with a cloche, or if in pots an inverted glass jar, remembering in both cases to lift for airing for ten minutes each day. Striking is hastened by inserting cuttings in a mixture of sand and ordinary soil and it helps to place the cuttings nearer edge of pot than in centre. Give some shade till struck. Do not be curious as to progress and do not coddle; as soon as growth starts give more air to avert damping off; a frequent cause of losing cuttings as well as seedlings.

Cuttings should be fairly long, say 8 or 10 in., of which half should be in the earth or pot, very firmly pressed in; a cutting merely thrust in is almost certainly doomed. Soft texture cuttings only need inserting to one-third length. Trim off lower leaves but do not strip off all, and do not put cuttings in too closely, leave room for root growth. Cuttings of roses are treated under that heading.

Some general hints may be given in addition to those above and where given under specific plants. Take cuttings from low down the stem. Leave an eighth of an inch below joint. Where hard wood cuttings are taken—with or without a heel—cut out intervening eyes of part inserted into soil. Cuttings from tender plants require the warmth of a greenhouse to strike, as in open wind would dry off the leaves. Shrubs can be struck in August or in autumn, but most successfully in spring. Sieve the sand and soil in which cuttings are placed to secure thorough mixing and sterilize soil to banish insect (*see* SEED STERILIZING). Hollow stem plants (as pansies) cannot be taken as cuttings; use the new growth by layering it. Cuttings of shrubs should be left in for a year as they are slow in making root. There has been a vogue for using recently discovered growth hormones sold under various names, and certainly the experiments with carnations, etc., have given remarkable results in the high percentage of successful striking. The solution in which cuttings are dipped before putting into pots has to be diluted with extreme exactness for differing varieties, and the amateur tempted to experiment should study directions carefully. Some explanation of the process is given under HORTOMONE, but it is advisable to consult an expert.

CYANUS. *See* CORNFLOWER.

CYCLAMEN. H.H.P.; 1 ft.; many colours; autumn.

This in one of the most artistic flowers for the warm greenhouse and reward the long patience needed to foster their slow growth from seedlings, during which time the corm is forming. Make the first sowing in August or first week of September and again in October for succession. Dibble the seeds about an inch apart and not more than a quarter of an inch deep. Place the ans in a warm and moist position in the greenhouse. When some seedlings are large enough for removal transfer to thumb pots, taking care not to insert them too deeply. As the plants develop, shift into larger pots. The Triumph strain may be gently forced, if required, in a temperature of 62° to 65° Fahr., with abundant moisture, under which conditions they flourish and keep their rigid self-supporting habit. The plants respond to soil containing well-decayed farmyard manure, old hotbed manure or moss peat. Lime in any form should not be used. Cyclamen that can flourish in the open have considerably smaller blossom; indeed they are dwarfs admirably suitable for the rockery. They are hardy, like a peaty soil, with leaf-mould, in which plant the corms 3 in. deep and 6 in. apart, in groups of ten or more as space admits. The flowers of these dwarf plants are claret and white.

CYDONIA. *See* QUINCE.

CYNOGLOSSUM. H.A.; 18 in.; blues; July.

Free flowering, character as Forget-me-not. Sow early for blooming same year, or August for next year's flowering, as the genus can also be treated as a biennial. The *linifolium* variety is one of the Venus's navel-worts.

CYPRESS. *See* CUPRESSUS.

CYTISUS (Broom). F.S.; 3 ft. and more; yellow, brown, mixed; April–August.

This beautiful flowering shrub is well worth cultivation and is most useful for clothing rough banks of dry or poor ground where many other plants would soon perish, but broom thrives. Its rich blossoms nowadays in mixed colours as well as yellow give a fine effect of colour, and by selection a succession of bloom may be obtained from early spring to late autumn. Many kinds will grow freely from seed, but seedlings require protection and staking in their early growth. Prune old wood very lightly in January. Good varieties are *sulphureus* (yellow), *albus* (white), *spartium janceum* (yellow), *andreanus* (yellow and brown mixed), *dallinorei* (rose purple); *Beanii*, a horizontal growing variety, flowering golden yellow.

D

DAFFODIL. H.P.; 18 in.; yellow; spring.

Classified among narcissi, which, however, include a wider range than "daffs." They should be put in in early autumn; do not use a dibber, but a blunt rounded piece of wood such as a bit of broomstick so that the bulb can rest on base of hole, which should be of depth according to class of daffodil, and have a little sand at bottom. A soil of good texture is better than one which is light and friable, as the latter will not hold enough moisture. It will result in better blooms and stronger stems if the bulbs are put in not less than 3 in. for smaller kinds and up to 6 in. for larger gradings. Classification of daffodils is into *Early Trumpets, Late Trumpets, Double Trumpets*, under which headings specialists have introduced a wide range of named varieties. *See also* general information under BULBS, for bowl culture and planting in rough grass.

DAHLIA. H.H.P.; 4 ft.; various and mixed colours; July–October.

Seed sown in February and started in heat will quickly develop into seedlings which will flower earlier than plants grown from tubers. Sow thinly in pans of ordinary compost and cover with a light sprinkling of earth. Pot off when about 1 in. high and gradually harden in frame for transfer to the open which should give flowers in June. The soil should be a good, rich hazel loam, deep dug. Lift the tuber roots at first frost, store in sand, protected from frost. In May, when shoots appear, plant out 18 in. apart. Cover over with leaf litter or cinders as a precaution against frost. Flowering should begin from the middle of July and continue until frosts cut down the plants if the seed heads are removed as soon as formed and at all times keep roots moist. The taller sorts need staking. Earwigs and insects which spoil buds can be trapped if small pots half filled with moss are placed inverted on the tops of stakes. The pots should be emptied daily into boiling water. There are many varieties, and constant additions are being made. The main divisions include *cactus, pompom, paeony flowered, stellates, collarette, fancy, singles, zinniastyle*.

DAISY (Bellis). H.P.; dwarf; red, white; April.

Planted in large clumps with excellent effect. May be grown from seed or by division of the roots in autumn. It flowers with little check when bedded-out, and will do well in most sunny positions and in any soil. The newest sorts have double scarlet, pink, or white flowers almost aster-like in form and size. Sow in June, put out October for next season's flowering.

DAISY BUSH. *See* OLEARIUS.

DAMPING OFF.

To prevent loss of seedlings by damping off in frame or greenhouse, a shallow seed-box of lime placed inside will prove effective. Lack of ventilation during misty and damp spells is the most frequent cause of the trouble, which arises from a minute fungus growth especially attacking seedlings which are too crowded. By sparse sowing and thinning at an early stage to avoid overcrowding damping off can to a great extent be prevented. Nothing can be done with affected seedlings; destroy them and dust the rest with flowers of sulphur. The incidental fungus can be guarded against by sterilizing the soil before sowing, *see* SEED.

DAMSON.

There has been much improvement in late years in growth of the trees and the start of fruiting has been speeded up. Plant as for fruit trees in general and treat as plums for culture. It is a few years before a damson bears and it has to be pruned regularly to encourage branch growth till the tree has a "head" mature enough and spreading enough to bear good fruit in satisfying quantity, such pruning being a winter-time operation. Once fruiting the trees need only rare pruning. A variety that has large fruit of distinctive flavour is the *Merryweather* and is best suited for the amateur, and should be planted with space of 10 ft. each way.

DAPHNE MEZEREON. F.S.; 4 ft.; rose, purple; spring.

Note that *Mezereon albo* is white. It flowers early, before the leaves appear, the bare branches bearing a mass of blossom which give place to foliage of a delicate green, in disc formation, darkening as they develop. The *grandiflora* variety blossoms in the autumn. *Blagayana* is dwarf, of trailing habit, white flowers. Plant firmly in good soil, with a little lime, unless it is present in the soil. They like a moist position. Reproduction from seed, which is poisonous.

DATURA. H.A.; 18 in. (*cornucopia*); 2 ft. (*chlorantha*); white and yellow; scented; late August.

Sow in spring in sandy loam. The blossom of *fastuosa* is unusually attractive, but it should be noted that the plant is poisonous. A shrub variety for the greenhouse, *suaveolens*, has double flowers, white in August, and can be increased by cuttings under a cloche.

DECEMBER GARDENING. See MONTH BY MONTH IN GARDEN AND ALLOTMENT.

DELPHINIUM. H.P.; 5 ft.; light and dark blue; June.

Seed should be sown in frame in May and transferred to the border in readiness for early bloom in the following summer. They will succeed anywhere, but a deep friable soil, well manured, is best. Every two or three seasons they should be raised, divided and replanted in early spring. A long continuance of bloom may be obtained by cutting off the spikes as soon as they have done flowering and helping with a little liquid manure. Slug damage may be avoided among seedlings, if started in open in boxes in leaf-mould and sand and sowed early July. Although of the same origin, Larkspur (*which see*) is now sold as a distinct annual variety. *Panticulatum* is an annual hardy, 2 ft., flowering a violet blue in August.

DEUTZIAS. F.S.; 5 ft.; white in full clusters; May.

The species is easy to grow in ordinary soil, in moderate sunniness. Benefit by pruning to remove old shoots after flowering; do not reduce new shoots. Increase by division. *Wilsonii* has larger flowers, standing erect instead of usual drooping clusters, and *longifolia*, a recent introduction, has rose-tinged blossom. A pruning diagram is given under SHRUBS.

DEW, VALUE OF. See WATERING.

DIANTHUS. H.B.; 8 in.; brown, crimson, variegated; May–August.

A compact biennial border plant of about 8 in. in height and flowering rather like a carnation, but not on spikes. The colours favour the dark reds and often are variegated. They bloom all the summer if the dead flowers are picked, and do well in light soil with some lime content and in a sunny spot. Plant not too closely, about 8 in. apart, and this will allow for runners to be brought along for increasing stock. They are easily grown from seed sown in April or preferably May, for blooming following season, but if sown in heat in January will bloom same year. The *Indian Pink* is a good variety. It should be noted that carnations and pinks come under this general classification, though listed by seedsmen under their respective names.

DIASCIA. H.H.A.; 9 in.; pink; July–September.

Does well in greenhouse, but also thrives in sunny position in border if not put out till May. The variety *barberae* is mostly grown. Sow in heat, prick out, and harden before planting out.

DIBBER.

A useful though simple tool used in planting out young vegetables and so on. The ordinary dibber has a pointed end shod with a cone of steel, the shaft and short cross-piece being of hard wood, about 1½ in. in diameter and 18 in. long. It is often a home-made affair from a broken haft of a spade, the part handle being kept and sharpened to a point. The steel cap is not vital so long as the shaving to a point is well smoothed with spokeshave and sand-paper, leaving no furrows to catch the earth as, in use, the dibber is withdrawn. A smaller size for seedlings in general is useful and can be 6 in. long, ½ in. in diameter and with a blunt end. In using this small size a hole is made of just enough depth to take seedling roots. For planting cabbages and brassica in general thrust the full-size dibber in to 4 or 6 in. and draw out with a slight turn so that the hole does not fall in. It is a good plan after lanting to make another dibber-hole a couple of inches away and use it in watering to make sure the young roots get irrigated properly till established. The dibber is useful for planting leeks, making a hole 6 in. deep, but not filling in the earth when the leek is planted; only let enough soil fall to cover fibres of root, the rest holds water and dew till leek is established, and automatically the earth gradually fills, thus saving earthing up for blanching.

DICENTRA. *See* BLEEDING HEART.

DICTAMUS (Burning Bush). H.P.; 30 in.; white, mauve; May–July.

A suitable border plant which is a curiosity because the stalks give an inflammable exudation, which becomes luminous after dark on a light being applied; hence the name. A bigger variety is *giganteus*

Didiscus Coerulas

caucasicus. Average soil will do, but give it a dry, warm position. It does not take kindly to division.

DIDISCUS COERULAUS. H.H.A.; 15 in.; blue; Summer.

Better known by its popular name, the blue lace flower, it is raised from seed under a cloche in spring, or in greenhouse, hardened off as soon as fourth leaf appears and brought on for planting out in May.

DIELYTRA. *See* BLEEDING HEART.

DIERVILLA (Bush Honeysuckle). F S.; 5 ft.; bright yellow.

An autumn flowering shrub the treatment of which is the same as *Weigela (which see). Rosea florida* is a robust variety.

DIGGING.

Whether in garden or allotment, digging must be thorough, especially if soil is being turned up for the first time.

The right time for digging is the late autumn, so that the winter

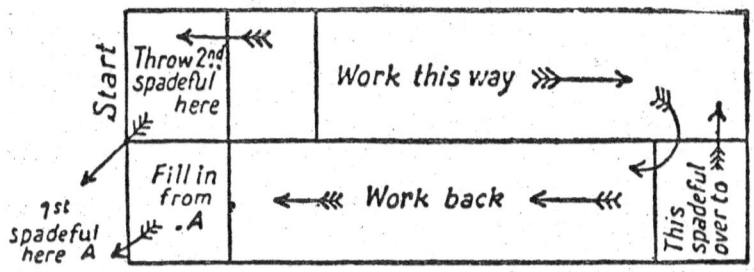

Surface plan of single spit digging

snows and frosts can purify (sweeten is the gardener's term) and break up the clods, making it easier in the spring to get the necessary tilth or fineness for sowing and for root growth.

Digging is of various kinds: single spit, double spit (a spit is a spade's depth); trenching; bastard trenching; skimming; ridging, as may best suit character of soil and what is to be grown.

Single Spit.— Where the soil is found to be of good quality and shallow-rooted plants desired to be grown on that particular plot, single spit digging can be adopted, though always double spitting is best. Or it may be the soil itself is shallow and there are stones below the depth of one spit. Dig out a spadeful and put it beside the line of working: the second spadeful is thrown into where the first one has come from and so on down the length to be dug. Having dug the length, put the soil of the first spadeful of return line into the vacant end of the first trench and work back. Start again at far end and continue till the required width is turned over. In single spitting, manure is simply dug in.

Double Spit.—Here the digging is to the double depth of the spade. Dig out one spit, put it aside as in single spitting, then dig, but do not bring out the second spit. Instead, turn it over, break roughly and dig in some rotted leaves or grass cuttings. Proceed in this way to full length, filling in as proceeding, and then bring the first spadeful to the end, continuing thus till plot is dug. By manuring the lower spit at this stage a lot of digging is saved in the spring, and only surface manuring will be necessary, whether by compost or artificials.

Trenching.—Here the digging goes to a depth of three spits. Instead of working a single width at a time, a double width is dug. Both widths are turned out for the first spit; when digging second spit, dig first the left spit and turn out on surface, fork over the spit below it (*i.e.* three spit lot) but do not remove, then dig right-hand second spit and put it on the left-hand over the disturbed third spit, dig the exposed right-hand third spit and so proceed with the whole plot in this way, filling in second and first spits as digging is done and bringing from starting-point the first spadefuls to complete at the finishing-point. Manure between third and second spits.

Bastard Trenching.—This proceeds on much the same lines as trenching, except that it is mostly done on clayey or heavy ground, and in consequence, to secure better drainage, small stones, broken brick and plaster are dug into the lower of the three spits before the earth from the second spit is thrown over it. Manure as in trenching.

A good deal of labour is saved by digging trenches where the peas and beans are to be grown and leaving them open to be half-filled with fallen leaves and shallow-rooting annual weeds. If this material is trodden down and the trenches are filled in with the excavated soil they will be ready for sowing in the spring.

Deep Digging.—The object of trenching and bastard trenching, *i.e.* deep digging, is to bring the best soil not right to the top but near enough to the surface for the roots to benefit. It follows, therefore, that where the undersoil is heavy clay or cold and stiff, deep digging is not recommended. For light or medium textures, even with marl and stones and sand in the sub-soil, deep digging yields excellent results.

Digging

Skimming.—This operation refers to the slicing off of turf where virgin soil is being dug. If the soil is shallow, the turves are placed face down and the dug soil of spit immediately below skimmed area thrown on top, the whole left to mature during the winter. Where there is a good depth of soil and particularly if compost is scarce, the skimmed turves are placed aside and stacked, grass down, in some corner exposed to the weather so that they can rot and provide compost for future use—not less than a year later—when they have rotted. The uncovered soil can be treated by any of the methods

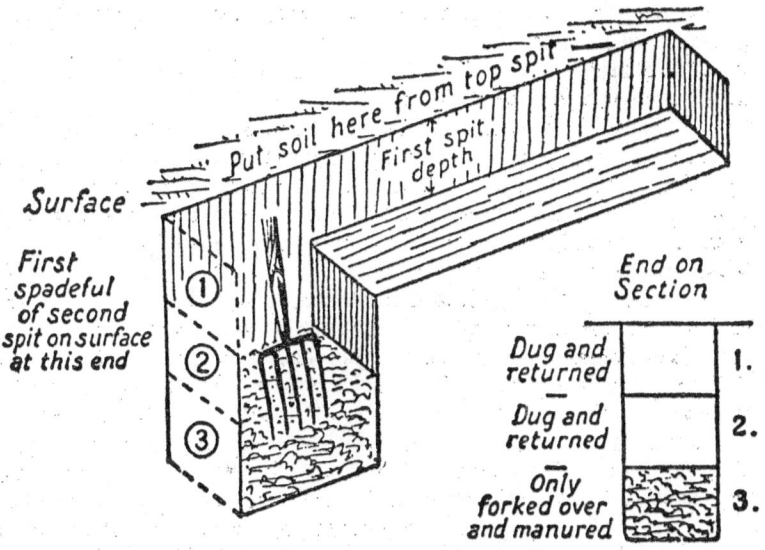

Bastard Trenching.

described for digging. To skim turf, cut with the spade to 2 or 3 in. through the surface for the width of the spade and for about 18 in. length of either side, insert the blade of the spade into the width-cut, easing up the turf till the spade can be thrust almost flatly along to free turf for the 18 in., to the depth of the grass roots only. Go on in this way till area desired is " skimmed."

Ridging.—This mainly applies to cultivated ground. After lifting crops, dig over but do not leave level. Work up into a series of ridges, much as when earthing potatoes, and so expose a greater area of soil to the beneficial effects of frost and weather.

In whatever class of digging, it is better to get rid of the weeds as proceeding. If ignored they will multiply so quickly as to make the labour tenfold the next year. Small weeds can be dug in, they then die, but those with large or deep roots must be extracted, roots and all, and burned. To sweeten ground spread lime, ½ lb. per square yard.

Inexperienced gardeners dig too long and too furiously. Do half an hour steadily at it, then rest the muscles by getting out the stones and deep-rooted weeds; do another half-hour, and then take another rest for ten minutes.

Always clean and polish the spade after use: it makes all the difference in working.

The Ministry of Agriculture, in a leaflet, advises on digging. The following is a succinct epitome:

When double digging any plot of regular shape, such as a 10-rod allotment, it is best to divide it lengthways into two sections. Begin by taking out a trench across the end of one section 2 ft. wide and 1 ft. deep. If turf is present, pare it off about 2 in. thick and, together with the excavated soil beneath, remove it to the adjacent section, where the work will finish.

The exposed sub-soil is then forked up to a depth of about 10 in. and on this the turves taken from the next 18-in. width of the land are placed grass downwards. The second 18-in. width of top soil is then dug to a depth of 1 ft. and thrown forward on to the inverted turves, and the sub-soil forked up. This process is repeated throughout the length of the first section, and the second section is then similarly dealt with. Complete the work by filling up the working trench with the soil taken out of the first trench on the first section.

The double digging of land already under cultivation proceeds in exactly the same manner except that, in place of the turf, manure, material from the compost heap or waste plant material is placed in the trench on top of the broken-up sub-soil.

It is important to remember that the digging of heavy clay soils should be done when dry in late autumn, so that the full benefit of frost action in breaking it down to a fine tilth can be secured. Loamy or sandy soils can be left later, but all soils are better for early digging so that they are well consolidated by sowing time.

DIGITALIS (Foxglove). H.P.; 3 ft.; various and variegated; June.

These are invaluable for shady spots, flowering best in moderate sunlight. They like a rich, leaf soil compost. The flower stem grows to 3 ft. or more, and the hybrids produce many lovely tints. The young plants rapidly spring up from self-sown seeds. It is poisonous to animals. If sowing from bought seed, note, they flower following season.

DIMORPHOTHECA (Star of the Veldt). H.A.; 1 ft.; salmon, orange, black-ringed; summer.

A quickly-developing plant, giving flowers six weeks from sowing, which should be in April. Either sow and thin out or transplant if started in seed bed. The flowers of *aurantiaca* are distinctive and profuse, allowing cutting till autumn. A half-hardy perennial species, *chrysanthemfolia*, is 2 ft., grows in the greenhouse. A dwarf variety is 6 in., apricot, March to April. Revels in sun and a dry situation.

DIPELTA. F.S.; 4 ft.; pink, white, yellow, brown; spring.

A compact and free-flowering shrub of the same habit as Weigela, but rather more varied in range of colour. One of the latest varieties is *yunnanensis*, pale pink; *ventricosa* has brown and cream, and *floribunda* gives white, pink and yellow bloom. Spring planting is usual in good average soil, giving plenty of room for bushing out.

DIPLADENIA. Greenhouse climber; crimson, white; late summer.

A free flowering hothouse plant which can be trained to creep round pillars, or from a tub on to a light framework. Its brilliant flowers grow in profusion if watering is kept up, though later but little is needed. They flourish in peat mixed with a smaller proportion of loam and sand. Re-pot in spring and syringe regularly. Cuttings in heat, placed in sandy peat, can be struck in spring.

DIVISION.

To propagate by division, separate plants either in October and November after flowering or in March and April as new growth starts. Lift the clumps, keeping the roots as intact as possible and, after lifting carefully, divide the plant into crowns with a sharp knife. By washing out the earth (putting clump in a pail) division is easier. Do not use a spade for this purpose. With herbaceous plants, such as Michaelmas Daisies, which throw out fresh shoots rooted just below the surface, carefully detach those on the outer edges and plant in autumn or spring. These make the strongest plants. In such plants as polyanthus and primulas the new shoots make root while still in the clump and can be more easily seen by washing out the earth when the old clumps are lifted and then teased out singly or in twos or threes according to the size of fresh clumps desired.

DODECATHEON (American Cowslip). H.P.; 6 in.; various; spring.

A beautiful hardy plant that is easily raised from seed or bulbs in sandy peat in a cool situation and appropriate for rockery, preferably in the shade. The blossom varies from rose, purple, white to lilac. Sow seed or divide in spring. A fine variety is *meadia giganteum*.

DOG'S TOOTH VIOLET (Erythronium). P.; dwarf; lilac, white; spring.

A hardy bulb well suited for the rock garden, averaging 6 in. in height, or as a spring edging to a border, as it is elegant in leaf and flower. Plant bulbs in autumn in peaty soil in a sunny situation. They should be planted 6 in. deep, 9 in. apart, and will bear division every two or three years.

DOGWOOD. *See* CORNUS.

DONDIA. H.P.; 6 in.; yellowish green; winter.

A useful rockery plant by reason of its flowering season. Grow in loam. It is increased by division.

DORONICUM (Leopard's Bane). H.P.; 1 ft.; yellow; April.

Showy, vigorous-growing plants, thriving in any soil. Useful as a covering for rough banks or for the wild garden, where its large, bright yellow flowers of daisy-like form are very effective in early spring. It can be easily propagated by division of the roots. The usual varieties are *caucasicum* and *austriacum*, but a May flowering sort, *Harpur Crewe*, grows to 2 ft., blooms profusely but only for a short time.

DRABA. H.P.; dwarf; yellow; spring.

As this only grows to 2 in., it is useful as a carpet plant which its lanceolate leaves as a foil to the yellow blossom makes effective. It grows best in sunny position; is not particular as to soil but prefers sandy loam. A 3-in. variety is *bruniaefolia*, of same colour and habit. Increase by division or seed sown in spring.

DRACAENA. Greenhouse.

A foliage plant which needs ringing (the cutting out round the stem, of a ring of the bark) to prevent legginess. From these rings roots soon show, which can be detached and made into new plants. Grow in small pots as they succeed best when roots are crowded, and give a soil of loam mixed with a third part manure and a little gritty sand. Press soil firmly, keep well watered and give plenty of light. Increase also by stem cuttings which root readily in heat at any season. As room plants they need frequent sponging.

DRACOCEPHALUM (Dragon's Head). H.A.; and H.P.; dwarf; blue; July.

Well suited for the rock garden or the mixed border in average soil. *Ruyschianum* is one of the best of the perennials and is a handsome plant with flowers of bright purple blue. Among the annuals are *Moldavicum* and *canariensis* (sometimes known as Balm of Gilead), the former being esteemed for the fragrance of its blue flowers. Perhaps the most beautiful of all, however, is *grandiflorum*, of dwarf habit, 6 in., with fine clusters of vivid blue flowers, eminently suited for the rock garden. *Rupprechti* is 1 ft. high. All may be raised from seed and the perennials increased by division in spring. Watch out for slugs.

DRAINING.

Where ground is normally too moist, drainage must be resorted to. It is best left to experts as amateur efforts often result in sunk lines of earth following the course where pipes are laid. It is an expensive expedient but effective.

DRYAS. H.P.; dwarf; yellow, white; June.

Attractive rockery plants of shrubby habit which grow well in a mixture of peat, loam, sand and a little lime, given a sunny situation. The white blossom is rather like minute strawberries. Increase by cuttings under a cloche or by division in spring.

DRYING FRUIT, VEGETABLES AND HERBS.

Certain fruits can be dried in the home quite simply and without expensive apparatus.

The fruits that dry best are apples, grapes, pears and stone fruits, but some varieties, especially of plums, are more suitable than others. Soft fruits and berries are not generally satisfactory.

All that is required is a number of trays made from four wooden laths nailed together to form a square that fits into the oven, drying cupboard or plate-rack. Wire gauze or canvas is nailed over the framework, and the trays are covered with muslin to prevent the fruit from sticking.

Great heat is harmful; scorching must be avoided; the temperature should never exceed 150° F. Drying can well be done with the heat that remains in the oven after cooking is finished, drying being continued on several days if necessary.

A plate-rack over the fire can often be used, but care must be taken to guard against smoke.

Fruits should be fresh and just ripe; dried at this stage, they retain their colour and flavour better. Most fruits should be halved or sliced, as this hastens the process. Grapes or small plums, however, are usually dried whole.

The fruit should be dried to a leathery consistency but not hard. The time required will depend on the temperature and may be anything from about four hours for apple rings, at a temperature of 140° F., to twelve hours or more for juicy varieties of plums. Occasional turning will hasten the process.

Vegetables for drying should be young and fresh, and most kinds first need blanching in boiling salted water for about five minutes. They are then put into cold water and drained well.

String beans should be sliced in the usual way and dried till brittle. Broad beans should be shelled. Only a few varieties of peas (chiefly the Marrowfats or Blue Marrow varieties, such as Harrison's Glory) are suitable for drying by artificial heat and they should be gathered when young and tender.

Surplus beans (haricot varieties) and peas of most varieties can best be air-dried.

Green pods should not be picked, but all allowed to ripen on the plants as far as possible. The whole plants are then lifted, tied in bundles and hung up to finish drying in an airy place before removing the seeds from the pods.

Dried fruits or vegetables should be left to cool before packing in jars, tins, boxes or paper bags. If sufficiently dried and kept in a dry place, they should keep well for many months.

When using dried fruits and vegetables they should be soaked overnight or longer before being cooked, until they regain their normal size. They should be brought to the boil slowly in the water in which they have been soaked and boiled until tender.

Sugar added to fruit should be put in just before cooking is finished; this prevents toughness.

Herbs should be gathered just before the plants flower, then should be washed, tied in bundles, protected from dust with a piece of muslin and hung up to dry near a fire.

The leaves of the larger kinds may be picked from the stalks, blanched in boiling water and dried in a cool oven at a temperature of 110° F. to 130° F. The leaves should be dried until quite crisp and then crushed or sieved to a powder and stored in bottles or tins away from the light.

Parsley keeps its colour better if it is placed in a very hot oven for one minute rather than dried slowly, but it must not be scorched.

E

EARLY VEGETABLES UNDER GLASS. *See* INTENSIVE METHODS; COLD FRAME CROPS; CLOCHE CULTURE.

EARWIGS.

Dahlias are the favourite haunt of these insects, but they take shelter in any flowers of sufficient size, as well as hidding in brassica. The best and simplest trap is still the small flower-pot, stuffed with a little dry moss or hay and inverted on the top of a stake. It should be examined every morning and evening and its catch destroyed by plunging it into boiling water. Another simple device is a roll of corrugated straw-board, one end thrust into a matchbox cover. *See also* INSECTS ON PLANTS, to destroy.

ECCREMOCARPUS. H.H.A.; climber; orange; July.

Sow in February under glass, space out seedlings to 3 in., pot on, harden and plant in open in May against arch or trellis giving a light but rich soil. The usual variety is *scaber*, a rich orange, and doing equally well in open or greenhouse, but there are also *roseus*, a red, and *longiflorus*, a yellow.

ECHINOPS (Globe Thistle). H.P.; 3 ft.; blue; summer.

A fine hardy plant, growing from 3 to 5 ft. high and useful for making ornamental groups in the wild garden. There are several varieties, *ritro* and *banalicus* being very good, but perhaps the best is *ruthenicus* with its round-headed flowers of beautiful blue. It is easily increased by division or raised from seed, and it thrives in any soil.

ECHIUM PLANTAGINEUM. H.A.; 15–20 in.; blue shades; June–July.

Of compact habit and profuse floriation. The red variety is *creticum* and *alba* is a white. A biennial variety is violet and grows to 3 ft.; *fastuosum* will thrive in the greenhouse.

EDGES.

Where flower borders or beds are cheek by jowl with grass verges, whether lawn or rough, growth of couch and bindweed is a constant nuisance. It can be prevented by cutting a spade-width channel 4 in. deep between verge and bed, as diagram shows. The collection of dead leaves which are blown into the verge is also much more easily removed and thus insects find no harbourage.

EGG PLANT. *See* AUBERGINES.

ELAEAGNUS. *See* WILD OLIVE

EMBOTHRIUM. *See* CHILEAN FIRE BUSH.

EMMENANTHE. H.A.; 1 ft.; yellow; July.

Grow from spring-sown seed sown in position in average soil and no special treatment.

ENDIVE.

Esteemed for salads. Generally speaking, treat as if growing lettuce. Sow in shallow drills in April for early use, or for late use in June or July. When 2 or 3 in. high transplant into friable ground or thin out 1 ft. apart. When nearly full-grown, they must be blanched, to be fit for the table, by gathering and tying the leaves together to exclude the light and air from the inner leaves, which must be done when quite dry, or they will rot. In three or four weeks they will be blanched. Covering with a flower-pot or whiting the inside of a cloche serves the same purpose. For winter cropping sow *Batavia* in August. Sowing should be in drills.

EOMECON. H.P.; 1 ft.; white; summer.

Suitable for a sunny situation in rockery or equally striking in border. Grow in leaf-mould and loam. It has roots which spread and these can be divided in spring to increase plants. It is known rurally as the Morning Poppy.

EPIGAEA. H.P.; trailer; white; summer.

Its foliage is evergreen and the flowers have a grateful fragrance. Give it a cool, sheltered position away from hot sun and keep watered. A good peat suits it. Increase by division in spring.

EPILOBIUM. H.P.; dwarf; white; July.

The dwarf variety has bronze green leaves which are so close to the ground that when in flower it looks like a copper mat studded with white. It is easy to grow from seed in average rockery mixture. The taller variety, *hirsutum*, will reach 4 ft. if grown in moist situation, preferably by a pond, and has purple-red flowers.

EPIMEDIUM. P.; dwarf; red, blue, yellow, white; May.

A good rockery plant with attractive foliage doing well in shade and sandy loam. An unusual variety, *nivenum*, has white flowers and shield-shape leaves tinted bronze. Increase by division.

ERANTHEMUM.

A winter-flowering plant with blue flowers which, at that season, is an attractive feature of the warm greenhouse, grown in an equal mixture of sand, leaf-mould, peat and loam and trained into bushiness by pinching out growths here and there. After flowering, re-pot and prune back. The best variety for amateurs is *pulchellum*, which can be increased by cuttings taken in spring.

ERANTHIS. *See* ACONITE.

EREMURUS. H.P.; 6 ft;: red, pink, yellow, white; summer.

It should be noted that it is some four years before the handsome flowers make a first appearance. They require protection, if in open, from cold, and do best in rich, friable soil, with loam as a principal constituent. Sow seed in spring in greenhouse, with bottom heat, and pot when fair size, then put into plot the next autumn. Keep an eye open for slugs. Varieties: *robustus*, silvery-rose; *elwesii* and *olgae*, are blush; *bungei* and *warei*, yellow; and *Himalaicus*, white. See also ASPHODEL.

ERICA.

The large family of Heaths (Heather) come under this category, of which many varieties are only successful in the greenhouse, while others are open-air subjects, growing slowly and requiring more than usual care in discovering what amount of water suits this or that variety. Plant in sandy peat; and in October for plants in the open; re-potting greenhouse species in February. Take cuttings under a bell glass in sand in spring. Most heathers run to 1 ft. or 18 in., but the tree Heaths grow to 6 ft. No Heath likes lime.

ERIGERON (Fleabane). H.P.; 12–36 in.; orange; June.

The border types grow from 6 in., although about 9 in. to 1 ft. is more usual. They should be planted not later than March, in a sunny position, for flowering from June, not being particular as to soil, and root growth is fairly rapid. The flowers vary in colour which may be violet, *roylei;* pale blue, *glabellus;* white, *coulteri;* or yellow, *aurantiacus*. The taller erigerons run up to 3 ft.; are of sturdy, upright growth and give grand massed effects in beds and borders.

ERINUS. H.P.; rockery; claret; May.

Grow from seed and transplant into rockery with well-drained sandy soil and sunny position. The sturdiest variety is *alpinus*, 6 in.; *albus* is white; *carmineus* is rose, and there is a new pink variety only 2 in. high.

ERITRICHIUM. Hardy alpines; blue, with yellow eye; summer.

Plant in a mixture of peat, sand, gritty loam and leaf-mould and porous stone chips. Care is needed to rear them. Increase by division in spring. The variety giving best chance of success is *nanum*, which produces beautiful blossom.

ERODIUM (Crane's-bill). P.; various; June.

Tiny rockery plants only 3 in. high (*chamaedryoides*), white; or 6 in. (*macradenum*), violet; and *guttatum*, which is white with a dark blotch. All prefer a light friable soil, well drained and in sunshine; unsuitable for northern gardens. Start seeds in warmth.

ERYSIMUM. H.B.; 18 in.; orange, mauve; July.

Although biennial, if sown in open early in spring it will flower the same year and does well in ordinary soil. The orange variety is *perofskianum*, the mauve is *linifolium* and is only 9 in. high, best sown in May, being more definitely biennial. It is allied to the *Cheiranthus* in habit.

ERYTHRINA. F.S.; 6 ft.; scarlet; May.

If grown in open put against a warm south wall; it is a useful conservatory plant, the shorter species being most suitable. It is called the Coral Tree because the blossom is in racemes and has that appearance. The outdoor variety is *crista galli* and requires a rich soil with sand and grit, and periodical treatments of liquid manure. Protect base in winter. Increase by heeled cuttings raised under an indoor cloche and with bottom heat.

ERYTHRONIUM. *See* DOG'S TOOTH VIOLET.

ESCALLONIA. F.S.; 5 ft.; red, white; July–August.

Likes a warm corner of the garden and some shelter, not being fully hardy. The hardiest variety is *macrantha*, with drooping clusters which appear in spring and continue till late summer. Another red variety, *rubra*, is in flower from mid-June to September, while *floribunda*, of the same flowering period, is white and not hardy. On the other hand, the white *Phillipiana* is both hardy and free-flowering in July and August. Put in well-drained sandy loam. Take cuttings in August.

ESCHSCHOLTZIA. *See* CALIFORNIAN POPPY.

EUCALYPTUS.

Hardy foliage tree only successful in warm districts, it being the Blue Gum of Australia. Often grown in tubs, when it reaches only medium height. The *citrodora* variety exudes a citron perfume. Grow in loam and peat and take cuttings in June, striking under a cloche in sand.

EUCHARIS.

A warm house, bulbous plant, much esteemed for its white fragrant flowers which bloom in profusion at Easter. They can be grown with success in the open in a warm situation in a rich loamy soil, but resent transplanting. Give soot water occasionally and re-pot every third year in March.

EUCRYPHIA. F.S.; 10 ft.; white; June.

The hardiest variety is *pinnatifolia* with yellow stamens. Grow in peaty loam and propagate from cuttings under glass. They prefer mild districts and in winter require protection if their situation is exposed to wind and weather.

EULALIA.

An attractive ornamental grass, 6 ft. high, and of graceful appearance. It does not require special treatment or soil and is increased by division in spring. A good variety is *japonica zebrina*.

EUNONYMUS. *See* SPINDLE.

EUPHORBIA MARGINATA. H.A.; 18 in.; variegated; September.

It is the foliage plant also known as "snow on the mountain." At best in September. Sow seed early in May. There is a wide variety of euphorbia, all with the quality of the sap being milky, some being perennial, others half-hardy, but the choicest is *marginata* and does best in loam.

EUTOCA. H.A.; 1 ft.; blue; summer.

Will grow robustly in average soil, sowing in open in April.

EVENING PRIMROSE (Oenothera). H.P.; 4 ft.; yellow; summer.

Whether treated as a perennial or biennial it will grow easily from seed sown in spring where wanted and later increased by division. It is less popular than formerly because of its straggling habit. A dwarf variety, *bertolini*, is 18 in. and large flowered.

EVERLASTING PEAS. Climber; white; purple; July.

Easily grown from seed in well-drained soil, preferably hazel loam, and increased after that by root division. A prolific grower with an abundance of flowers; useful for covering porches or sheds; rather old-fashioned, but make a fine show, especially the *White Pearl* variety. Its catalogue name is *lathyrus latifolius*.

EVERLASTINGS (Immortelles). H.H.A.; 36 in.; mixed.

Grow in sheltered warm position in open and thin out, cut before fully out for use indoors as winter decoration, after hanging in dry shed to mature. The finest variety is *helichrysum*, salmon, scarlet, orange, copper; *acrolinum* is rose, white; *Rhodanthe maculata*, is 1 ft., a bright rose, white centre, and a purple *xeranthemum*. They all prefer a light, sandy loam; fuller directions are given under their respective names.

EXACUM. H.H.B.; 9 in.; H.H.A.; 18 in.; violet; winter.

The biennial variety, *affine*, has a scent and if sown early will flower the same season, and by taking cuttings in spring with bottom heat is virtually perennial. The annual is *zeylanicum macranthum* and flowers in autumn from spring-sown seed. Both are for the warm house, and prefer a hearty soil of loam, peat and beech compost.

EXHIBITION HINTS.

There are rules for every species, detailed in regulations for the various shows, but in general it will be useful to note that quality and perfection of type are more important than size though this, of course, counts.

Exhibition terms mean: *kinds*, distinct types; *varieties*, particular sorts of one thing; *amateur status*, where no money is earned by gardening.

Packing, etc.—Put flowers in water as soon as cut and then as soon as they reach the show. If using maidenhair fern, it is best to pass stalk ends through a flame to seal and then to immerse the whole fernery in water till needed. Flowers must not be packed wet; use tissue paper crumpled, not cotton wool, as transit packing.

Despatch.—Send exhibits in wooden boxes with air holes; label clearly, giving full address, and put your own full address inside.

EXOCHORDA. F.S.; 6 ft.; white; May.

Give a sheltered position in average soil. A tall variety, *alberti*, grows to 10 ft.; *grandiflora* is a handsome variety. Increase by suckers taken in spring or by layering in autumn.

F

FATSIA (Aralia). F.S.; H.H.; creamy white; November.

Grow in sheltered situation in loam or in cool greenhouse. Plant in spring or autumn and propagate by cuttings in bottom heat, with sand. It can be increased by ringing as described for the Dracenia. The best variety is *japonica*.

FEBRUARY GARDENING. *See* MONTH BY MONTH IN GARDEN AND ALLOTMENT.

FELICIA (Kingfisher Daisy). H.H.A.; 6 in.; gentian blue, yellow discs; June–August.

Follow half-hardy culture. The variety *bergeriana* is best for the rockery, in a mixture of peat, loam and coarse sand. Increase by cuttings under a cloche.

FENZLIA. H.A.; dwarf; purple; July.

Grow from seed in open in April in light loam. It is of the same family as Gilia, which, however, is a taller species.

FERNS.

The varieties number more than 3000, and therefore no attempt is here made to deal with the needs and habits in more than general terms though some are given elsewhere under their botanical names. For potting, a mixture of loam and peat as principal ingredients, with a little humus and sand added. So long as they have adequate moisture there is no need to plant in shade. They do not like being disturbed at the roots. Therefore, with pot ferns the annual re-potting should be done carefully, the roots being kept in a ball of earth while the rest of the soil is renewed. Room ferns need ventilation without draughts, and watchful watering by tapping the pots for sound; once a week is enough in winter; in summer use judgment and include a syringing or sponging of the foliage with tepid water. Ferns in hanging baskets should be lined with moss to retain the compost. Propagation of ferns varies; a number are increased by spores which show in the under side of the leaves, the leaves being detached and pressed only slightly, spores downward, into the surface of fine soil, and when the new growth starts, potting off singly. Maidenhairs are propagated by root division.

FERTILIZERS.

Manuring is the use of decayed garden refuse, animal humus (*see* HUMUS), bonfire ash, etc. (*see* MANURING). Fertilizers are the modern equivalent, used where natural compost is difficult to obtain. They give quicker results, are easier to obtain and can be applied with less labour.

Fertilizers are mainly of three classes, each possessing distinctive cultural functions: potash promotes growth, nitrogen increases yield, phosphate strengthens roots and ensures more full ripening.

The average proportions for all classes of fertilizers is 1 oz. (1 tablespoonful) to the square yard, but see special table overleaf.

The method of using is to mix in small proportions with the tilth and to scatter over the ground among growing plants.

For use in the vegetable plots, phosphates are scattered over the dug areas a week or two before sowing seed. Give an annual dressing for 10 rods (an average allotment) of 30 lb. superphosphate, and 20 lb. sulphate of potash, applied at the beginning of the season. A dressing of 1½ lb. of sulphate of ammonia per rod will be needed, but this should be applied to the growing crops. Green crops and potatoes require an additional dressing of sulphate of ammonia. Basic slag is a satisfactory alternative to superphosphate if applied during the winter at the rate of 50 lb. per 10 rods.

Another method of applying fertilizers is as the trenches are dug for putting in the young vegetables. A scattering is made—bone meal, dried blood, and so on—along the bottom of the trench and covered with earth, so that the young roots do not get to the fertilizing material till they are established and need extra nourishment to make sturdy growth.

Different plants, flowers as well as vegetables, have their preferences, and while a general fertilizer is always beneficial, mixtures can be obtained from seedsmen to suit this or that particular need.

Although these fertilizers are generally known to gardeners as artificials, they are in reality the concentrated elements of natural soil.

It is because of the different chemical needs of varying classes of vegetable produce that the system of Rotation (*which see*) is so usefully employed.

From the American *Fertilizer Review* comes the advice that when putting in fertilizer prior to seed sowing it is better to place it along the seed drill rather than below. In dry weather, it says, capillary attraction draws the fertilizer upwards and so damages young roots, but if at the side it remains till the roots reach there and benefit from it just when they need help. For certain classes of plants more or less than the average, 1 oz. per sq. yard may be required and this, for varying areas, works out as here given:

Per Sq. Yard	Rod	Rood (¼ acre)	Half-acre	Acre
½ oz.	1 lb.	38 lb.	76 lb.	1½ cwt.
1 oz.	2 lb.	76 lb.	1½ cwt.	3 cwt.
2 oz.	4 lb.	1½ cwt.	3 cwt.	5½ cwt.
3 oz.	6 lb.	2 cwt.	4 cwt.	8 cwt.
4 oz.	7 lb.	3 cwt.	5½ cwt.	11 cwt.
8 oz.	15 lb.	5½ cwt.	11 cwt.	22 cwt.
16 oz.	30 lb.	11 cwt.	22 cwt.	43 cwt.

The following general advice for special purposes is given by an expert:

For Vegetable Crops.—A few days in advance of sowing seeds or planting out, rake the fertilizer well into the soil, allowing 3–4 oz. per sq. yd., or 7 lb. per sq. pole. Supplement this, during the period of growth, by a top-dressing at the rate of 1–2 oz. per sq. yd., choosing showery weather. The top-dressing may be either raked in close round the plants or applied in liquid form, using 1 oz. of the fertilizer to 1 gallon of water.

For Gardens generally.—For all general garden crops apply a good-grade fertilizer containing organic and inorganic materials during the preparation of the ground, 2–4 oz. per sq. yd.; as a top-dressing 1–2 oz. per sq. yd. The fertilizer should not be allowed to come into contact with the foliage. The plants will gradually reap the benefit of such treatment.

For Potatoes.—A fertilizer should be sown in the bottom of the drills at planting-time, using 6–7 lb. per sq. pole, or 3–4 oz. to each sq. yd. When dung is also used, a rather smaller quantity of the fertilizer will generally suffice. Rake the artificial in so that it is not brought into contact with the tubers; give another light dressing after the tops of the haulm are through the soil. The artificial must not be allowed to touch the foliage.

For Flower Borders.—To develop strong healthy foliage, with well-formed bloom of good colour, and long-flowering, mix fertilizer with potting soil, 3 lb. per cwt. of compost. As a top-dressing, artificials should be applied, 1–2 oz. per sq. yd. periodically. If used in liquid form use 1 oz. to 1 gallon of water, stirring well at time of use.

For the Greenhouse work, 1 teaspoonful to a 5-inch pot, or 1 dessertspoonful to a 7-inch or 8-inch pot is sufficient for a single application. Before applying and watering in, gently stir the surface of the soil to assist the absorption of the fertilizer and prevent clogging.

How to use Mineral Fertilizers

Basic Slag.—2–4 oz. per sq. yd. as top-dressing. Acid and heavy soil. Apply in autumn and winter. For all crops except when soil rich in lime, but do not mix with farmyard manure or sulphate of ammonia.

Kainit.—2 oz. per sq. yd. Forked in, light soil. Apply in autumn. Cheap form of potash.

Nitrate of Potash.—½–1 oz. per sq. yd. as top-dressing, all soils. Apply in spring. Stimulant.

Nitrate of Soda.—½ oz. per sq. yd. as top-dressing, light soils. Apply in spring. Do not mix with farmyard manure nor apply to peas or beans. Very quick action.

Nitro Chalk.—2 oz. per sq. yd. Forked in. Heavy and acid soil. Apply in spring and summer. Quick acting but lasting. Keep in the dry.

Sulphate of Ammonia.—½ oz. per sq. yd. as top-dressing, not on acid soil. Apply in spring and summer. Do not mix with lime or basic slag.

Sulphate of Potash.—½–1 oz. per sq. yd. as top-dressing. Heavy soil. Apply in spring and autumn. Mixes well with other fertilizers.

Superphosphate of Lime.—1½–2½ oz. per sq. yd. Forked in. Not on acid soil. Apply in spring and autumn. Acid manure, good for nearly all crops.

FIG.

Its free growth does not fit the fig tree for culture in small gardens, but, if space admits, a good fruiting variety such as *Brown Turkey* yields plentiful and delicious figs. Where there is a warm corner of a walled garden, it can be grown successfully as an espalier but needs protection against chill winds and frost. Under favourable conditions it will yield two crops in a year. With a young plant, let it become almost potbound, and when planting out, usually in

Flax

February, crowd rather than spread the roots, and mix lime, a generous supply, with average soil but of firm texture, without adding manure, but a mulch is useful in May. Water well in hot weather. If first crop is ready in June another may be picked in August. Prune old wood in October, and earlier, say beginning of September, trim back fruit-bearing shoots to half a dozen leaves. As root restriction is important, keen growers line the root area with stones or rubble, and even cement the base of the hole.

FLAX. *See* LINUM.

FLOWER-POTS.

These are made in graded sizes, indicated by their inside diameter. The smallest are called "thumbs," and are 2 in. across, the sizes increasing therefrom as follows. They are ordered in recognized numbers called "casts," which also are given:

Casts	72	72	60	60	60	54	54	48	48	40
Sizes (inch diameter)	2	2¼	2¾	3	3½	4	4¼	4¾	5	5½
Casts	32	28	24	16	12	8	6	4	2	1
Sizes (inch diameter)	6¼	7	7½	8½	10	11	12½	14	15½	18

Seed-pans follow the same dimensions and casts.

Sea Kale pots are in two sizes—16 by 16 in. and 13 by 12 in.

Rhubarb pots are 16 by 24 in. deep.

FLOWERING CALENDAR.

It is possible to have a floral display in the open all the year round by growing shrubs, perennials, herbaceous plants, bulbs and annuals of one sort or another as the following selection will show. This does not take account of rockery specimens or alpines. Neither is it a colour guide, for so many plants have varieties of differing colours that it would not be helpful. Such variations are given in the general alphabetic descriptions.

NOVEMBER—DECEMBER—JANUARY

During the wintry months, main reliance for display must be on the flowering shrubs, which, with some bulbs, give a splash of colour even in the hardest weather: the yellow of winter jasmine and the lilac pink of laurustinus and viburnum fragrans, the clusters of yellow hamamelis and the scented yellow blossom of chimonanthus fragrans. Then there are the rich red berries of holly and cotoneaster horizontalis and the blossom of such perennials as winter aconite, which has yellow blossom with a green fringe of leaf cup; the hellebore, known as the white Christmas rose; in not too severe winters the blue and white of chionodoxa; the varied blossom and bronze leaves of lonicera, and petasites (winter heliotrope), white.

As the year advances, the selection increases until spring and summer brings a considerable choice in colour, height and beauty of foliage and blossom. The selection here given will provide a satisfying variety, yet leaving very many others, well known and not so well known, from which to choose according to personal preferences:

FEBRUARY

Annuals	Perennials or Bulbs	Shrubs
	Anemone	Daphne mezereum
	Scilla	Garrya
	Snowdrop	
	Wander Primroses	
	Bulbocodium	

MARCH

	Bellis	Coluta
	Primroses	Forsythia
	Violets	Magnolia
	Crocus	Almond
	Wallflower	Kalmia
	Arabis	Andromeda
	Primula	Rosemary
		Camellia
		Arum (Easter) Lily

APRIL

	Bleeding Heart	Amelanchier (Snowy Mespilus)
	Flags	Kerria
	Corydalis	Ribes (Flowering Currant)
	Aubrietia	Viburnum
	Narcissi	Pyrus Maulei
	Tulips	Azara
	Hyacinths	Mahonia Japonica (Barberry)
	Forget-me-not	Skimmia
	Polyanthus	Arum Italicum
	Megasea (Saxifrage)	

MAY

Annuals	Perennials or Bulbs	Shrubs
	Monkshood	Broom
	Burnt Candytuft	Deutzia
	Golden Alyssum	Weigela
	Anchusa (light)	Rhododendron
	Columbine	Syringa
	Arabis	Tamarisk
	Asphodel	Laburnum
	Burning Bush	Azalea
	Euphorbia	Berberis yunnansis
	Heuchera	Lilac
	Iris	Choisya ternata
	Lychnis	Spiraea
	Catmint	Wistaria
	Onosma	
	Iceland Poppy	
	Sidalcea	
	Tradescantia	
	Lupin	
	Freesia	

JUNE

(The annuals here listed for June, July and August are arranged in their flowering order)

Annuals	Perennials or Bulbs	Shrubs
Cacalia	Achillea	Coluta
Annual Chrysanthemum	Agrostemma	Genista
Nemophila	Anchusa (dark)	Tree Lupin
Phacelia	Anthemis	Philadelphus
Anthemis	Borage	Calycanthus
Asperula	Cornflower	Buddleia globosa
Bartonia	Valerian	Coronilla
Clarkia	Gaillardia	
Collinsia	Potentilla	
Collomia	Spiraea	
Convolvulus	Verbascum	
Star of the Veldt	Fuchsia	

JUNE—(continued)

Annuals	Perennials or Bulbs	Shrubs
Echium	Scabious	
Erysimum	Delphiniums	
Eschscholtzia	Columbine	
Eutoca	Nemesia	
Gamolepis	Nigella	
Gilia		
Gypsophila		
Layia		
Leptosyne		
Linaria		
Linum		
Night-scented Stock		
Nolana		
Platystemon		
Saponaria		
Shortia		
Silene		
Omphalodes verna		
Virginia Stock		

JULY

Annuals	Perennials or Bulbs	Shrubs
Acrolinum	Antennaria	Catalpa
Calandrinia	Clematis	Ceanothus
Calendula	Erigeron	Potentilla
Campanula	Geum	Prunus
Candytuft	Sweet Rocket	Abelia
Cheiranthus	Lavatera	Hypericum
Clarkia	Lilies	
Centaurea Cyanus	Veronica	
Cynoglossum	Antirrhinum	
Hieracium	Pentstemon	
Larkspur	Everlasting Pea	
Mignonette		
Nasturtium		
Oenothera		
Annual Poppy		
Salvia		
Saponaria		
Silene		

JULY—(continued)

Annuals	Perennials or Bulbs	Shrubs
Sweet Sultan		
Alyssum		
Argemone		
Godetia		
Stocks		
Sweet Pea		
Zinnia		
Helianthus		
Brachycome		
Viscaria		

AUGUST

Annuals	Perennials or Bulbs	Shrubs
Coreopsis	Acanthus	Hibiscus
Delphinium	Helenium	Hydrangea
Haura	Red Hot Poker	Tamarisk
Helichrysum	Sweet Bergamot	Escallonia
French Marigold	Phlox	Buddleia variabilis
African Marigold	Cosmea diversifolius	Olearia
American Cornflower	Montbretia	
Love-in-a-Mist	Canterbury Bell	
Salpiglossis		
Datura		
Rudbeckia		
Scabious		
Nicotiana		

SEPTEMBER

Annuals	Perennials or Bulbs	Shrubs

(Several blooming in August continue flowering in September)

Annuals	Perennials or Bulbs	Shrubs
Blue Salvia	Chrysanthemum uliginosum	Bush Fuchsia
Aster	Helianthus	Eunonymus
Anagallis	Golden Rod	
	Michaelmas Daisy	
	Monkshood	
	Anemone Japonica	
	Cimicifuga simplex	
	Astilbe	
	Boltonia asteroides	
	Liatris	

OCTOBER

Annuals	Perennials or Bulbs	Shrubs
Rudbeckia (Autumn glory)	Funkia	Berberis Thunbergi
Aster (Angliae and cordifolius)	Prairie Sunflower	Pyracantha
	Polygonum affine	Symphoricarpus
	Colchicum	(all berries)
	Physalis	
	Helenium autumnale	
	Saxifraga Geum	
	Sedum spectabile	

It should be emphasized that these flowering periods fluctuate according to district climatic conditions and the mellowness or bleakness of prevailing temperatures, and whether, in the case of shrubs and perennials, they have been divided in autumn or spring; autumn is better as progress is not retarded.

FLOWERING SHRUBS.

There are at least fifty flowering shrubs which are robustly hardy, can be cultivated with ease, by ordinary methods, providing a rich variety of colour and elegance of foliage which for many years can add grace, beauty and distinction to any garden. Some are bushes, others of taller growth, and a few attain to the height and girth of small trees. Most of these find place in this work, and will be recognized by F.S. after the name. *See also* SHRUBS.

FLOWERS, chief divisions.

For propagation purposes the gardener can roughly divide plants into:

Annuals, which grow from seed, bloom and die all in one season.

Biennials, which grow the first year, bloom and die the second season.

Perennials, which continue to grow from year to year, producing blossom and increasing with age.

Of flowers for the open plots, two other divisions are:

Hardy, seed which can be sown with success in the open.

Half-Hardy, where seed has to be sown under glass, or during the heat of summer.

These two divisions are mostly marked on the seed packets.

FLOWERS, to keep fresh.

An aspirin or a little starch dropped into the water in which flowers are placed will keep the stems upright.

Flowers will last longer by cutting a small piece off the stem every day and splitting hard woody stalks about 1 in. from the bottom. Do these operations with a sharp knife, not scissors. Add a little soda and salt to the water to freshen the flowers. Several sheets of damp newspaper should be wrapped loosely round flowers sent by post.

FORGET-ME-NOT (Myosotis). H.P.; 6 in.; blue; early summer.

Once started sows itself freely and gives a profusion of blue flowers, making delightful contrast against the dark leaves. Stronger plants result from a June sowing every year and put in position in October for flowering the following spring. A strong blue variety is *alpestris*; *dissitiflora*, light blue, and *alba*, white.

FORSYTHIA (Golden Bell). F.S.; yellow.

The *viridissima* is erect, growing sturdily, 6–10 ft., with many branches stretching upward, all of which bear a profusion of blossom in March to April before the leaves appear. Give plenty of room, not less than 5 ft., and prune immediately after flowering. They like a good soil. Easily grown from long cuttings planted deeply in June. The *suspensa* variety is of trailing habit, very graceful for arches and walls. These can be propagated by layering shoots, which readily root.

FOXGLOVE. *See* DIGITALIS.

FRAGRANT GARDEN.

A grateful addition to be placed where prevalent winds can blow in direction of dwelling. Such a plot can contain clove carnations, nycterinia, night-scented stock, mignonette, sweet verbena, sweet bergamot, wallflowers, evening primrose, nicotiana, scabious, heliotrope, jasmine, mock orange (*philadelphus*), schizopetalon walkeri and scented roses.

FRANCOA. H.H.P.; 30 in.; white; July–September.

Popularly known as Bridal Wreath by its graceful pendent spikes of bloom. It is at best in the cool house, but can grow in open in warm districts, after being raised from seed sown in heat and gradually hardened and given a mixture of loam, sand, leaf-mould and matured humus. The variety most grown is *ramosa*.

FRANKENIA. P.; dwarf-trailer; pink; summer.

A densely-growing rockery plant suitable for "carpeting." Grow in sandy loam and peat, and give warm situation. It flourishes best in coastal districts. Increase by division.

FREESIA. H.H.; greenhouse bulb; white, yellow; winter and spring.

This has flowers of delicious fragrance. Raised from seed sown in a rich compost, but as the roots are very brittle, use care in transplanting. Seed sown in February or March will give flowers the same year, while a further sowing in August will supply plants for the following spring. When established, bulbs will give offsets which can be detached and planted in pots an inch below the surface in July. In warm districts they will grow in a sheltered sunny border.

FREMONTIA CALIFORNICA. F.S.; 6 ft.; rich golden yellow; June.

To succeed a sunny position, with some shelter, is necessary, and it should be set in well-drained, chalky soil, bolstered by a proportion of leaf-mould. Increase by cuttings well bedded in sand and under glass in spring.

FRENCH BEANS. *See* BEANS.

FRITILLARIA (Fritillary). H.; dwarf and tall; lilac, yellow; March.

A bulbous plant of the lily tribe, one species of which is *meleagris*, snake's-head, lilac flowers, and looks well in a rockery, being of drooping habit. The stately member of the family is *imperialis* (Crown Imperial), growing from 3–4 ft. high and bearing masses of bell-like flowers. There are several varieties of this species, with flowers ranging from pale yellow to deep orange and fine red and gold-striped foliage. Delicate beauties are *aurea* with pale yellow spotted flowers, *latifolia* with pendulous flowers of various shades of purple. All are quite hardy and will grow in deep loam. Plant in autumn. Increased by division every three or four years, lifting in autumn and re-planting immediately in fresh soil.

FROST.

The vital time to counteract frost damage to fruit blossom is

April to the middle of May. A sure sign of frost is a low day temperature when east or north winds are blowing, yet at the same time the glass is high, and particularly if the night is clear and calm. Give protection in any way you can—litter, bracken, covering fruit bushes with paper over the buds, or use a sack with side seams cut to give greater covering. For early seedlings, cover with flower-pots.

A motor radiator lamp is enough in the average greenhouse or cold frame. Protection can be given in the greenhouse, or even in the open to choice plants, by grouping together and then putting a boxing of boards on all four sides, with a motor radiator lamp in centre (consumption 1 pint a week) and a sheet of brown paper over all.

Frost fatalities can be avoided among such small plants as polyanthus. They are best divided in spring, as autumn division results in loss because the frost forces roots to the surface with fatal results unless watched and pressed back and protected. The same applies to seedling anemones, lupins, etc., if sown late.

To revive plants which seem to have died through frost-bite, water with cold, not lukewarm water, and mostly they will soon recover.

FRUIT.

Bushes.—The culture of bush fruits is given under each kind. It may generally be stated that only by intensive cultivation will the maximum amount of yield be secured. Fruit trees trained on trellis by the sides of the path will yield satisfactory crops. Blackberry and loganberry will thrive on arches, a rough support of poles or a fence.

The bush and cane fruits—gooseberry, currant and raspberry—are very profitable and well suited to allotments. November is the best month for planting. No time should be lost in preparing the land in good time by digging it about 2 ft. deep. It is necessary also to order the bushes so that they are delivered for planting in autumn.

First-rate sorts are: blackberries, *Bedford Giant* and *John Innes;* raspberries, *Norfolk Giant* and *Lloyd George;* black currants, *September Black* and *Davidson's* Eight; red currants, *Laxton's Perfection;* gooseberries, *Lancer* and *Whinham's Industry.*

Protecting the fruit from birds is important. A simple plan is to run a thread of stout black cotton from branch to branch all round the bush. The cotton being black, the birds do not easily see it

Fruit

and, alighting on a branch, their claws become entangled and they are so alarmed that they shun the spot for the future. The same method may be usefully applied to protect the young shoots of peas.

Another good method is to dust the bushes with a mixture of quicklime and soot immediately the leaves have fallen and several times afterwards in the winter. The birds will not then touch the buds.

Yet another plan is to place on the ground beneath each bush a shallow pan kept filled with water. If the birds have free access to water which they can drink and splash about in without danger, they will refrain from attacking the buds for their moisture. The same also applies to the ravages made by birds on ripe fruit.

Trees.—Under the several species general directions are given which gardeners can follow to satisfaction, but for fuller details of management, etc., books specially devoted to fruit growing will afford a wider range of specialist information.

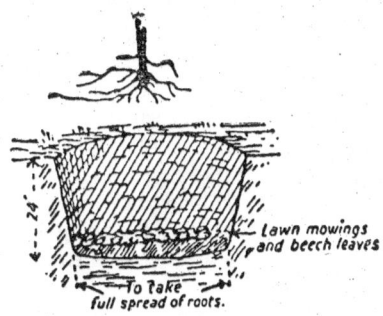

Planting Fruit Tree.

In general it may be said, where several trees are being put in it pays to dig the whole area two spits deep, rather than make separate places for each tree, but where only two or three are being put in, the accompanying planting diagram will guide, remembering that chalky soil must be replaced by good average soil, not heavily manured. Plant in October or not later than November; plant firmly, stake strongly before putting in the young tree, the tying being on the stake and where round trunk put webbing to save rub. Spread out roots and keep a good distance: standards, 20 ft.; half-standards, rather less; cordons, 30 in.

Fruit trees resist heat and drought more readily if, when planting, a little greater depth is given, and the hole filled with alternate layers of hedge clippings and soil, each of about 6 in., and the top soil well pressed in. A fortnight later add more soil to replenish that filtered down among the clippings.

It is contended as fully proved that best results are obtained by transplanting fruit trees at night. The earth about the roots should be disturbed as little as possible.

Grease-band fruit trees during September, also stakes.

Do not grow vegetables, particularly the brassicas, between fruit trees.

Fruit trees should be sprayed with nicotine or derris insecticide in May to reduce the plague of pests.

Remember that fruit trees are there for years of growth; therefore allow adequate room for a start, not less than 15 ft. between, each way.

Pruning.—On the matter of pruning see that entry, but some general notes may here be useful. In regard to the summer pruning of cordons: in July shorten each shoot to within say four to six leaves of its base to cause the sap to act on the remaining stipulary "eyes" or buds, so that they may plump up, and some may next year form fruiting buds, particularly the lower or basal ones, where the wood is more robust. After this summer pruning, the "eyes" at the tips will push forth fresh secondary growths in a further effort to extend the main side-shoots. Do not prune all of any one cordon at the same time; do it gradually over a space of ten days and thus prevent a setback in growth. Start with the well-developed shoots. Very soon those growths lagging behind will catch up, and these in turn may receive attention. Another time-hint is to do the pears before the apples.

When summer pruning, the leaders must not be done, but in the autumn when attending to the side shoots, the sappy growth may be cut and the length of each leader halved.

Autumn pruning may go ahead when the leaves of fruit trees have fallen. Those on walls need attention first. The general practice in pruning apple and pear trees is to shorten the side-shoots to within two or three buds of the base of the past summer's growth and to reduce the length of the leading shoots.

The pruning of fruit trees has the following general procedure: Nearly all fruit trees would bear heavier crops of better fruit if more branches were cut away, particularly from the middle of the trees, to let in more air and sunshine. The chief pruning of fruit trees is done between leaf fall and the bursting of the buds in spring. That is the time to inspect them to see which branches ought to be cut out. If the main branches are 12 in. apart all will be well. If they are not, any that seem ill-placed should be cut right out. Then prune on the following lines: the leading shoots which extend the main branches are cut back by one-third or even one-half if they are not vigorous, and the long side-shoots are pruned to within about three buds off the base. Shoots which are short and possess fruit buds need no pruning. It is easy to distinguish between blossom buds and leaf buds. The former are large, somewhat rounded and conspicuous; the latter small, pointed and pressed closely against the shoots. To improve set of next year's branches prune just above a bud that points outwards, for that helps to keep the middle of the tree free from useless and hindering branches. Apple, pear, plum and sweet cherry are each pruned in much the same way, but plum and cherry are most satisfactory when pruning is light.

To free fruit trees from gum, scrape it off and then wash with a mixture of horse-manure, clay and tar.

To remove moss from fruit trees, the branches should be washed with strong salt water or solution of lime. Burning the prunings of fruit trees and ornamental trees and shrubs is also a wise proceeding.

Summer Pruning of Fruits.—*Currants* (red and white): shorten side shoots to three leaves in mid-June. Do not touch leading shoots. *Pears:* pinch in mid-June instead of giving summer prune. Take out side-shoots to reduce number and pinch back to three or four leaves those that remain. Leave leaders alone. *Cherries* (sweet): shorten side-shoots to four leaves in mid-July. *Plums* (wall): late in July shorten side-shoots of main branches to four leaves. Keep a few young shoots. *Apples:* early varieties, mid to end of July; mid-season varieties, early August; lates, mid-August. All shortened to three leaves.

In tree fruit follow the pruning with a dressing of sulphate of ammonia.

In recent years the Lorette system has come into vogue for pruning fruit trees, which briefly consists of an intensive summer pruning to stimulate the more vigorous production and development of fruit buds. In April or May the leading or extension shoots are pruned, and later, sometime during June to August, according to district, type of fruit tree and particular varieties, the new wood, as it approaches a ripe condition, is hard pruned. The appropriate time is when the wood is of pencil thickness and just beyond half-ripe. It is contended that these operations (which are fully detailed in a book on the subject) direct the sap definitely to the development and strengthening of buds, thus considerably speeding up the production and maturing of fruit. See other general fruit-pruning hints under APPLES.

FUCHSIA. F.S.; 6 ft.; red and purple.

Given a well-drained, rich loam and due attention to watering, the bush fuchsias will flourish and flower freely in July to August. Once planted they will grow freely, though they require cutting down to the ground every year, but in some cases, where old established, it is only necessary to cut back to the main branches, especially in the South and near the sea where they will grow to upwards of 12 ft. A specially hardy variety is *Riccartonii; macrostemma* which is seen beside rural cottages, grows bushily, its country name being Lady's Ear-drops; *gracilis* is of slighter build and better suited for formal gardens. Fuchsias in winter often look quite dead, but will burst into bud in spring. It is quite easy to raise fuchsias from seed, which, if sown in January or February, will produce plants ready to bloom in July or August. Early sowings must be made in heat, and for the soil in which the seedlings are potted off a mixture of cow-dung is advised. Cuttings taken at joints after flowering will root in sand under glass.

A prevalent trouble is that buds fall off, which is due to careless watering. In very dry weather water daily; in overcast conditions twice a week is enough. If a pot plant, immerse in water once a week.

FUMIGATION OF SOIL. *See* SOIL.

FUMITORY. *See* CORYDALIS.

FUNKIA (Plantain Lily). H.; 1 ft.; lavender, white; July.

These make a good show in the front of the border, as the leaves are most attractive. Grow in light, sandy soil and for preference in a shady position. Increase by division and plant in autumn.

G

GAILLARDIA. H.A. (16 in.) and H.P. (3 ft.); red, brown and yellow; July–September.

The annual gaillardias revel in sunshine and a sandy loam for root run. Their dark crimson or yellowish flowers borne on stiff stems above the pointed, light-green foliage are distinctive. Sow in April to flower in July or August until November. Gaillardias are quite easy to raise from seed by sowing thinly in sandy soil. They dislike crowding whether as seedlings or fully grown.

The perennial gaillardias should be planted in March to produce a supply of large, daisy-like yellow and crimson flowers throughout the summer. A sandy loam suits them and a sunny position. The clumps should be lifted and divided every spring. Suitable for large borders.

GALANTHUS. *See* SNOWDROPS.

GALAX. H.P.; 6 in.; white; summer.

The variety *aphylla* has pretty foliage as well as pretty flowers and graces the rockery. It thrives in a moist situation, in peat mixed with grit and manure. Increase by division in autumn.

GALEGA. H.P.; 4 ft.; blue, white, lilac; July.

Any soil suits and they thrive in any part of the herbaceous border. Increase by division in autumn. The white variety is *alba;* the lilac *officinalis, hartlandii,* has variegated foliage and blue and white blossom.

GALTONIA. H.P.; bulb; 4 ft.; white; August.

The flowers are tubular and of drooping habit. Grow in clumps, planting 9 in. apart and 4 in. deep in friable soil, enriched yearly with leaf-mould and humus. Divide in March. The popular name is Cape Hyacinth; the variety *candicans* is known as the Spire Lily.

GARDEN ARRANGEMENT.

It is a good thing to study colour and height when arranging the flower borders so as to get harmonious grouping according to individual taste, with variation of height to break monotony of line. This is as effective as putting all the tallest at the back and height grading forward to dwarfs on the edge of the border. The time and duration of blooming is also a factor to be considered (*see* FLOWER-ING CALENDAR). As a rule it is more pleasing to mass together plants of the same kind and colour rather than dotting them about here and there, mixed with others, patchwork fashion. The diagram " Planning the Plot " under BEDDING OUT, can be studied with benefit.

Trees and Shrubs.—The position of trees and tall shrubs needs consideration, for if they overhang a neighbour's property he is entitled to cut to the boundary fence, if on request it is not done. Also it is well to note that on all but freehold property all trees become property of ground landlord unless a protecting clause is inserted in lease.

Legal Points.—A greenhouse must not be fixed to house with nails, but screws, as these latter are considered to make the erection portable, neither must it be set in ground in cement or on bricks and mortar, but only rest on a rubble or breeze foundation. An occupier, however, has liberty to gather any fruit from his trees which falls in a neighbour's garden, but is liable for trespass if he does damage in doing so.

Where the garden is not attached to the residence and is almost wholly devoted to the production of vegetables and root crops for home consumption it is legally an "allotment garden."

The tenant of an "allotment garden" who receives six months' notice to quit expiring outside the cropping season is not entitled to compensation, but if his notice expires on September 29th or October 11th, or between those dates, he may remove his crops within twenty-one days after the termination of his tenancy. Before the termination of his tenancy he may remove fruit trees or fruit bushes provided and planted by him, and any erection, fencing or other improvement erected or made at his expense, making good any injury caused by such removal.

The tenant of an "allotment garden" whose tenancy is terminated in the cropping season (after April 6th and before September 29th) or on whose allotment re-entry is made for building, etc., is entitled to compensation for crops growing on the land in the ordinary course of cultivation and for manure applied to the land.

It is worth noting that no rates can be levied on an allotment garden or a plot, not exceeding ¼ acre.

GARDEN BONFIRES.

To get a bonfire going is an art as the garden refuse is seldom dry. Get two bricks, invert a large flower-pot on the bricks to make a draught chimney, build the rubbish round, start the fire with paper and the draught created will do the rest.

GARDEN, YEAR'S WORK. *See* MONTH BY MONTH IN GARDEN AND ALLOTMENT.

GARDENIA. Hothouse; double white; summer.

Of less esteem nowadays either as a flowering plant or for the buttonhole, perhaps because of its strong and peculiar perfume. It is a greenhouse plant, grown in 6-inch pots in rich soil with some sand, potted very firmly and kept moist. In winter they need a temperature of 65°. Take cuttings in spring for striking under a bell cloche in warmth for renewing stock annually, then discarding old roots.

GARDENING.

Throughout this book the manifold activities of gardening, flowers or vegetables, will be found under their most appropriate headings. Thus, the first operation of breaking the ground is detailed under "Digging," fertilizers under F, the main divisions of flowers under F, the raising of annuals under A and so on. Directions for the growing and propagation of individual plants also appear in normal alphabetic order: thus Antirrhinum under A; Zinnia under Z; or in vegetables, Broccoli under B and Vegetable Marrow under V.

In this way the gardener will be able to discover all he wants to know about flower and vegetable gardening with the added satisfaction that the instruction is dependable and up to date.

GARLIC.

A kitchen herb, bulbous and having a pungency like, but stronger than, the onion. It is grown in the same way as shallots. The bulbs are called " cloves " and planted 1 ft. apart in late winter.

GARRYA. F.S.; 15 ft.; white; December–February.

A striking feature of any garden of large dimensions, for its racemes of white catkin style blossom 6 in. long foiled by an intense dark and glossy foliage forms a picture seen to best advantage when igiven plenty of space. As the flowers fade they form black berres in masses that continue its picturesqueness. They prefer shelter from cold winds and make good porch or wall shrubs. A good ordinary soil suits them; they do not require a moist situation, and treated thus, are hardy. Do not transplant. Take cuttings in late summer and strike in a frame. They are unisexual, and cuttings from the male shrub give the handsomest result. The best varieties are *macrophylla* (large leaf), *elliptica* and *Fremonti*.

GAURA. H.P.; 2 ft.; white sprays; August.

Better grown as an annual, sown in the open in average soil in spring. The variety *lindheimeri* has rose and white flowers, grows to 3 ft. and prefers a place in the sun.

GAZANIA. H.H.P.; 6 in.; orange; summer.

An attractive border plant with conspicuous flowers ringed with black spots. They should be put in a sunny position in light soil.

Cuttings may be taken in August and struck in sand under a cloche or in the frame. The most satisfactory variety is *splendens*, which likes chalky soil.

GENISTA. F.S.; varying height; yellow: June.

Easy to grow from seed and flourishes in poor, dry soil preferably sandy, similarly to broom, to which it is allied. They like the sun. *Aetnensis* is slender and grows to 14 ft., as also does the straggly *cinera*. For rock gardens *pilosa* and *sagittalis* are suitable, and for the border *tinctoria* (2 ft.) and *tinctoria floreplena* (18 in.). The only pruning needed is when young to create bushiness. Take cuttings in summer to strike in frame and grow on in pots till big enough to pot out during autumn as they do not take kindly to transplanting.

GENTIAN. H.P.; 6 in.; blue, white; spring onwards.

For the Alpine and rock garden the beautiful little gentians seem almost indispensable, and though the dwarf kinds which are those most suitable for the rock garden and edging are less easily grown than the larger sort, they need but a little care to establish them in healthy tufts. They must not be overshadowed by taller plants; fresh air and sunlight are essential to their welfare and they must be very firmly planted. The Vernal Gentian likes a soil of sandy loam but cannot endure much drought, and will benefit therefore, by a few pieces of broken limestone being so placed as to retard evaporation. The Bavarian Gentian with its flowers of iridescent blue is another lovely example. It demands a moist, peaty soil—as bog-like as possible. Gentians may be raised from seed by sowing in pans in spring and planting out. The variety *asclepiadea*, blue and white, is 1 ft.; *lutea*, yellow, is 2 ft., and some which flower in August are *purdonii* and *lagodechiana*.

In early spring growing gentians are nervous of wind; to counteract, fill all round patch with leaf-mould and crushed egg-shell grit, well worked in and firmed, leaving shoots only visible. They will respond readily and be good specimens by May.

GERANIUM. H.P.; 24 in.; red, white; summer.

Sow under glass in March or August, or in the open in April. Increase by cuttings of matured side-shoots struck in August in a frame. They seldom withstand frost unless protected. Plant well apart in light, well-drained sandy soil in the full sunshine and water freely. The old plants can be lifted and stored for winter. For the Zonal geraniums *see* PELARGONIUM.

GERBERA. H.P.; 18 in.; scarlet; July.

Though hardy, it responds better to a warm outdoor situation, and is at its best in a greenhouse, where it will be in flower for the whole season. Scarlet daisy-like flowers come from *Jamesonii*, and hybrid varieties give orange and intermediate shades. Plant in a sunny south border in March in well-drained loam and peat. Protect plants in winter, or lift carefully and take into greenhouse. Raise from seed in moist sand and in warmth under glass in spring, or cuttings in autumn will root freely in the greenhouse.

GESNERA. P.; warm house; 1 ft.; scarlet and white; purple spotted.

Grow from tubers started in heat in loam with some good beech leaf-mould, sand and dry cow-dung, giving plenty of moisture till in flower, then ease off. Put into 6-inch pots. They flower profusely. *Cardinalis* is red, *maculata* purple and *refulgens* violet, all having white mixed with the colour and growing on long stems.

GEUM. H.P.; varies 6 in. to 2 ft.; orange, yellow, scarlet; June.

The flower spikes rise well above the spreading foliage. They are not particular as to soil or situation. *Mrs. Bradshaw*, crimson, is still a favourite, as is *Lady Stratheden*, a yellow. Newer varieties are *rossii*, yellow; *boresi*, scarlet, and *chiloense*, yellow and scarlet, which rises to 2 ft. Sow seed in cool place in summer for next year's flowering, or in spring in frame for flowering same year. Also increased by division.

GILIA. H.H.A.; 1 ft.; purple, black and white tricolour; August.

Often grown as biennials and started from seed under glass in winter for planting out in June. The annuals are *californica*, pink, 24 in.; *liniflora*, white, 1 ft., and *capilata*, mauve, 15 in. The variety *coronopifolia* is 1 ft., 30 in. rose and summer flowering. The species is allied to Fenzlia.

GILLENIA. H.P.; 2 ft.; red and white; June, July.

Ordinary soil is suitable and *trifoliata* is the best variety. It is increased by division.

GLADIOLUS. H.P.; 30 in.; various colours; July–September.

A light, friable loam, enriched with well-rotted manure, is best, and the situation should be fully open to the sun but sheltered from wind. Plant in March and April, as the corms then planted produce flowers in August and September. Stake well. But if early flowering kinds are desired, set in November, and protect from frost by suitable litter. Take up corms in October or November, and store in frost-proof place till re-planting time in spring. It is a good plan to decide

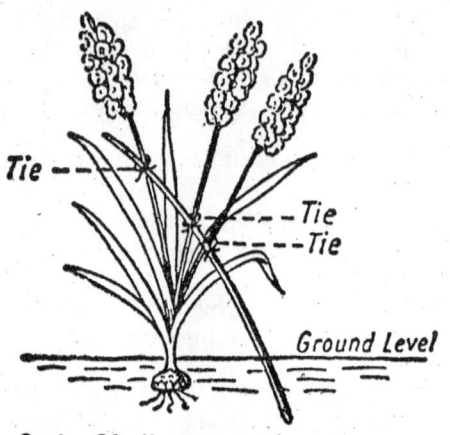

Stake Gladioli to avoid roots.

in the autumn where the plants will go, and give a spit-deep manuring in advance. Plant 3 in. deep and 15 in. apart. The corms are liable to wilt disease; any attacked are useless, and the rest should be sprayed with a 2 per cent. solution of formalin prior to planting. Increase by keeping the young off-set corms, storing in paper bags and starting in boxes or pots in spring.

GLAUCIUM (Horned Poppy). H.B.; 18 in.; red and white; summer.

Will flourish on a poor soil. It is of the poppy family, sown about May to provide vigorous plants for the following year. Handsome foliage of silvery white. *Luteum* has large orange-red flowers, while another variety, *Asia Minor*, bears flowers of bright scarlet.

GLOBE THISTLE. *See* **ECHINOPS.**

GLOBULARIA. Greenhouse shrub; trailing; blue; summer.

The shrub is *cordifolia*, which has a white as well as a blue variety, and grows best in sandy loam. Increase by autumn division. The family includes a herb species, increased by cuttings in spring and appropriate for display in the rockery.

GLORIOSA. Hothouse; twining habit; orange, yellow and red; summer.

The flowers are curious as well as attractive, and a good soil mixture of loam, peat and sand is best, taking note only rarely to disturb plants and then in January. Water well in hot weather. Increased by off-sets.

GLOXINIA. P.; 1 ft.; violet; claret blotch on white; July-August.

These lovely plants though chiefly for the greenhouse may be used in bedding for summer and autumn flowering, but only in warm situation. They can be brought into bloom at practically any season in heat. Give a rich fibrous loam, peat and silver sand compost, and be most careful to leave the root ball undisturbed. Once the plants are in flower do not give liquid manure but in the early budding state it is helpful. Gloxinias are of compact growth, the handsome, large flowers, of many brilliant colours, growing singly on thin stems. Increase by division, or more certainly, from seed sown in pans in sand in heat, any time.

GODETIA. H.A.; 30 in.; pink, white, mauve, etc.; July onward.

There are two distinctive types, the bushy and the tall, both of which flower freely throughout the summer. Sown mid-March. The bushy types are about 1 ft. high, the tall from 18 in. to more than 2 ft. The latter should be staked. May be sown in pans or where they are to bloom; transplant with 6-8 in. each way. The cone-shaped flowers have generally dark blotches of colour at the hearts, and some are shades of pink, red, mauve or lavender. They do not thrive in the shade, but otherwise have no preferences of position or soil. A September sowing in frame will give flowers in May.

GOLDEN ROD (Solidago Virgaurea). H.P.; 5 ft.; yellow; late summer.

A useful plant for hiding sheds, being tall and having profuse feathery yellow blossom, etc. It is propagated by root division; it flowers in the autumn and will grow in any kind of soil. It is distinctive in the herbaceous border, but needs keeping in hand.

GOOSEBERRIES.

Plant in autumn 5 ft. apart in deeply-dug, heavily-manured soil. Give a manure mulch in spring, after pruning, and keep roots moist. Every third year the soil and surface should have a thorough manuring, either with rich compost or basic slag (4 oz. to sq. yd.). In pruning leave last season's growth at full length, though it may be shortened if it extends beyond the space at command. Thin annually by cutting out old limbs which have any sign of decay and any young wood which obstructs light and air, cutting back this young wood to within a few buds from the stem. Any suckers which may appear should be carefully eradicated from the very base and not merely cut back to the surface of the ground. The digging of the ground between gooseberry bushes should never be done with the spade, a gentle loosening of the earth with a fork to the depth of 6 or 8 in. and an occasional use of the Dutch hoe to keep down the weeds is quite sufficient. Good sorts are: white, *Langley Gage;* yellow, *Early Kent* or *Yellow Champagne;* green, *Green Hedgehog;* red, *Whinham's Industry.*

Where space is limited, gooseberries can be grown successfully as cordons, inserting 15-inch cuttings in October; the buds should be removed for 5 in. to which length insert them and firm in, 6 in. apart. When growth starts train leading shoot to a stake and pinch out side-shoots. Put into permanent position the next autumn.

GORDONIA. H.P.; F.S.; white, late summer.

Rather difficult to start, but once established in loam, leaf-mould and sand, give fine blooms. Plant in spring in sheltered position and increase by layering in sand, not disturbed for six months. A 10-foot variety, with fragrant blooms continuing till autumn, is *lasianthus*, and one which shows golden stamens is *pubescena*, which grows to 8 ft.

GORSE. F.S.; 4 ft.

Hardly needs description; it is the *Ulex Europoeus*, has profuse golden blossom from April to June, and continues to flower till the autumn. Its foliage is spiky and evergreen. Grow from seed in position in poor but dry soil in as much sun as possible.

GOURD. H.A.; climber.

Train over arch or pergola. Fruit and pods distinctively ornamental. Sow in May in a rich soil, and warm position; preferably start seed in heat unless in warm southern district.

GRAFTING.

An interesting process mainly for the purpose of putting new life, as it were, into old fruit trees, by inserting a tongue-like wedge (*see* diagrams). The old tree, the "stock," is cut down to a couple of feet from the ground; into the side at the top a cut is made that is wedge-shaped, with the point downwards; the incision cuts through the bark, wedge-like at top and tapering to a point as it goes downward. The inserted tongue is called the "scion," and this is taken from a robust tree or one of better quality, to achieve the aim of rejuvenation. These scions should be buried in sand in a shady place for a week to keep them backward till wanted. The scion should be taken from a sturdy young branch of last year's growth, contain two or three healthy dormant buds, be not less than 6 in. long and of little-finger thickness. Taper the lower end exactly to fit the

Two wedge cuts in stock, each tapering

Side View Front View
Scion, lower part is tapered to fit into stock

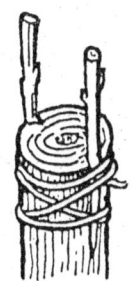
Grafts strongly bound in

cut in the stock, then insert it so that it presses firmly everywhere against the bark. This will leave that part of the scion not tapered sticking up beyond the stump or stock. It is usual to make two grafts, one on each side of the stock. After grafting, bind all round with raffia, and cover the whole with grafting wax so as to facilitate the wedding of stock and scion by excluding the air. A recommended grafting wax can be made in the following way: Take 4 parts of pitch and resin, 2 parts beeswax and 1 part tallow; melt and mix the ingredients together and use when just warm.

GRAPES.

A vine should be about 6–8 ft. long when purchased, and put in during the autumn, after which cut down to a bud which gets full light. This cannot be arbitrarily fixed as it depends on the size and situation of the greenhouse, for the best chance of a crop of satisfying grapes is by growing under glass, a lean-to for preference. In planting, tread down the soil very firmly, and if more than one vine is put in leave 5 ft. between each, and put them in at the front of the lean-to, so that they can be trained upward to the wall side of the top glass. Prepare a bed for the roots by digging at least 3 ft. deep, putting in, over a layer of broken brick for drainage, decayed turves almost to the surface, in which lime and bone-meal are mixed, and then filled up with good average soil, but take care the drainage is good. Cut back first year's growth to a little more than half its length so as

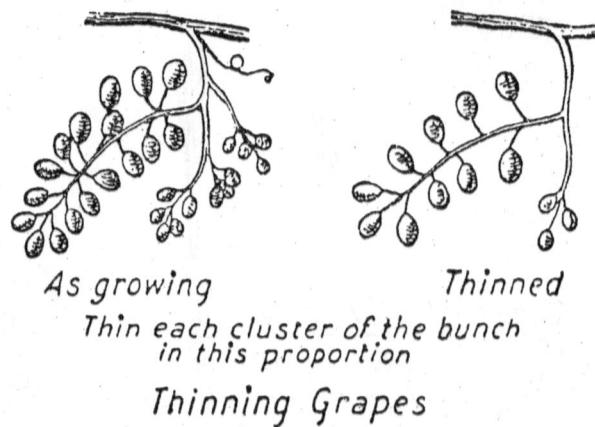

As growing   Thinned
Thin each cluster of the bunch in this proportion

Thinning Grapes

to increase the girth and stability of the main stem. This should be done in autumn and will result in really sturdy top growth during the second year. Prune off side-shoots up to the basal buds; from these the third year's lateral shoots will burst. It is really only in the third year that fruits form, though some immature bunches may form during the second year and which are best removed before taking strength from the young vine. Three-year-old vines can be purchased for fruiting first year of planting. The third-year crop will be from laterals from the main rod, and burst about 1 ft. from each other. Do not let the laterals run wild; when the bunch has formed pinch off lateral at a couple of leaves beyond, and after gathering, cut lateral back to a bit more than half in the autumn. The question of heat depends on kinds and when bunches are wanted; the earlier, the greater temperature advisable; for ripening in August the heat of the sun will materially help. During the time the fruit is forming an average temperature of 70° is needed. Do not neglect airing; both ventilation and watering are factors in success; keep the air fresh, keep it moist and syringe at intervals. Open the ventilators during hot spells, but don't forget to close them at the cool end of the day. When the bunches form, relentless thinning is necessary. If inexperienced get someone who knows to show how it's done, but if you do it yourself it will be satisfactory if the reduced bunch of young grapes is thinned to extent of diagram. Use long-pointed scissors for snipping and steady the bunch with a forked stick. If scalding and scorching shows, pay more attention to ventilation. If red spider appears it is because the air is too dry—keep it moist and the trouble will not arise. For mealy bug, paint with methylated spirit.

Many growers, where space allows, have the root outside and bring it into the house by removing a brick from the side. This allows for more effective manuring and secures the benefit of weathering. The manured root area is kept free of other growth. To minimize the risk of attacks of mealy bug, some gardeners adopt the long and tedious operation for vines under glass, of carefully paring off all the outer husk growth from the whole of the branches, doing so in January. It has to be done gently and with care not to cut into the under layer of bark, and then a paint, made of clay moistened to coating consistency and some Gishurst compound mixed in, is applied.

GRAPE HYACINTH. *See* MUSCARI.

GRASS.

Good grass seed should contain qualities which are at their best during different parts of the year and so secure a continuity of rich grass. A recommended mixture for lawns on light soil is one containing Agrostis, Crested Dogstail, Fescues and Goa which are all dwarf varieties. If the ground is on or approaching the heavy side an addition of rye grass should be made, while for tennis courts the seed of rye grass is supposed to prevent the ball from skidding in play.

A lawn-keeper of long experience destroys dandelion, plantain and other strong weeds by the use of ordinary creosote such as is applied to fences and stakes. For young weeds of this character the tops are pulled off and a drop of creosote tipped on the root. For older weeds, dig out the tops, thrust down well into the root a spike—an old screw-driver for instance—and in the hole, re-thrust the screw-driver three times after dipping it each time in creosote: a tedious process, but always effectual as it kills the root.

A little nitrate of soda dissolved in water and sprinkled over the surface occasionally will be found of great assistance in keeping grass green. *See also* LAWNS; and for treatment of grass verges *see* EDGES.

GREEN FLY. *See* APHIS.

GREENGAGE.

The culture and treatment follows that of plums, *which see*.

GREENHOUSES.

There are three: the cold house; the warm house; the hothouse. The first is a glorified frame so far as cultural possibilities are concerned, though the range is greater, and in coldest weather frost can be kept at bay by slight heat, say 50°, such as a motor radiator lamp, which burns very slowly but maintains a regular heating capacity. The warm house is one which can be heated all the year round by pipes from one or other heating apparatus, of which there are various types using differing heating mediums. The temperature should never fall below 60°. The hothouse has air always in a state of warm or hot moisture, varying in degree according to what is grown.

In construction each follows the same method, a foundation, brick or wooden, preferably cedar, walls of say one-third the height of the whole surmounted by four glazed sides, with windows mostly opening horizontally, and an apex glazed top, also with ventilation. The staging runs along each side and the back and is slatted, not solid boarding. The cold and warm greenhouse can also be of the lean-to type, which may be described roughly as half a greenhouse, because it is built against a wall or the side of the dwelling-house, but otherwise follows the same principles of construction. Latterly, iron-framed greenhouses have come into use.

Appropriate plants for each class of greenhouse are given throughout this book, but many other special classes are grown, either in flowers, while for starting plants, either vegetable or floral, the cold or warm greenhouse provides scope for intensive cultivation on lines given under "Intensive Culture" and as recommended for numerous individual plants.

Scrupulous cleanliness must be the rule to prevent invasion of insects, fungi, etc., and precautions must always be taken against damping-off, *which see*. The interior and staging should be lime-washed annually and means provided by white-spraying the glass or by other protection to prevent the sun making the interior air too hot.

The use of sterilized soil is recommended, especially for the seed boxes; for the method *see* SEED.

In the summer the greenhouse, if not bare, is sometimes lacking in brightness. Sown early, say in February in box and transferred to pots in due time, a very few seeds of this or that annual remedies the drabness by a pleasing and varied summer display at little cost or trouble. The Swan River daisy (*brachycome*), kingfisher daisy (*felicia*), rhodanthe, nemesia and petunia are some of the most suitable kinds to raise from seeds in February in slightly-heated greenhouse or in March if no artificial warmth is available.

During the winter also there is a break in brightness, especially where heating facilities are not readily obtainable or it is difficult to keep heat going. Here, too, even an unheated greenhouse can be kept bright with flowers in winter and early spring.

Reliance must be placed chiefly on hardy plants, but a few others may be included in the collection, for instance, the perpetual-flowering carnation, primula malacoides, primula stellata and Indian azalea.

Certain hardy plants may be lifted from the garden in November or December and potted for the cold greenhouse—wallflower, polyanthus, pansy, viola, violet, primrose, forget-me-not, and even snowdrop and other early bulbs. Keeping the ventilators closed for a few days will help the plants to become established, but the greenhouse ought to be ventilated freely in mild weather.

Owners of frost-proof greenhouses should sow seeds of a quick-growing cabbage in February for early planting out. They will be ready to cut in late summer and thus help to maintain an almost unbroken supply of this vegetable.

A supply of winter salads is obtained by taking up and potting seedling lettuces and placing them in the cold greenhouse.

Another way of making use of an unheated greenhouse in winter is to sow seeds of some of the hardy annuals, *e.g.* larkspur, love-in-a-mist, godetia, annual chrysanthemum and clarkia. The seeds are sown on a bed of soil, the seedlings being planted out of doors in spring.

GREEN MANURING. *See* MANURING.

GREVILLEA. F.S.; 6 ft.; red, yellow; June.

The red variety is *rosmarinifolia* and in appearance is rather like rosemary, while the yellow variety, *juniperina*, is more like a juniper. The flowers are in clusters and stand variations in climate, though in winter they need some protection. A foliage variety, *robusta*, the *Australian Oak*, is more suited for the greenhouse. Half and half loam and peat, with some sand, suits all varieties.

GROWTH HORMONES. *See* CUTTINGS and HORTOMONE.

GUELDER ROSE. *See* VIBURNUM.

GYPSOPHILA. H.A.; 18 in.; white, rose; July.

The annual type is *elegans* and its flowers are single or double. The delicate foliage is a general favourite for use in table decorations, or as foliage to mix with other cut flowers. The perennial variety is *paniculata*, much more bushy, with neater blossom in great profusion, and has a tuberous root. Dwarf varieties are: *sundermannii* (pink), *cerastioides* (white). An average soil suits all varieties, a little chalk being an advantage.

H

HABERLEA. H.P.; 6 in.; lilac, white; spring.

A rockery plant preferring the shade and to be grown in peat mixture. The lilac variety is *rhodopensis;* and the white, *virginalis*. They look best in a crevice, and welcome some protection in winter.

HAEMANTHUS. Bulb; 1 ft.; red; May and August.

A warm-house subject which should be very firmly potted in sand, loam and peat in equal proportions. Keep well drained, but give copious water in hot weather and none in winter, giving a top-dressing of fresh soil, taking away an inch of the old, every spring. Increase by offsets.

HALESIA. F.S.; 10 ft.; white; July.

A quite hardy, deciduous shrub, the flowers of which droop, which accounts for its rural name Snowdrop Tree and in other parts Silver Bell. Plant in spring in well-drained loamy soil in sheltered position, and only prune to keep neat. Take root cuttings, struck in frame in spring.

HAMAMELIS. See WITCH HAZEL.

HAREBELL. See CAMPANULA.

HARICOT BEANS. See BEANS.

HAWKSWEED. See HIERACIUM.

HEATHER. See ERICA.

HEBENSTREITIA COSMOSA. H.A.; 18 in.; white; fragrant; July.

The flowers are on spikes and have orange spots. Sow in mid-April in average soil and thin out.

HEDGES.

Used as windscreens in suburban and rural gardens, largely privet, whitethorn, laurel, etc. In America a low hedge takes the place of the English fence or wall, much to the communal satisfaction of garden lovers.

Various types used for hedges require individual treatment, but all should be trimmed pyramidically so that the lower growth gets light, air and moisture and does not become unsightly near the ground. All, too, benefit by clipping periodically, not only for the fashion of keeping a close and even appearance, but seasonally in May and September for the good of next year's robustness. There are two dozen species in popular use; and each have points of preference according to taste, district and purpose.

Where the roots of privet and other hedge shrubs invade the border and interfere with the growth of flowers, a simple way of root pruning is to strike the spade vertically and sharply into the ground, so severing the roots. Done 6 or 9 in. from the stem, it will not injure the hedge.

HEELING IN.

May be described as a half-way house to planting. It is done where it is inconvenient immediately to plant such as shrubs, fruit and rose-bushes, standards, herbaceous perennials or trees received from nurserymen. A shallow trench is dug, sufficient to take the roots, and the plants are laid in on the slant with the roots covered. They can so remain with safety till removed to permanent quarters. The practice is also adopted to complete the ripening of bulbs or onions which have to be lifted before the " grass " has fully withered in order that the ground they occupied can be put more quickly into successional cultivation.

HELENIUM. H.P.; 2 ft.; yellow, brown; July.

Hybrid varieties are attractive and they have a lengthier flowering season, the flowers, borne on stems standing well above the foliage, being in good supply from July onwards. They prefer sunny positions but thrive in any good soil. The root clumps do not increase very rapidly, and should be planted by mid-March to bloom the same year. Divide occasionally.

HELIANTHEMUM (Sun Rose). H.A.; dwarf; various; June.

Bright flowers in many colours make this rockery plant a favourite. It likes the sun and a mixture of sand in light soil. Increase by cuttings in a frame or by seed. *See also* ROCK CISTUS.

HELIANTHUS (Sunflower). H.A. and P.; 3-8 ft.; yellow; autumn.

The sunflower may be divided into two classes—the perennial (sometimes called *Harpalium*) and the annual, both quite hardy. The perennials are of such vigorous growth and increase so rapidly that they should not be introduced into a small garden without consideration, but in the wild garden and in shrubberies they are especially valuable because they flower in late autumn. *Decapetalus*, a bushy plant some 4 or 5 ft. high, with abundance of rich yellow flowers, *giganteus*, often attaining a height of 10 ft. and bearing large flowers of deep yellow 2 or 3 in. in diameter, and *rigidus*, one of the best-known and flowering very freely, are all good examples. Of the annual sunflowers there are many varieties, averaging 4 ft. in height and liking moist soil, including an outstanding species, the *Red*, the petals of which are a deep brownish crimson; *soleil d'or* has double blooms; *maximus* has large flowers; *cucumerifolius* has black centres. Sow seed of any variety about Easter and increase perennials by division, being ruthless in discarding old clumps.

HELICHRYSUM. H.A.; 3 ft.; white, red, yellow, pink, cream; August.

For cultural directions *see* EVERLASTINGS.

HELIOPHILA. H.H.A.; 18 in.; blue; summer.

An interesting border plant in which the blues range from azure to purple, with a white heart. Start under cloche and give a warm place in border in average soil.

HELIOTROPIUM (Heliotrope or Cherry Pie). H.H.P.; 18 in.; blue; summer.

Often more wisely treated as an annual, as by sowing in heat early in March the seedlings will be ready for planting out at the end of May. They need a good dry soil, and by their delightful fragrance and delicate tints of colour they are rightly highly esteemed. Many new varieties have been introduced from time to time, such as *Roi des Noirs*, a very dark shade; *Anna Turrel*, a beautiful light kind; and the *White Lady*, pure white; while the old fashioned *peruvianum* still holds its own. It makes a good greenhouse pot plant.

HELLEBORUS (Christmas and Lenten Roses). H.P.; 3 ft.; white, colour spotted; winter.

Of much value in the garden, as it flowers in the open when little else is in bloom. The variety *niger* has for its bloom the well-known flower, Christmas Rose, beautiful in its waxy-white and delicate blush tint; but we now have other varieties with blossoms of dark purple and ruby red, such as *colchicus* and *abchasicus*, and with foliage of marked beauty. The variety *orientalis* is the Lenten Rose. All kinds are content with ordinary soil but will do better in well-manured fibrous loam mixed with coarse sand, for stagnant moisture is not good for them. Propagation may be made by division, July being the best time, when the plants are in full vigour; and they may also be raised from seed sown under glass, the seedlings being pricked out into a shady border of rich soil as soon as they are large enough to bear moving. In the following year they may be transplanted to their permanent quarters, and by the third year they should bloom. The white or false hellebore is veratrium (*which see*).

HEMEROCALLIS (Day Lily). H.P.; 30 in.; various; June–September.

Although in flower for the long period indicated, each blossom lasts only a day, but during its life it has a delicate perfume, and as new blooms continually form, six or more on a spike, the lily is well worth a place in the border. Plant a foot apart in autumn in a sunny position in good average soil and increase from offsets. The colours of respective varieties are: *kwanso* (bronze); *flava* (lemon); *fulva* (orange); *aurantiaca* (orange). Among its hybrids are: Sir Michael Foster, Gold Dust, Apricots—all good specimens.

HEPATICA. H.P.; 4 in.; blue, white; winter.

A free-flowering rockery plant; also effective if planted under trees and left to spread. As is obvious, it thrives in shade and is not difficult to raise in any soil. It is best left undisturbed; therefore increase by seed rather than division. The double white is beautiful.

HERBACEOUS BORDER.

A good wide strip is recommended; if ground can be allocated, 10 ft. enables a bold display and gives scope for artistic grouping. (*See* diagram "Planning the Plot" under BEDDING OUT.) The border is called herbaceous because it should be occupied by plants which lose their leaves in winter; which are robustly perennial and which are profuse in flowering, such as Michaelmas daisies, golden rod, delphiniums, pentstemon, helianthus and a great number more as described under their own names. The greater number are increased by division, which should be done every year, taking the young shoots from the outer circumference. It hardly needs to be advised that the taller plants should be at the back of the border and height graded downwards to the front, but it is effective to break the height line by an occasional tall specimen among those of lesser height. These outstanding taller plants, not having the wind-break of surroundings of equal height, must be well staked, but the support can be almost invisible by using pea-sticks as here illustrated. It will be observed that the upper part is free because the spread of the pea-stick gives sufficient support, while not obtruding upon the sight. The same

Staking Herbaceous plants with Pea Sticks.

--- Pea stick

method for staking can be recommended for general use. Due forethought as to season of flowering and harmony of colour schemes will have its reward, and it is well to bear in mind that three or four of the same kind and colour grouped together is better than scattering single plants here and there along the border. A hint given by an experienced amateur is that in tall plants which throw out blossom at sides as well as tops of stems, the tops of their front growth can be shortened so as to have " floral pillars " instead of a lot of bare stem.

HERBS.

Culinary.—There is sufficient variety in the herb family to provide seasonings to suit all tastes. The following are the principal sorts, and a corner in the garden should be reserved for their culture. All can be treated as perennials, and a root to start with, planted in April, will soon give good clumps from which to draw supplies. Sweet marjoram, chervil, parsley and fennel are best treated as annuals and grown from seed. Tansy, rue, sage and rosemary do best from slips; thyme, balm and basil by root division. Sow basil, fennel and dill in May; other herbs in March. The leaved herbs can have their leaves picked and dried and stored for winter use and, of course, can always be used freshly plucked from spring till late autumn. The list includes mint, basil, chervil, parsley, thyme, fennel, marjoram, sage, chives, rosemary, rue, savory, tarragon, horse-radish, sorrel, balm.

Medicinal.—Unlike our grandparents, we tend to ignore the medicinal value of the many wild herbs of the countryside, as we do numerous familiar cultivated herbs. The list is extensive, but some of them, with their uses, may be given. A little observation and inquiry of countryfolk will soon familiarize one with these healing herbs of the woods and hedgerows, sufficient to gather them with intelligent recognition. In the main the leaves, flowers and roots are dried in the sun after thorough cleansing and powdered or ground for use. The usual way to prepare is by simmering a handful in a quart of cold water for about one hour and taking the resulting liquid. The letters in brackets in the following list indicate whether root, leaves or flowers are the effective parts. Coltsfoot (1. for colds), dandelion (r.l. for blood conditions and liver and kidneys), gentian (r. general tonic), marigold (f. induces perspiration), burdock (r. skin troubles and kidney complaints), bryony (r. coughs and colds), blackberry (l. diarrhoea), catmint (l. induces perspiration), marshmallow

(r. coughs), camomile (f. neuralgia), watercress (l. blood purifier), raspberry (l. tonic and ease for dysentery), celery (seed, rheumatics), plantain (rub leaves on stings), thyme (l. flatulence), yarrow (l. reduces temperature), elder (f. sore throat and inflammation) and many more.

Storage.—Herbs should be gathered on a dry day and just before they flower. Cut off the roots and wash if necessary. Dry either in a slow oven or in the sun till crisp but not brown. Pick off the leaves and rub to fineness between the hands or pass through a coarse sieve. Store in a well-corked bottle for use.

HESPERIS (Rocket). H.P.; 18 in.; purple, white; June–July.

This old garden favourite has sweet-scented spikes of purple or white flowers. It blooms freely, but to bring it to perfection it needs a rich, moist soil, and even then is the better for yearly division and transplanting into fresh ground. Seeds should be sown in spring in a sunny situation and the seedlings transplanted in due course. The variety *matronalis* is the Dame's Violet with purple flowers and a grateful fragrance; it is at its best where chalk is worked into the soil or is present. A double white variety is known as the Scotch Rocket, and a biennial variety, night scented, is *tristis* which, however, is variable in colour.

HEUCHERA (Alum Root). H.P.; 18 in.; deep red, white, pink; May–June.

Start from seed and thereafter increase by division. Grow in good, light soil in sunny position. The foliage is dwarf, the flowers rising on tall spikes in the same way as London Pride. The coral-red variety is *sanguinea* and this is most popular.

HIBISCUS. F.S.; 4–6 ft.; various colours; August–October.

A compact free-flowering variety is *syriacus*, its blossoming being blue, white or pink. They have no fads, but need planting in a loamy soil, well drained and in a warm situation. Give plenty of space. The variety *trionum* is an annual, 18 in., yellow flowers having claret centres, blooming in August.

HIERACIUM (Hawkweed). H.A.; 18 in.; white, yellow, pink; July onwards.

It grows well in ordinary soil and can be increased by division though an annual sowing gives best results. A variety only 1 ft. in height is *villosum*, while *auranticum*, 18 in., is orange.

HOEING.

The hoe is not used so often as it should be in keeping plots in good condition. Its value is to keep the soil from cracking and getting hard and so delaying growth. The Dutch hoe is easily thrust through the surface at a slight angle and so keeps the tilth loose for air and moisture to benefit roots. It is also invaluable for keeping down small weeds which gather closely round plants. The draw hoe has its blade at right angles and, as its name implies, has its use in

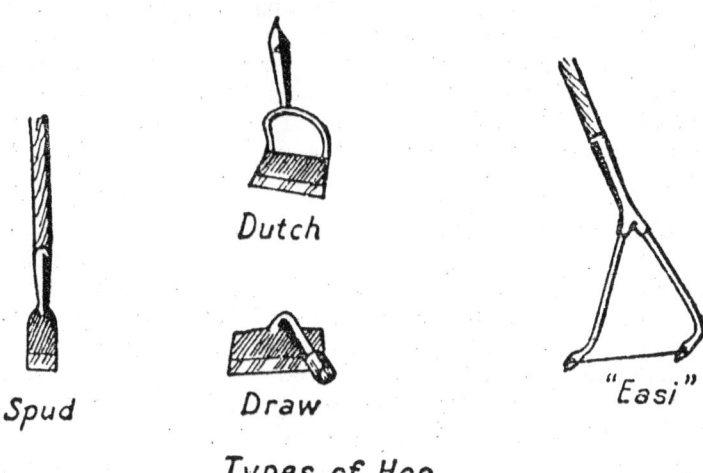

Types of Hoe

keeping soil level, breaking lumps, and drawing soil round roots where rain or wind have loosened. After digging and in preparing ground for sowing, some prefer it to the rake. A novel hoe more useful for weeding near roots than the Dutch hoe can be made by fixing a fern trowel on a long handle. The spud is a miniature thrust hoe about 2 in. wide and usually fixed on a walking-stick. The modern form of the Dutch hoe, instead of the usual blade, has a high-tensile steel wire stretched taut between the prongs of a spring steel fork. It allows a continuous draw hoe action as well as to and fro; slices off weeds below the surface, and in loosening the tilth does not heap it.

HOLLY. H.P.; red berries; winter.

Propagation is by cuttings of half-matured wood struck in August in a cold frame or by layers in summer. Plant in May or September and prune in April. Growth is very slow. When planting remember it loves chalk, and if the soil is not of that character a few lumps dropped round the hole will give a flourishing bush especially if the bottom soil is beaten hard before filling up.

HOLLYHOCK. H.P.; 8 ft.; various colours and doubles; July.

Its bold and stately growth renders hollyhock suitable for backgrounds, where large effects are required. Its main requirements are deeply trenched soil, abundant manure and frequent watering. Always stake stems. Sow seed in rich ground in open—June—and add some potting soil for first roots to feed on; these can be planted in October, choosing a dry day to establish during winter, if given some protection from frost. If sown in heat in January they will flower in the autumn of the same year on being planted in open in June.

HONESTY. *See* LUNARIA.

HONEYSUCKLE. H.P.; climber; cream and rose; early summer.

The honeysuckle is useful as a climber having, in addition to its fragrant blossom, the advantage of leafing early. It thrives best in a deep, light, loamy soil. The bush varieties may be increased from rooted suckers, cuttings (which take a year) or layers (in autumn), as well as by seed. Plant in November.

HORMINUM. H.P.; 10 in.; blue; June onwards.

Grow in sunny border and dry position in average soil. It is rather bushy and suits the rockery. Divide in spring.

HORTOMONE.

A new chemical solution by dipping cuttings into which it is claimed rooting can be made almost a hundred per cent. certain. A body, the National Plant Hormone Committee, has much information available to inquirers. The material is obtainable under various trade names. For a description of these "growth hormones," as they are called, *see* CUTTINGS.

HOTBED.

Where there is no greenhouse, seedlings can be raised much earlier on a protected hotbed than in the open ground, and so plants are a week or two ahead of those from seed sown in the open.

Sow the seed on the surface soil of the hotbed, give protection from frost, give air on warm days, and when in fourth leaf harden for transplanting to cold frame, or if late spring, to the open ground.

To make a hotbed, dig out a square 6 ft. each way (or such size as will suit individual requirement) to a depth of 3 ft. Make the bottom firm, lay on stable manure, out of which the first fierce heat has gone, till level with the ground, then surround with a wooden frame, and let settle for a day or so. Then put a layer of leaves or grass cuttings and top the lot with fine earth to form seed-bed, press

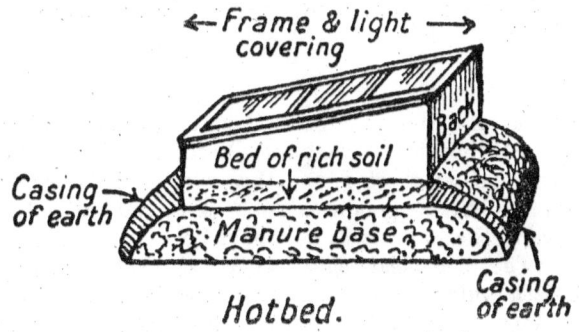

Hotbed.

down and level off to 6 in. below the top of wooden frame, cover with the glass top of a cold frame. In this the seed will grow quickly, especially half-hardy varieties. If an old window-frame, still glazed, is available, the whole thing could be made to adjust to it in size.

When all the early seedlings required have been raised, the frame and light can be removed (and used elsewhere as a cold frame) and vegetable marrow seeds sown in May. They will germinate without protection and flourish in the richness of the hotbed. The life of a hotbed is not more than a month and a half. Don't start it too early —begin say February or March, according to locality—so as to have its benefit till frosts are over. Eight inches of soil will suffice.

HOUSELEEK. *See* SEMPERVIVUM.

HOUSTONIA. H.P.; dwarf; blue; summer.

Grow in light loam with a little lime and increase by division in spring. In the rockery it clings closely to the surface. A lavender variety is *serpyllifolia;* blue, *caerulea.*

HUMEA. H.H.B.; 4 ft.; rose-red; summer.

A bedding or greenhouse plant attractive by its plumed blossom and its fragrance. Start seed in frame, prick off and pot on twice till in 6-inch pots for inside, or in warm border when spring is in, in loam, sand and manure.

HUMULUS JAPONICUS.

This is the annual hop, hardy and suited for pergolas as it is a rampant climber whether in sun or shade. The *Variegatus* has leaves with silver and cream markings. In *aureus* the leaves are golden. Sow seed in open in April, or increase, same time, by division.

HUMUS.

The name for stable or farmyard manure, not so freely obtainable nowadays. It has to be well rotted, sometimes for over a year, by stacking and weathering, and then spread in the earliest months of the year so that its goodness can soak in and yet not be washed down beyond the root levels as would be the case if put on in the autumn. The beneficial chemical constituents of humus are—lime, potash, nitrogen and phosphoric acid in this order of proportion. Cow manure is only three-quarters as strong as humus, and pig manure one-fifth stronger than humus, but contains only one-third the proportion of potash. *See* MANURING, *also* FERTILIZERS.

HUTCHINSIA. H.P.; rockery; white; spring.

All right as a perennial, but best results are from annual sowing in spring. It likes sandy soil with a little lime or limestone environment. The best variety is *alpina*, which is a mass of white blossom like a carpet.

HYACINTHS. H.P.; 1 ft.; red, white, mauve, yellow; spring.

The hyacinth is quite hardy and will thrive in ordinarily good soil, but a well-drained, rich, sandy loam is preferable. For outdoor blooming, plant bulbs in a sunny position from September to November, 3 in. deep and from 5–10 in. apart. Lift the bulbs when the leaves have withered, dry in the sun, and store on dry sand or coconut fibre till the following year. For culture in pots, plant in succession from August to November (to bloom from December to April). Place three bulbs in a 6-inch pot containing two parts turfy loam and one of well-rotted manure, leaf-mould and sand. They are less suitable for bowls, which are mostly too shallow. There are various excellent strains in each colour; one for each is named: white, *L'Innocence;* yellow, *City of Haarlem;* pink, *Gertrude;* blush, *La Franchise;* blue, *Enchantress* (light), *King Menelik* (dark). For forcing is *White Roman*, which plant in August and a little later for succession, and reliable doubles are: *La Tour d'Auvergne* (white); *Laurens Koster* (blue). For the Grape Hyacinth see MUSCARI.

HYDRANGEA. F.S.; 5 ft.; pink; June.

A shrub found more in the South to greater height, and notable for its abundant clusters of pink blossom, though where iron is present in soil, or by artificial means, the flowers show blue. The variety called Chinese guelder rose is *hortensis* and is most general; *Veitchii* is a white variety, and *panticulata* distinctive, white tending to pale pink; *petiolaris* is of climbing habit, and *Schizophragma hydrangeoides* more so, going up to 25 ft. with small white flowers. Give a warm, rich soil (same applies to growing in capacious tub), and in winter dress with manure. In the South it is best to try *hortensis*. Increase by cuttings of the summer wood, in gentle heat, and give plenty of water till rooted, then plant in a light soil with plenty of sand. Renew mould every year if plants are potted. Protect roots during winter with a covering of loose straw.

HYDROPONICS.

A scientific method of growing plants without soil by suspending in water. A tank of concrete or metal is constructed, size according to need or space available, but of a depth of only 8 in. The water, which has minerals in solution, occupies half the depth, and across its surface is stretched a wire-mesh net on which rests a bed of vegetable litter with sawdust or peat merely for the purpose of giving a hold for the upper parts of the roots. Thus supported, the roots grow down into the culture liquid from which it draws sustenance (*see* diagram). In this way a continuous food supply is provided, which can be adjusted in strength and constituents to suit the needs of any particular group during each stage of development. The minerals dissolved in the water include phosphates, nitrates, sulphates, calcium and other special elements, and can be regularly renewed and regulated as to strength with a scientific accuracy which produces astonishing results, whether seed is sown in the litter belt, or the start is made from seedlings.

The advantages claimed are: (1) during the whole period of development a plant has all the food it can absorb; (2) plants can be grown close together as enough food is always available; (3) there is freedom from bacteria; (4) the culture medium never "sours" as does soil. Experiments with tomatoes have shown that the yield is so great as to equal 1750 tons per acre, and a tank one-hundreth of an acre in superficial area yielded 1480 lb. of potatoes. Flowers grown in this way have shown similar precocity.

It is a scientific accomplishment, but one definitely suggesting an interesting hobby for amateurs willing to install a tank. It will

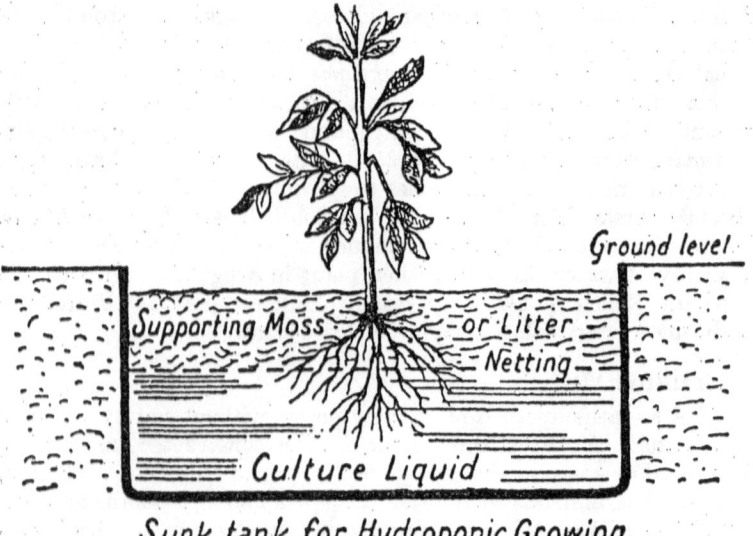

Sunk tank for Hydroponic Growing.

be appreciated that, first, by this system water takes the place of soil as the vehicle of growth and, secondly, it follows that as plants vary in their needs the tanks must contain components to satisfy each, or a series of tanks used for plant groups having similar requirements. Some flourish in limy places, others in sand or gravel, others again in peaty soils from all of which the extractable foods can hardly be the same. If the needs for the perfect development of each plant are known they can be more effectively met by growing the plant in a watery solution containing certain appropriate chemicals than in the soil where constant changes are in progress. In effect the liquid becomes a nutrient solution and, provided the aeration needed by all plant roots is assured, the result should be perfect. As growth proceeds, the chemicals will gradually be absorbed by the roots and eventually exhausted, so they need renewal from time to time. The practical application of hydroponics has already been tried out in this country over a period of two years by two amateurs in their London garden and they were not disappointed with the results achieved in the production of vegetables. As a commercial adventure the future of hydroponics is well worth watching.

The system was first experimented with on a wide scale in California where it yielded an extraordinary abundance of croppage, thus establishing its value as a new method of intensive production.

HYPERICUM (St. John's Wort). F.S.; 3 ft.; yellow; August.

Members of this class are also known as *Aaron's Beard* and *Rose of Sharon*. This free-growing shrub is useful for covering banks and even as hedge-division, where its brightness of leaf as of flower gives a touch of originality. The tall variety is *elatum;* also *aurum*, 4 ft. gold-edged leaves and fine blossom late into autumn. The old variety is *Androsoemum*, free flowering, vigorous in growth, and also known as *Tutsan*. A June flowerer is *calycinum;* a variety with red anthers, *triflorum*, is distinctive but needs sheltered situation; *Moserianum* is a dwarf. Prune all in spring.

Any ordinary soil suits if well-drained, but give more than average water. Take cuttings in August, in frame in sandy mould.

I

IBERIS. *See* CANDYTUFT.

ICELAND POPPY. *See* PAPAVER.

ICE PLANT. H.H.A.; trailing; red; May–July.

The gardener's name is imposing, for the ice-plant is the *crystallinum* variety of the *mesembryanthemum*. Its leaves are fleshy and ice-blue in colour, while its blossom is in varying shades of red, and is excellent in the rockery or as a carpet plant in the border, growing best in sandy loam having a little lime and leaf-mould. Increase by heeled cuttings struck in sand, after being dried for an hour or so in the sun. The variety *criniflorum* flowers in a variety of colours, and is also known as the Livingstone daisy.

IMMORTELLE (Acroclinium Helichrysum, etc.). *See* EVER-LASTINGS.

IMPATIENS. P.; greenhouse; dwarf and 18 in.; red; winter.

The species includes the Balsam (*which see*), and also *sultani*, dwarf, with deep red flowers in profusion, which bloom very shortly after cuttings are well rooted if potted in a mixture of peat, loam and sand. An orange-scarlet variety, *Holstii*, is often treated as an annual, is red, 18 in. high, and can be put in the border in sunny position after the frosts have gone.

INCARVILLEA. H.P.; 18 in.; rose and yellow; summer.

This attractive plant shows full bell-like trusses the whole period of flowering, especially the variety *delavayi*, which also does well in the greenhouse. An average soil suits, and increase is from spring-sown seed under a cloche, or by division.

INDIAN MALLOW. *See* ABUTILON.

INDIAN PINK. *See* DIANTHUS.

INSECTS ON PLANTS. *See* PESTS. *See* **also** ANTS, to destroy; APHIS, to remove from rose buds; EARWIGS, to destroy; PLANT LICE (Aphides), to destroy; ROSE TREES, to clear from blight; TOBACCO WASH, to prepare; WIREWORM, to destroy.

INTENSIVE CULTURE.

The value of intensive methods in the production of salads and certain vegetables is that they are ready for use some weeks earlier than if grown in the open. Instead, they are grown or started under glass and, where needed, with artificial heat. Although a greenhouse, heated or cold, is an advantage, if the amateur does not mind the trouble, such crops are obtainable without a greenhouse or heating apparatus. The use of cloches (*which see*) takes the place of the greenhouse, and the manure or compost heap, made up into a hotbed (*which see*), supplies the necessary degree of heat. A frame (*which see*) is necessary to enclose the hotbed, and the cloches are more convenient if of the lean-to or barn type, rather than bell glasses, as these can be added to as required to make continuous rows, and when one kind of crop is sufficiently forward, these cloches can be moved to cover new plants which mature later. The secret of tenderness in early produce is quick growth. Soil, therefore, must be rich, free from bacteria (*see* SEED-BED for sterilizing procedure) moist and not hard packed, so that roots can have a free run. Constant vigilance in giving air, protecting from cold snaps, watering, and watching every stage of growth is the price of success. For general guidance the following instructions are given: *Beet.*—Sow globe variety under cloches in January, 1 in. deep, at 6-inch intervals. *Carrot.*—Sow thinly in frame in three fortnightly successions starting first week January *Cauliflower.*—Sow January in hotbed, transfer at fourth leaf to cold frame, then to open, end of March. *Celery.*—Sow thinly on hotbed February, prick off early in leaf-mould and sand, put out under cloche mid-April, then gradually harden. *Chicory.*—Same as for seakale from crowns raised from summer-sown seed. *Endive.*—Sow seed in open, September, transfer to cold frame, November, then place on hotbed end of January. *French Beans.*—Sow in March, transfer to open in May; or sow under cloches March and remove gradually when foliage fills cloche, usually in May. *Leeks.*—Same as onions. *Lettuce.*—Sow in frame October, transfer to hotbed in January or in open under cloches. Give air to earliest growth in frame, to save damping off. Cover cloches with straw at nights till lettuce established. *Mustard and Cress.*—Sow cress two days before mustard, sow both thickly, and keep on hotbed all the time, sowing in second box as soon as first forms leaf and so on for succession. *Mint.*—Take existing roots from outside in March and grow quickly in hotbed, near glass. *Onions.*—Sow in January in hotbed and only remove when setts in strong growth, 6 in. high, to open, covering with cloches. *Peas.*—As for French Beans. *Potatoes.*—For a small crop of new potatoes, plunge a box of seed-potatoes in hotbed in January; when leaves show transplant carefully to sunny spot covered with continuous cloches till haulms touch glass, then remove cloches. *Seakale.*—Take a root with healthy crowns, put in a pot, cover with another inverted, and bed deep enough in hotbed to allow frame to close. Water after potting. *Tomatoes.*—For summering in open start from an April sowing in boxes on hotbed in rich soil arranging good drainage. *Turnips.*—Same as for carrots. *Flowers.*—Earlier plants can be secured by sowing seed in shallow pans placed under frame on hotbed, but extra care in hardening off must be taken.

INULA. H.P.; 18 in.; yellow; July–August.

It grows in any fertile soil, preferably a friable clay. Increase by division. *Hookeri* is a pale yellow; *glandulosa*, a deep yellow.

IONOPSIDIUM ACAULE. H.A.; dwarf; lilac; summer.

For the rock garden this is a charming little plant, hardy, dwarf in its growth (about 2 in. high), and although classed as an annual its pretty tufts of flowers spring up year by year from self-sown seed. *Acauli* is a good variety. Sow where it is to bloom in spring.

IPOMAEA. H.H.P.; twining climber; blue; summer.

The variety *hederacea* will flower in the open, but most of the species are better in the hothouse, such as *bona-nox*, which is white; *horsfalliae*, rose, and winter flowering; *learii*, blue, autumn flowering. Annual varieties, sometimes listed as *Mina Lobata*, are *versicolor* and *quamoclit*, scarlet, which is half-hardy and grows to 3 ft. All kinds need a rich soil on the light side, with sand and leaf-mould. The perennials are increased by cuttings struck in heat. Thin the hothouse species after flowering.

IRIS.

This plant may be divided into two groups, the bulbous and the non-bulbous (*rhizomatous*). The varieties have increased of late years both in beauty of colour, height and habit. All are hardy and perennial. The English irises are *Xiphioides*. The Flag Iris will flourish in almost any soil, and flower year after year. *Black Prince*, with large, fragrant flowers of light and dark purple and yellow markings; *Mme. Chereau*, having white flowers tinged with soft blue; and *Pallida dalmatica*, a fine variety, with tall stems of delicate blue flowers and splendid foliage. The Spanish Iris (*Xiphium*) includes white, blue, yellow and striped. It likes a light, well-drained soil and a warm, sheltered situation, but plenty of sunlight, and should not be disturbed. Most of the iris family flower in June, the Flags a month earlier and the dwarfs in February and March from October planting; *alata* (blue) flowers in winter. The *oncocylus* group, known as the Cushion Irises, are outstanding in beauty of colour, but are considered difficult subjects. Plant in November in sunny position. The Bearded Iris, belonging to the Flag group, requires plenty of sun, and some lime in the soil; otherwise it is content with ordinary soil and treatment. The *Pallida dalmatica* mentioned above is bearded, and others are: *Variegata*, yellow mixed with some darker shade; *neglecta*, various shades of lilac or purple; *plicata*, white stippled purple; *sambucina*, bronze. When iris leaves turn yellow, and have wet rot just above the root, give a dressing of superphosphate. The old custom of dusting around the plants with lime has been discarded as ineffective.

IXIA. Bulb; 1 ft.; lavender blue; late spring.

Well worth cultivating for its dainty blue flowers, either in the greenhouse or the open garden in a warm border of southern aspect. For early flowering, the bulbs should be planted in September or the beginning of October, in a light, well-drained soil, and some protection from the frost, such as bracken litter, should be given as soon as the new growth appears. For greenhouse culture grow three in a 5-inch pot, well-drained, usual bulb mixture.

IXIOLIRION. Hardy bulb; 1 ft.; blue; June.

Average garden soil with some sand is suitable for planting bulbs in October. Put them in 3 in. deep and leave undisturbed for some years. A sunny situation is recommended, particularly for *montanum*, 18 in., and for *pallasii*, the flowers of which are larger. Increase by offsets.

J

JACOBAEA. H.A.; 18 in.; various colours; July.

They have single and double flowers in a wide range of colours —mauve, purple, rose, crimson, white. Though hardy, the seed germinates better sown in winter under glass and planted out in May in fertile soil. A favourite variety is *senecio elegans*.

JACOB'S LADDER. See POLEMONIUM.

JANUARY GARDENING. See MONTH BY MONTH IN GARDEN AND ALLOTMENT.

JAPANESE MAPLE. See ACER.

JASIONE. H.P.; 1 ft.; blue; July.

A rockery plant in the scabious flower category, which should be planted in light soil, either in November or March. It is increased by division.

JASMINE. H.P.; climbing rambler; white (spring), yellow (winter).

Increase by layers or cuttings of ripe wood struck in a warm frame in a mixture of light soil and sand during the summer. Plant out from October to March in fertile soil, in which they do best, though they will thrive in ordinary soil. The yellow or Winter Jasmine blooms when the stalks have no leaves, while the spring-flowering white rambler has the foil of dark foliage to increase its beauty. Prune shoots after they have bloomed.

JERUSALEM ARTICHOKES. *See* ARTICHOKES.

JEW'S MALLOW. *See* KERRIA.

JONQUIL. *See* NARCISSUS.

JULY GARDENING. *See* MONTH BY MONTH IN GARDEN AND ALLOTMENT.

JUNE GARDENING. *See* MONTH BY MONTH IN GARDEN AND ALLOTMENT.

JUNIPER.

A foliage shrub or tree of the conifer class, evergreen, which grows best on moist deep-dug loam having a percentage of lime. They are used for lawn or drive decoration, should be planted in April, require no pruning and increased by cuttings under a cloche in August. Certain varieties, including *Bermudans* are only for the conservatory.

K

KALANCHOE BLOSSFELDIANA. P.; 18 in.; scarlet and orange; May onward.

This greenhouse plant flowers a year from seed-sowing, which should be in May, in heat, and pricked out into 5-inch pots as early as it is possible to handle it. It is in bloom for nearly three months and vividly beautiful. It requires leaf-mould and sand in the main potting of loam, and the pots should be well-drained with small crocks.

KALE. *See* BORECOLE.

KALMIA. F.S.

This is of the nature of laurel, is evergreen and runs from 2 ft. height up to about 10 ft. in bushy thickness. The *Stagger Bush* is the sheep laurel and the *Calico Bush* the mountain laurel, while *glauca* is the pale laurel. Of these, the first averages only 2 ft. in height, with purple flowers in May; the second, 10 ft., pink blossom, very profuse, in spring; the last, rose-tinted blossom, April to May. Do not plant in chalky soil; give them peat and leaf-mould; keep them moist. Propagation is best by seed under glass (the seed is tiny) or by cuttings under glass.

KANSAS GAY FEATHER. *See* LIATRIS.

KAULFUSSIA AMELLOIDES (Cape Aster). H.A.; 6 in.; blue and crimson; August.

Suited for edgings, and flowers are freely produced in about four months from sowing in early April in good garden soil and a sunny position. One of the fern family is also named Kaulfussia.

KENTIA.

A genus of palms which are only for inside growth and mostly under warm conditions. They need a mixture of loam, peat, leaf-mould and sand, and need 6-inch or larger pots, only changed when pot-bound. Give good drainage, and in summer water well; very little in winter. Leaves require occasional sponging with dilute fungicide to prevent scale.

KERRIA (Jew's Mallow). F.S.; 6 ft.; orange; May–July.

The favourite variety is *japonica flore pleno*, giving a plentiful show of double rosettes of orange-hued blossom from May to July. It is bushy but not woody, robustly hardy, not particular as to soil and best planted in autumn. Take cuttings July or divide clump in August. All the pruning required is to prevent overcrowding.

KILLARNEY FERN. *See* TRICHOMANES.

KINGFISHER DAISY. *See* FELICIA.

KITCHEN GARDEN.

The many vegetables, root crops and herbs will be found under their own names. The Allotment (*which see*) is the modern equivalent if garden space is limited. All cultural directions are given under their appropriate headings.

KNIPHOFIA (Red Hot Poker). H.P.; 3 ft.; orange, scarlet; July onwards.

The striking blooms are held on high stalks well above the foliage and are best planted in groups, with some attention to background, in well-drained, deep sandy soil, with loam mixed in, though they do not mind a clayey patch. Increased best by seed in spring. Varieties to grow are *nobilis*, orange red; *rufa*, coral red; *tuckii*, bright yellow; and *Lemon Queen*. Red Hot Poker is also known as *Tritoma*.

KOCHIA (Summer Cypress). H.A.; 24 in.

A foliage plant which turns red in autumn; it has no leaves in the ordinary sense, but thread-like panicles in profusion like a massive beard at first a delicate green turning in autumn to a deep rich crimson. Ordinary soil, but lime-free, suits it. Sow in open in warm spot in May, or treat as half-hardy and start in heat in early April. The best variety is *trichophylla*.

KOHL-RABI.

Grown for their edible stems, the lower parts of which thicken like turnips. They should be gathered young. Sow seed end of March, transplant in rows 2 ft. apart, 1 ft. between each. Good rich soil, sunny position, general culture as cabbage. It does not run to seed.

KOLREUTERIA. F.S.; 12 ft.; yellow; summer.

A recent species, *paniculata*, is growing in popularity, by reason of its attractive feathery foliage and long terminal spikes of flowers followed by capsules in autumn. It prefers a sheltered position in friable loam. Increase by layers in autumn, or by cuttings in spring in sand under a cloche.

L

LABURNUM. Tree; yellow; May, June.

Where there is room, this is an attractive feature of the garden for its dainty foliage and graceful racemes of flowers, which are in profusion. A good strain is *alpinum*, which should be planted in October in a sunny position and average soil, staking well and keeping well watered till established.

LANTANA. H.H.P.; dwarf and tall; orange, red, white; summer and autumn.

Grow from seed, then cuttings each season, which are started in heat and transferred to larger pots if kept in greenhouse, or planted in sunny border in average soil. They are in clusters of florets, rather like Heliotrope. The variety *salvifolia* is mauve and grows to 3 ft. In the greenhouse it blooms late in the year.

LARKSPUR. H.A.; 2 ft.; blue, white, pink; July onwards.

Likes good soil and warm position, but will do well anywhere. Sow seed sparsely in January in open, as germination is slow, transplant when 1 in. high; give plenty of room. It is the annual form of Delphinium, than which the foliage is more graceful.

LAUREL. F.S.; 6 ft.

Though it is a flowering shrub its creamy, fluffy blossom is insignificant and the shrub is mostly grown as hedges or windscreen because of the density of the foliage. There are ten varieties, of which the cherry laurel and the Portugal laurel are best known, the latter being increased from seed, the others by long cuttings almost wholly buried. A warm, loose loam suits them. *See also* KALMIA.

LAURUSTINUS. F.S.; 6 ft.; white; winter.

This is the *Tinus* division of the viburnum, and the floriation in December to March is followed by red berries up to June. *Lucidum* is in flower in April; *variegatum* has golden leaves. It will thrive in any soil, but doesn't like cold winds. Strike cuttings of half-ripened shoots in sand.

LAVANDULA. *See* LAVENDER.

LAVATERA (Tree Mallow). H.A.; 4 ft.; white, pink; July.

These show up in the rear of the border. They are sown in March. Plant 18 in. apart and two or three in a group. The flowers have a satin-like appearance, some white, *splendens*, but the majority shades of pink. *Arborea variegata* has variegated blossom, but is not fully hardy.

LAVENDER (Lavandula). H.P.; 2 ft.; blue; scented capsules in autumn.

Plant slips in pots during March or April, and leave in a shady place till rooted. Then expose to the sun till strong enough for transplanting to permanent position. The true English lavender is the variety *spica*, which can be raised from seed. Dwarf forms are *nana*, *nana alba* and the *munstead* varieties.

LAWN MAKING.

Taken all round it is far better to make a lawn with sown grass rather than with turves, because it is permanently more pleasing to the eye all the year round, and also saves the interminable back-aching job of weeding. Grass suitable for garden lawns, or for tennis courts, is a mixture of various kinds and it therefore pays to get it from a reliable source. Leading firms select seed from a number of varieties, which are at their best at different times and so the lawn does not lose its beauty at any time of the year. A mixture containing rye grass is recommended for heavy or medium soil and for light soil one of the dwarf grass mixtures of a reputable seedsman. The same expert mixing is necessary for producing a lasting and responsive tennis court as indicated in a later paragraph. *See also* GRASS. In making a new lawn the site, which is more successful if it has a north aspect, must first be levelled, after digging, breaking up, removing weeds and stones. The late summer is the best time, so arranging progress that the actual sowing is done during August or September, thus giving the grass a good start before any weeds that may still be in the soil, or get into the prepared plot by way of wind-blown seed, start germinating in the spring. The temperature of the soil is low in the early spring and, in consequence, germination is slow and it is not at all unusual for the young grass to take three weeks or a month to appear above the ground, as against five to ten days if autumn sown, so unless the season is open and genial a patchy germination and trouble from weeds may be expected by spring sowing.

Preparing the Ground.—An important point which needs stressing is that new grass will only grow in top-spit, which must be borne in mind in levelling the ground. Where, after removing surface rough grass, if any, the contour demands removal of top-spit, keep it aside for putting on again when levelling is done. Where there is existing grass it must be skimmed off, the spade only taking to the depth of roots, putting the turves on the compost heap and freeing the top-spit from couch-grass runners and roots of deep weeds.

Drainage.—When the plot is stripped examine the nature of the soil for drainage. If water will not soak away readily the site must be drained by a layer of stones and rubble, well firmed down, or if the expense of laying pipes can be borne, this is the best way and should be done under expert advice.

Levelling is the next process and the accompanying diagram will help. Work from the centre-to-be, put in a couple of stakes 6 ft. apart, on the top put a length of wood, and a spirit level. Then with a mallet hammer in one or other of the stakes till the bubble of the level is at the marked centre, which gives the level, when both stakes should be an inch above surface. Then put other stakes 5 ft. farther off on all four sides; lift one end of levelling plank to next peg, which

Lawn levelling pegging.

drive in to level, and repeat to outer edges. It will then be seen where it is easiest to remove soil by noting the gradients. When this is roughly done, go over again to adjust stakes to final true level, thoroughly firm down the area with a light roller, remove stakes and score with a rake for the sowing process. Note to have this surface composed of top-spit only. In any case there should be at least 2 in. of good loamy soil, and the addition of a grass fertilizer will assure a good even growth—3 oz. to the square yard will be about right.

Sowing should be at the rate of seed of the highest quality; otherwise sow more thickly as germination is less dense. If the soil is poor a thicker sowing is also recommended. For the formation of a new lawn sow 2 oz. of seed per square yard to ensure a close turf in the shortest possible period. Where time is not of the greatest importance, however, a seeding of 1 or 1½ oz. per square yard should eventually produce a sound turf. A thick sowing greatly contributes to success, not only by rapidly covering the ground with grass and the closeness of the resulting new grass mutually protecting from the weather, but by the suppression of weeds. For renovating, 1 oz. of seed per square yard should suffice, unless the turf is very thin.

Tennis Courts.—For tennis courts the ratio of seed should be 2–4 oz. to the square yard. In preparing for sowing it is a good plan to mark out the plot in square yards. Sow the seed on a calm, dry day (not a windy, nor wet one). The seed should be sown as evenly as possible and be lightly covered with soil—not deeper than $\frac{1}{4}$ of an inch—by carefully raking the surface in two directions, after which the whole should be rolled and cross-rolled with a light roller. Protect from birds by crossings of black thread. When the grass has grown to 2 in. above the ground it should be cut, either with a scythe or sharp machine, and should be kept short. Roll frequently with a light roller.

A Turved Lawn.—If it is decided to lay turves, they should be obtained as free from weeds as possible and of a reasonably fine texture. The turves are usually cut to a thickness of 2 in. and 3 ft. long by 1 ft. wide, each being rolled for removal. It will often be found that greater satisfaction will result from cutting the turves to a smaller size, say 1 ft. 6 in. by 1 ft., and keeping them flat. The soil is levelled and prepared in the same way, made reasonably firm by rolling. It is important that it should be given a thorough soaking with water before the turves are laid and though top-spit is not imperative with turves, they should rest on good soil. The whole of the site should not be watered at once, but a piece at a time, so that it is thoroughly sodden when the turves are put down. The roots will then become established much earlier than they would otherwise. After the turves are laid they should be well rolled, and at intervals over the space of a few weeks.

Lawn Upkeep.—It is hardly necessary to indicate that a lawn must be regularly mown; now and again during winter keep the grass short enough to save scything when growth renews in spring; then in March start once a week and continue mowing at weekly intervals. Keep weeds down. Renew worn patches. During the winter when the ground is soft the roller should not be used, though on light subsoil a rolling now and again can be given where ground is comparatively dry. In spring and summer roll after mowing; do it up and down, and also from side to side. After October regular mowing can cease till March except, as is stated above, to keep length manageable for spring mowing. Lawn sand is best put on in October, with another scattering in March. The grass will show colour patches but will soon resume its greenness. It is a tonic and mildly poisonous to such weeds as daisies.

Lawn Repairs.—Irregular worn patches are best renewed by cutting out a square and re-sowing or laying turf, rather than merely patching up the worn part. The idea is shown in the diagram, and will be found to be more sightly as well as more certain.

Weeds.—To free from dandelions, docks and plantains. Young weeds can be removed with a minimum of disturbance to the turf by using a potato peeler. More established weeds, however, should be cut to the ground in spring and immediately have gas tar or a little salt put on them, or with a skewer thrust a drop or two of creosote into the heart of the root.

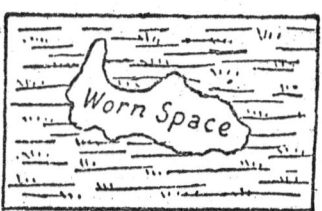

Take out a squared turve as this.

Patching worn turf

Worms.—To kill worms add 2½lb. freshly-slaked lime to about 8 gallons of water. Allow to settle and use the clear liquid on the lawn.

Lawn Mowings.—As well as making valuable compost, they protect roots of tender plants from strong sun-heat if strewn around them.

Lawn Sand.—A reliable home-made lawn sand can be compounded from 12 lb. fine sand, ½ lb. sulphate of iron, 1½ lb. sulphate of ammonia; mix well and scatter at the rate of 1 oz. per square yard.

LAYERING.

Propagation by layering is usually done in July so that roots are sturdy before the frosts. Make an upward cut just below a joint in a lower shoot. The incision should pass half-way through the shoot and should be from 1–3 in. long according to the size of the plant. Peg the shoot securely into the soil, keeping the "tongue" as open as possible, but be careful not to break it, see diagram. Place underneath a little grey sand, cover with earth and, after a couple of days, give plenty of water. Cut away from the parent plant when the layers are finely rooted, in soft-wooded plants such as carnations this occurs in about six weeks, but do not sever till growth is in good activity.

LAYIA. H.A.; 1 ft.; yellow, edged white, July.

Sow in open in May in good average friable soil, selecting a sunny position. *Elegans* is the best variety.

LEADWORT. *See* PLUMBAGO.

LEAF-MOULD.

To make quickly available, dry off (sun or heat) oak and beech leaves, and work through a sieve. The resulting "dust" is splendid for potting and is more quickly absorbed. The ordinary way of piling leaves in a heap covered with earth takes at least a year to be ready, and beech leaves (the best leaf-mould) rather longer. All leaf-mould is better plant food if mixed with sand and is particularly useful on clay soil.

LEEKS.

Make successive sowings, February, March, April in open on deeply dug, well-matured ground. Water the ground a day before sowing. Do not sow thickly, nor cover with much soil; water well

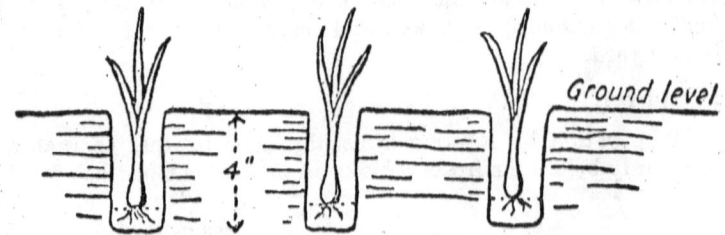

*Plant young Leeks in dibbled holes.
Do not fill in: only cover roots.*

and thin out when about 3 in. high. Transplant into rows 1 ft. apart. The bleaching can be done by Nature if the young plants are dropped into deep dibbled holes, these holes not being filled, but only enough soil thrown in to cover the roots, and then the hole filled with water. Do not allow to go dry or caked, using hoe for this.

For an early crop sow seed in boxes early in February on a moderate heat for an early crop. Prick out when about 2 in. high, transfer to a cold frame in April, and harden off and plant out in May. They can be lifted as required for use.

LEGAL POINTS FOR GARDENERS. See ALLOTMENT, *also* GARDEN ARRANGEMENT.

LENTEN ROSE. See HELLEBORUS.

LEOPARD'S BANE. See DORONICUM.

LEPTOSIPHON. H.A.; dwarf; mixed colour; June.

Sow where it is to flower as soon as frosts have gone. Used in rockeries and for edgings as it is only 3 in. high and is free flowering.

LEPTOSYNE. H.A.; 18 in.; yellow; all summer.

Very quickly raised from seed sown in a frame and transplanted when hardened or in open ground in May. It will blossom in five weeks, keep in display till autumn and requires only average soil. The variety *stillmani* (Golden Rosette) has double flowers.

LETTUCE.

The tender crispness of these easily-raised salad plants can now be enjoyed nearly all the year round. For an early crop sow half an inch deep in February on a slight hotbed, and transplant in April on a sheltered border; again in the middle of March and in succession every fortnight. For winter and spring use sow the varieties *All the Year Round*, or *Continuity* (a bronze leaf). The first week in August and in September, plant in good rich garden soil, 1 ft. apart each way, and during dry weather give a liberal supply of water. The seedlings from the last sowing should be transplanted 4 in. each way under a south wall, for planting out in early spring. For very early use *see* INTENSIVE CULTURE. Frequent sowings avoid a glut one month and none the next. Treat for quick growth by having soil well matured and so that when ready they are still tender. The cabbage lettuce is mostly grown nowadays, thus doing away with the labour of tying up, as the cos lettuce demands. Dust with Derris to combat greenfly. Among the best lettuces for sowing in April are *Brittle Ice* and *Wonderful*. The first makes large heads of pale green crinkled leaves and the name is appropriate. It should be thinned to 1 ft. apart. The latter stands well in a dry season. Lettuces do not transplant well when the season is advanced.

LEUCOJUM. Bulb; dwarf; white; March and later.

This hardy and attractive bulbous plant is like a snowdrop with green edges, 4 in. high and can be planted in groups, in the rockery, in autumn 2 in. deep. The early flowering variety is the Spring Snowflake (*vernum*) and the later, the Summer Snowflake (*aestivum*). Increased by offsets. A particularly beautiful variety is *vageneri*, and in *carpathicum* the blossom is yellow edged.

LEWISIA. H.P.; dwarf; rose; summer.

A suitable alpine or rockery species, 4 in. only in height. Give them a sunny position in well-drained loam and sand mixed with good compost. One variety, *rediviva*, often looks dead, after flowering, but is only dormant. A pink variety, flowering in August, is *tweedyi*. Increase by division.

LIATRIS. H.P.; 4 ft.; purple; August.

Plant in light soil in dry situation, starting seed under a cloche or in greenhouse in spring. The flowers open first at the top of the spike and work downwards. Varieties: *spicata* and *pycnostachya* (both purple); *graminifolia dubia* (rose-purple). Increase by spring division. Its popular names are Kansas Gay Feather and Blazing Star.

LIBERTIA. H.H.P.; 18 in. and 36 in.; white; April.

Responds to the care it needs; it wants a position apart to show it off, plenty of summer sun, and in winter needs to have the roots protected. It is evergreen and the blossom is like an Iris, of satiny texture. They should be planted in March in well-drained friable soil containing peat. Increase by division. The heights of respective varieties are: *formosa* and *paniculata*, both 18 in.; *grandiflora* and *ixioides*, both 3 ft.

LILAC. F.S.; 10 ft. to tree height; white, red, purple, pink, lilac; spring.

There are so many varieties that only those in most esteem need be mentioned. They are of the syringa family, and *vulgaris*, the common lilac, is single and the true lilac colour. Of the double lilacs, *Alphonse Lavalée* is most general, and despite its name is a British plant with blue spikes. For a short specimen try *persica*, about 6 ft., with neat lilac spikes. *Chinensis* is deep violet and free flowering. *Marie Legraye* and *Mme. Lemoine* are single and double whites respectively. *Charles Joly* is a double dark red. Too many lilacs are grown in odd corners and in far too close hedges, with poor result from being robbed of air, sunlight and growing space. Give them room and average loamy soil and they will flourish generously if not over-watered. They want the root suckers cut out every season. Layering in July is surest and easiest way of increasing.

LILIES.

Lilies do best in deep-well-dug soil or in a fibrous loam which is well drained and contains decayed leaf-mould and gritty sand. Plant in October, 5 or 6 in. deep (a good rule is double the depth of the bulb) and do not take up oftener than once in three years. This in general applies to most varieties, which are numerous, except the hothouse types, which few have facilities to cultivate. A handy plan is to buy lilies in pots in the late spring and sink the pots into the border, not in too much sun, in suitable groups according to ideas of colour. If the pots are small for the root growth, be very careful when re-potting into larger size to use a soil without the addition of humus or lime. Lilies throw out roots above the bulb as well as below; it is therefore wise to plant low in pots to allow for adding soil as needed. If in the plot, keep an eye open for this habit and cover these upper roots in good time. Among the great number of varieties *candidum*, 4 ft., is the Madonna Lily, and should be planted in August for next summer's flowering. The Trumpet Lily, *longiflorum*, 3 ft., is planted in spring. *Martagon*, 3 ft., purple, its variety *chalcedonicum*, being scarlet, and there is a beautiful white Martagon, each flowering in July. The Orange Lily is *croceum*, 3 ft.; while *davuricum luteum*, 2 ft., is yellow with black spots, both flowering in June. A newer type is *regale*, white and yellow marked brown, 3 ft., July flowering, two years from planting. *Speciosum rubrum* and *Harrisii* are also suitable sorts for bedding out.

Some lilies do well in a shady situation, with moist soil; among them are *canadense*, yellow, 3 ft.; *superbum*, orange, red, 6 ft.; *parryi*, yellow, black spots, 3 ft.; *grayi*, red and purple, 4 ft.; *burbankii*, crimson, 5 ft. All these flower in July. Also are *roeztii*, yellow-spotted purple, 3 ft., and *parviflorum*, orange marked black, 30 in., both June flowering. A new hybrid *Maxwell* will stand wide climate variations.

To guard against disease all bulbs should be well dusted with powdered sulphur before planting, but no cure has been so far found for the virus affecting lilies and it cannot be detected in the bulb.

Lilies are increased by their offsets, and in some varieties also by the scales on the bulbs.

The *Arum* is not really a lily but popularly included; its proper name is *richardia*, it is not hardy, is mostly grown in the greenhouse to flower in winter and spring, and nearly all are white, the exceptions being *pentlandii* and *Elliottiana*, both yellow. They follow general lily culture, and could be brought into the open (in pots plunged in border) in summer and taken back in September. It is the Easter Lily. The Scarborough Lily is entered under *Vallota purpurea*; the Mariposa Lily under *Calochortus* and the Day Lily under *Hemerocallis*.

Adequate support should be given to all tall lilies, especially where high winds are experienced. *Parryi*, for instance, will need support or those with flowery heads will topple over in the wind. Generally, *regale* does not need support and only a few lilies like the variety *Wilmottiae* ask for support at more than half their height.

LILY-OF-THE-VALLEY (Convallaria Majalis). H.P.; 6 in.; white; May.

The prime necessity for the production of a good bed of lilies-of-the-valley is a well-manured soil, soft and loamy, with plenty of sand, while a shaded south aspect, free from draughts, is the satisfactory position. The crowns should be planted in early autumn, singly and 2 or 3 in. apart, and the surface covered with a mulching of well-rotted manure. As soon as the new growth appears a weak solution of liquid manure should be applied occasionally, and for protection from spring frosts a light covering of fern litter is very useful. They will come up every year, and should be divided every three years. They do very well as pot plants in the greenhouse, making an attractive front line on the staging. For April display put not more than six crowns into a 5-inch pot in autumn, using friable soil and leaving the tips visible. They can be plunged in bulb fibre, which need not be done till the late autumn. Patience is required as they will not start till early spring. For greenhouse culture use *Berlin* crowns, and for growing in the open *Fortin's Giant*.

LILY-OF-THE-VALLEY TREE (Clethra). F.S.; 4–6 ft.; white; August.

Both *alnifolia* and *arborea* are white, the former being the shorter and hardier. It is better to grow *arborea* under glass. A dwarf variety is *C. Minor*. Increase by cuttings or layers in autumn or spring.

LIME.

An average lime dressing is 8 oz. to the square yard for early winter application and for spring 4 oz. to the square yard, but where the soil is poor use double. Clay soil particularly benefits by liming.

To test soil for lime, half fill a large glass jar with the soil to be tested, add dessertspoonful sodium salicylate, cover with water to half-inch above soil, leave for twenty-four hours; then, if water is brown, lime is needed.

As well as purifying the soil, lime sets free mineral manures that otherwise would not fertilize plants and crops.

In January dress the plot intended for cabbages, etc., should the ground require liming, at the rate of 20 lb. per rod of ground with carbonate of lime or ground chalk, or 15 lb. per rod of hydrated lime. Ground intended for green crops to carry through winter should not be disturbed; clear any spent crops or weeds, apply lime to the surface of the soil and hoe in to prevent loss by wind.

LIMNATHES. H.A.; 4 in.; yellow; June–July.

A free-flowering, fragrant specimen of which *douglasii* is 6 in. Sow early in average soil.

LINARIA. H.A.; 1 ft.; scarlet, white, orange, mixed crimson and gold; June, September.

Sow in March and in June in open to get a flowering succession. Thin out. They are not particular as to soil so long as it is light and the situation sunny. The white variety is *bipartita;* *alpina*, with violet and yellow flowers, is for the rockery, being only 6 in. high, as also is *cymbalaria*, lilac, and preferring a warm crevice in the rockery. Some of the taller varieties are perennial.

LINDELOFIA. *See* CYNOGLOSSUM.

LINNAEA. H.P.; dwarf trailer; pink; June.

A trailing evergreen which flowers freely and has fragrance. It is suited to the rockery if given a shady position and planted in peaty soil. Propagate by division.

LINUM (Flax). H.A. and H.P.; 18 in.; red, blue; summer.

A family which includes several useful plants for the garden, some of them being perennial but better treated as annuals. A friable soil in a not too sunny plot suits them well. The variety *grandiflorum* is both hardy and showy, and by sowing in autumn as well as spring a succession of bloom may be had throughout the summer; there are two kinds, one with deep scarlet and the other with bright rose flowers. *Narbonnense* is also very good and gives a copious supply of large light-blue flowers, beautifully veined. *Flavum* is a smaller but hardy plant with flowers of a peculiarly soft hue of yellow. Both these varieties are perennial.

LIPPIA. H.H.P.; 2 ft.; red, blue, white; June–September.

This is the lemon-scented class of the verbena, or aloysia, the particular variety being *citriodora*, which should be planted in spring, in the south, but in more rigorous districts treated as a greenhouse plant. It needs a mixture of loam, leaf-mould and nearly half sand; can be raised from autumn-struck cuttings in frame.

LIQUID MANURE.

Immerse in a dozen gallons of rain-water, a sack containing a half bucket each of sheep, goat, fowl and cow manure and soot. Stir occasionally during a month, then use as liquid manure, diluting till pale amber in colour. For qualities for various kinds *see* HUMUS.

LIVINGSTONE DAISY. *See* ICE PLANT.

LOBELIA. H.H.A.; dwarf; H.P., 30 in.; blue, white; all summer.

This dainty plant may be roughly divided into three classes— the compact or dwarf kind, the free-growing, spreading kind and the tall perennials. It is the dwarf kind which is chiefly used for bedding out, being sown in winter under glass and transplanted into boxes until sufficiently established for bedding-out. The spreading varieties are raised for filling hanging baskets and providing edgings for window boxes. Various shades of blue as well as white may be had in both these kinds—*Grandiflora* and *Magnifica*, *Prima Donna* (a red variety), *Speciosa*. Fine examples of the tall perennials are *syphilitica* (blue) and *cardinalis* (red), and they are very valuable for the garden as autumn flowers. But they are only fairly hardy and need some protection during the winter. Therefore lift them after flowering and store them in a dry place till spring. Lobelias need a rich, free soil and plenty of water during the summer.

LOGANBERRY.

Plant at least 5 ft. apart in October in a deep, rich loam which is moist but well drained. Thin out the clumps in June, cutting away all but about half a dozen young shoots, which should be fastened to supports such as trellis work or wire fencing. Cut away old branches after the fruit has been gathered and tie up the new shoots in their place. It can be increased by division or by layering in September; when rooted and separated in spring, it will take three years to

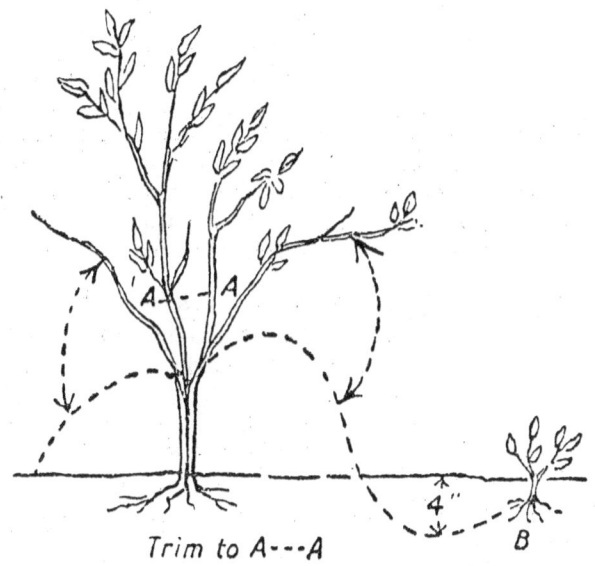

Layering and trimming Loganberries.

fruit. Be rigorous in pruning as the logan is strong and quick in growth. It is not generally known that logans can be propagated from the leaves. At the famous East Malling Experimental Station a carpet of leaves is made in August in a cold frame, each leaf-stalk being firmly pressed into sand. A callus forms before autumn, roots begin to develop and from each a young plant is soon in growth.

LONDON PRIDE. H.P.; 1 ft.; coral; summer.

Most useful for border edgings, its pink spikes making beautiful compact masses when grown in natural clumps. Will grow in almost any soil and needs little attention. It rapidly increases by offset suckers, and so should be reduced severely. It is in the *Robertsonia* class of the saxifrages.

LOVE-IN-A-MIST (Nigella). H.A.; 18 in.; blue, white; August.

Has attractive feathery foliage through which the dainty blossom is seen. Seed should be sown in March and twice later for succession in light soil and in the place where the plants are intended to bloom.

LOVE-LIES-BLEEDING. *See* AMARANTHUS.

LUNARIA (Honesty). H.B.; 2 ft.; mauve, white; summer.

A charming, old-fashioned plant very useful for the wild garden or for rough banks, where its blossom and, later, its flat, silvery seed-pods may be made very effective. The seed-pods can be dried in the sun and used for indoor decoration. Seed should be sown in spring or early summer and the seedlings thinned out so as to ensure strong plants for the following year. Its natural soil is chalky ground, but it is perfectly hardy and will thrive almost anywhere.

LUPIN. H.A. and H.P.; 3 ft.; various colours; May, July.

The annuals have a good range of colours, and present no difficulty in raising. Sow where wanted, giving plenty of room for bushing, stake low, with branching twigs to give support without being obtrusive. The perennials are as versatile in colouring. Sow March for autumn show or in summer for next spring flowering. A fairly new strain, *Russells*, are of exceptional beauty in various pastel colours. Any good soil suits lupins, though a rich, light soil having no lime will secure better results. Give positions in sun. They seed prolifically; cut these off rigorously, allowing only a couple of pods to remain on each to ripen for next year's seed. Lupin seedlings are very attractive to slugs. A good plan is in July to sow in deep boxes, not less than 6 in. and plant out in late autumn.

LUPINS, TREE. P.; 4 ft.; cream, yellow and mauve; summer.

The seeds need soaking for an hour or two before being sown where it is to grow. The variety *payeni* is 6 ft. Deep, average soil and a sunny situation.

LYCHNIS (Campion). H.P.; 24 in.; scarlet; June–August.

The popular *chalcedonica* is from 18 in. to 2 ft. high and bearing large dense heads of bright-scarlet flowers; there is a white variety, *vespertina*, but it is not so good. *Grandiflora* is a handsome plant (with several varieties) bearing fine clusters of large flowers with fringe-like edgings, and varying in colour through many shades of red to white. All do well in a warm situation and on a light soil. They may be raised either from seed or cuttings, and are improved by occasional transplanting. Another variety is *Lagascae*, a charming little plant for the Alpine garden, profuse in flowers of a bright-rose colour; it thrives best in a sandy soil and sunny position. It is easily raised from seed. Agrostemma (*which see*) is akin to Lychnis.

LYSIMACHIA. H.P.; trailing; yellow; summer.

This variety of Lythrum (*which see*) is our old friend Creeping Jenny, which thrives in any soil, prefers moisture, and is increased by division.

LYTHRUM. H.P.; 4 ft.; rose; summer.

Does well in any good soil so long as it is in a moist situation. The purple variety, *salicaria*, is also known as Loosestrife. Increase by division in spring.

M

MACROGLOSSUS (Cape Ivy).

A greenhouse specimen belonging to the *senecio* family, with yellow flowers during summer, is a climber growing in average soil and requires attention in watering.

MAGNOLIA. F.S.; 7 ft. and upwards; white and purple; spring.

Nearer the tree category than shrub, but very beautiful in spring, flowering with a wealth of bold white and purple blossom. The earliest to flower is *Stellata* (*Halleana*), March, while *grandiflora* blooms in August. *Lennei* has rose-purple flowers. A hybrid, *conspicua*, white, is the Yulan. Most varieties are in flower in April. Plant young specimens late spring or autumn, in leaf-mould and peat, in full sun and some shelter from north and east winds.

MAIDENHAIR. See ADIANTIFOLIUM.

MAIZE GRASS. See ZEA.

MALLOW. See LAVATERA; *also* MALOPE.

MALOPE. H.A.; 24 in.; various colours; summer.

Will flower freely from a sowing in the open ground in April and May. Sow thinly in a sunny spot. The height is 1–3 ft., and the growth fairly upright. The flowers are violet, crimson or pink, or white. They prefer a heavy soil. The variety, *trifida grandiflora* is dark rose. The Tree Mallow is described under LAVATERA.

MALVA MOSCHATA (Musk Mallow). H.P.; 3 ft.; rose; late summer.

It thrives in average soil. Sow in March, in greenhouse, put in border in April for flowering August. Increase by division.

MANURING.

On light and free working soil it is advisable to apply stable or farmyard manure in the spring in a partially-decayed condition, when it can be lightly dug in. On heavy and sticky soils, however, it is best to apply " strawy " manure at the autumn digging. When this is done the action of the weather makes the surface of the soil friable and suitable for seed-sowing in the spring, improves the texture of heavy soils, increases the warmth, and makes them easier to work. It renders all soils more retentive of moisture.

Since the increase of mechanical transport, stable manure is scarce and to some extent this is replaced by providing decayed vegetable matter in the soil. All decayed vegetable matter except cabbage stalks and potato haulms, which can be burned and the ash added to the compost heap, should be kept in a heap or pit. Wood ash, soot, cow, sheep, pig and poultry droppings are also valuable manures. *See* COMPOST and LIQUID MANURE.

Green Manuring.—Wherever there is a piece of the plot or garden which is clear by the end of August or early September and is not required for another crop before the end of the year, it is a good plan to sow some Mustard broadcast after the ground has been lightly pricked over. This should be dug in when it is beginning to show flower, and before severe frost sets in; it will help to keep up the stock of humus in the soil. Lupins, from surplus seed, do the same.

Closely allied to manuring is the changing of positions for vegetable crops. Vegetables should be arranged in groups, and one crop, or group of crops, should be followed by another making somewhat different demands on the soil, and leaving the soil in best condition for the next crop. This will keep the soil in a better-balanced condition, improve the quantity and quality of the crop. *See* ROTATION; *also* CROPPING PLAN. For artificial manures, *see* FERTILIZERS.

MARCH GARDENING. *See* MONTH BY MONTH IN GARDEN AND ALLOTMENT.

MARGUERITE. H.P.; 3 ft.; white, yellow; August.

The marguerite family is large and has many different names. The tall, large, white daisy with yellow centre is popularly known as the marguerite, and it grows freely, making a grand show in the herbaceous border. Increase by shoots or cuttings in spring or autumn. It likes a sunny position and is not particular as to soil. A good white is *Mrs. F. Sander*, and a yellow, *Étoile d'or*, while a blue species, really *agathaea coelestis*, is included by amateurs.

MARIGOLDS. H.H.A.; 18–30 in.; orange; late summer and autumn.

Marigolds love a sunny position, are well able to sustain drought, and will thrive in a poor soil. Sow in March and plant out in the usual way. They are the *officinalis* variety of calendula, *which see*.

As well as the homely species are the *Tagetes*: African and French varieties, the latter having rather smaller flowers, and being striped and blotched with brown on the orange. A dwarf variety, *signata pumila*, is 9 in. and free flowering. Sow in boxes, start under a cloche and harden off, or do not sow till May, and put into border in June.

MARIPOSA LILY. See CALOCHORTUS.

MARJORAM.

This herb is raised from seed sown in spring in the open and increased by division. See HERBS.

MARROW. See VEGETABLE MARROW.

MARTYNIA. H.H.A.; 2 ft.; crimson; summer.

The attraction is the perfume, most pronounced in *elegans*. Sow under glass in spring, and pot up into loam, sand and leaf-mould.

MARVEL OF PERU. See MIRABILIS.

MASK FLOWER. See ALONSOA.

MATTHIOLA BICORNIS. See NIGHT-SCENTED STOCK.

MAY GARDENING. See MONTH BY MONTH IN GARDEN AND ALLOTMENT.

MEADOW SAFFRON. See COLCHICUM.

MECONOPSIS. H.P.; 3 ft.; blue, yellow; summer.

Remembering the seed takes a month or more to germinate, sow in February under glass, and again in a fortnight for later flowering. Sow sparsely as they resent crowding, and thin out. They start best in sandy loam and when fairly forward prick out into pots, having compost added to the loam and put into shady place till established. Use either for flowering in cool house or in the open where sheltered from strong sun. The species comprises various poppies: the Welsh Poppy (*Cambrica*), 1 ft., yellow, and good for rockeries; Himalayan Poppy (*Wallichii*), 3 ft., blue drooping heads; Chinese Poppy (*integrifolia*), 3 ft., primrose. The Welsh Poppy has a fine double variety, *plena*. It is a growing custom to make annual sowings, so securing finer bloom.

MEGASEA.

The large-leaf, pink-flowering, spring Saxifrage (*which see*).

MELIOSMA. F.S.; 6–10 ft.; white; summer.

An interesting spiraea type, which has a delicate fragrance, succeeds in average soil, and is increased by rooted suckers. Autumn or spring planting as convenient. The hardiest variety is *Myriantha*.

MELON.

Can be grown in a frame if in good sun, given free air and planted in a rich compost of loam, sand and leaf-mould in good firm texture, well tilthed, and, if conditions are favourable, melons may be cut four months after sowing. Sow seed, one in a pot, in winter, plunge in a box of manure for warmth to start germination and when roots established set in 5-inch pots and later give a top-dressing: when 1 ft. high plant in the frame soil. Their habit is like the vegetable marrow and general treatment for fertilizing the female flowers, which have swellings (*see* sketch in CUCUMBERS) that are the incipient melons, must be given. Remove surplus shoots, add compost if roots show through. Give plenty of water. Greenhouse culture is much the same, training them up strong wires or canes by the glass. They can also be grown in the open, after starting in a frame, if put on a rotted turf pile or an old hotbed. Good qualities are *superlative*, with red interior; *Imperial Green-flesh* is juicy and good tasting; *Blenheim Orange* is suitable for growing in the frame. Do not be afraid to stop shoots, as this lessens the number of male flowers.

MERTENSIA. P.; dwarf; blue; May.

A good rockery plant flourishing in any soil providing it has some peat and sand and is given shade. *Sibirica*, 1 ft., has blue and white blossom; *peniculata*, 18 in., is darker blue; *virginica*, 1 ft., inclines to purple, and *echioides*, a deep blue, is 6 in. Divide in spring.

MESEMBRYANTHEMUM. *See* ICE PLANT.

MEXICAN ORANGE. *See* CHOISYA TERNATA.

MEXICAN SUNFLOWER. *See* TITHONIA.

MICHAELMAS DAISY. H.P.; 5 ft.; various; September–October.

It belongs to the perennial asters or starworts, hardy, bush-like, prolific in flowering. The best effect is achieved by allowing them to grow in masses and support each other. All varieties may be raised from seed in autumn for planting out in the spring, or they can be sown under glass in February to flower the same year. More often they are increased by division from outer shoots in spring. A fine variety is *subcoeruleus*.

MIGNONETTE. H.A.; 1 ft.; gold and red; summer.

The delightful fragrance of this plant assures its welcome. Of the various varieties, *Machet*, with its bold spikes of flowers, is a general favourite, especially as a pot plant. For winter flowering indoors the seed should be sown about August in a compost of sandy loam and leaf-manure, taking care to sow thinly, and add lime when planted. For summer flowering sow in early May in a warm spot. It will not transplant.

MILDEW.

To remove this fungus from plants syringe either with a solution of 1 oz. nitre to a gallon of water or with a mixture of 1 oz. flowers of sulphur to 2 gallons of soapy water.

MILFOIL. *See* ACHILLEA.

MILLA. Bulb; 18 in.; white; spring.

Either for cool house or warm border outside in sandy loam, *biflora* being a favourite white variety, and *violacea* a violet. Increase by off-sets.

MIMOSA. *See* ACACIA.

MIMOSA PUDICA (Sensitive Plant).

Its rose-coloured flowers are less the attraction than the peculiarity, which gives it its popular name, of a touch of the hand causing its leaves to droop. Grow from seed in heat in spring and pot up in a mixture of peat, loam and sand.

MIMULUS. H.H.P.; 6–18 in.; scarlet; June–August.

Grow in fertile soil in moist situation and let them winter under protection. March is the best time for planting; start seed in warmth during winter and pot on till ready for the border, hardening before putting out. *Cardinalis* is scarlet, *cupreus* is orange; *ringens*, 1 ft., is blue; and *radicans*, 6 in., is white blotched violet.

MINA LOBATA. H.A.; climber; white; summer.

A free-flowering blossom, changing to creamy white from buds that are first red then orange. Sow in position, warm, in May. This is the annual variety, *versicolor*, of *Ipomoea* (*which see*).

MINT.

Grow in moist friable soil in half-shade, planting roots from suckers in spring and cut back stems on old plants if not done in September. It wants keeping under by hoeing off surplus suckers below the surface. Never spread wood or fire ash on mint as it may kill off young plants.

MIRABILIS (Marvel of Peru). H.H.P.; 2 ft.; various colours; July.

A tuberous, fragrant perennial which may be treated as a half-hardy annual and raised from seed by sowing early in the year in heat, pricking off the seedlings to harden in a cold frame and planting out in June into an ordinary soil, where they can get plenty of sun. The variety usually grown is *jalapa*, a handsome plant some 2 or 3 ft. high and developing into a dense bush covered with flowers varying in colour from white to yellow, red and purple in many shades; *multiflora* is a smaller plant with fine clusters of bright reddish-purple flowers, while *longiflora* is remarkable (as its name indicates) for its long tubular flowers, which are enriched with centres of brilliant red.

MITELLA. H.P.; 6 in.; white; June.

Grow in a moist peaty soil in rockery or border and increase by division in autumn. The variety *diphylla* has cream-coloured blossom.

MITRARIA. F.S.; H.H.P.; 4 ft.; scarlet; July.

Requires a sheltered position and shade in fibrous peat and sand. Increased by shoots started in warmth in summer under a cloche.

MOCK ORANGE. *See* PHILADELPHUS.

MOLES.

Hydrogen peroxide or calcium cyanide is very effective for killing off moles. Soak a piece of cotton-wool with the above and apply to the run for about five minutes, morning and evening. The irritation of the human skin produced by this treatment may be soothed by afterwards rubbing in a little lanoline.

MONARDA DIDYMA (Bee Balm, Sweet Bergamot). H.P.; 2 ft.; red; July.

It thrives in any soil, bearing whorls of deep red flowers which last a long time. A larger and more showy variety with flowers of brilliant crimson is *kalmiana*. In both cases the best effect is obtained by massing the plants together in bold groups. Increase by division in spring.

MONKSHOOD. *See* ACONITUM.

MONTBRETIA. Bulb; 18 in.; brown, yellow; August.

Not particular as to soil, but prefers shade and moisture. The flowers start from long spikes. They spread rapidly and should be divided each year. Some growers winter the plants in the greenhouse. There is a wide range of varieties.

MONTH BY MONTH IN GARDEN AND ALLOTMENT.

Of the dozens of jobs always possible any day, at any time of the

Cut offset at 1.

Pot in soil and sand up to 2.

Increasing Montbretia.

year, in the garden or allotment, the following are the more imperative for the month indicated. *Note* that in northern districts and in bleak and exposed positions the work is better done a week or ten days later than in average temperatures, and that—so far as sowings are concerned—if cold winds persist it wastes no time to wait till it is a bit milder and heavy night frosts are over.

January.—Burn rubbish and vegetable stumps: wisdom in this prevents pests multiplying. Protect artichokes from frost. Prune fruit trees and top-dress round about them. Protect roses with bunches of straw and bracken. Get on with digging, turn over if dug earlier, work in compost. Put in a few broad beans for early supply. Sow cauliflowers in frame. Protect celery from frost. Plant out earliest cabbages. Examine stored potatoes, parsnips, carrots, etc.; throw out as needed.

February.—When not frosty do some deep digging, three-spit trenching, and manure soil in readiness for early peas and beans. Where soil is heavy, work in sand, wood ash, leaves (especially beech), fire ashes, to lighten in time for root crops. Prepare onion bed for sowing late in month. Plant shallots, divide chives; stir top soil of mint bed, trim runners to stop spreading unless more mint is wanted to grow. Make sowings of spinach, parsnips and early carrots if ground not too hard from frost. Start rhubarb under large pots. Get a hot-bed ready for hastening cauliflower seedlings. Spray roses and fruit-tree buds. Sow sweet-peas in warm corner for later transplanting. Look over seed potatoes. Clear up decayed rubbish; burn it. Make plans for garden lay-out and the rotation scheme for vegetables.

March.—Plant rose trees, make ground very firm. Sow tomatoes under glass. Pot rooted chrysanthemum cuttings. Trim up herbaceous border, pinching out weak new growth from perennials, stir and mulch ground around them. Plant out onion setts. Sow the hardier annuals and any new perennials. Get in early potatoes. Sow leeks. Give an eye to young peas, protect with ash, and put light twigs about to scare birds. Keep the weeds down or they will get out of hand. Slightly prune creepers, removing dead ends. Plant gladioli. Any new grass plot to be prepared and levelled, dug and raked to fine tilth for sowing as soon as frosts go. Strawberry runners should be laid for sprouting ends to root; cut off runners that show no new leaf. Raspberries that fruit in late summer should now be cut down to 6 in., leaving a couple of buds; fresh shoots will grow in good time; canes planted in autumn will not fruit till following year. Pot on chrysanthemums, and where stock wants increasing take old clumps into greenhouse for hastening new shoots, which can be taken for cuttings. Roses should now be pruned if weather not bleak, the hybrid perpetuals not being cut too hard back.

April.—Plant out late-blooming lilies. Any fruit-tree grafting necessary ought to be done. Any new roses must not be planted later than first half of April, preferably first week. Sow most of vegetables now; if earlier sowings, put in more for succession. Put in a few more potatoes and make a sowing of carrots. Lawn mowing may now start or grass will get too long for easy work. Regular sowings of mustard and cress can start. Remember the value of the cold frame for sowings of annuals and half-hardy kinds, as well as for bringing along seedlings in protection from cold winds. The hardy annuals can be sown in open border where wanted to remain, thinning out later. Any re-potting of perennials such as azaleas and other flowering shrubs ought to be done now. Do not forget to roll the lawn at intervals, as the ground is not now too soft. Sow beetroot, globe and taper; also dwarf French beans. Keep the hoe going among the young plants before weeds get vigorous and stifle flowers or vegetables; also keep the earth loose round new growth by using the hoe regularly. Plant out pansies and violas, trimming off dead growth from those which have survived the winter. Any lawn turfing for renewals should be done not later than this mid-month. Main-crop vegetables can be sown and any thinning of earlier sowings should be kept in mind. Spray fruit trees and the larger shrubs. Paths heed attention to make them tidy for the summer; rolling, levelling, removing worked-up stones and regular weeding.

May.—The flower garden now demands close attention if fine plants are to develop. All annuals will be in vigorous growth, any weaklings can be sacrificed; allow plenty of growing space; tie up sappy shoots; watch out for insects; loosen soil round stems; give weak manure water; and where buds are showing pick off any showing blight or wither. The herbaceous border is in vigorous growth and some weaker shoots can be sacrificed, particularly the Michaelmas daisies; the flowering will be all the stronger. In the vegetable garden runner-beans can be put in, putting in the stakes at the same time, deeply enough to stand high winds. Sow vegetable marrow and cucumber in warm spots. Seedlings of these raised earlier can be planted out if covered at nights to protect from frost, pots will do. Codlin-moth now starts to trouble; also American blight. Succession sowings of vegetables, roots and the lighter green stuff, as lettuce, can be made. Next year's perennials, wallflower, forget-me-nots, sweet-william and so on can now be sown and until mid-June, as well as biennials. Don't neglect the spraying of fruit trees. Spring-flowering shrubs can be pruned when the blossom has died down. Manure rose trees.

June.—If the dahlias were not started last month do so now. Take the tubers from where stored for winter, put into good light soil mixed with sand, till the shoots are 4 in. high, lift gently, divide with a piece of tuber for each shoot, and plant in flowering quarters late in June, putting a few lettuce leaves about the spots to save them from slugs; keep down green fly. Take advantage of a warm spell to clean out and fumigate the greenhouse. Herbaceous border plants could do with surface manuring, either liquid or one of the powder fertilizers. In the vegetable plot vigilance is needed to keep pests at bay with dustings of Derris powder or one of the special insecticides put up for particular plants or root crops. Do not overdo watering, but when done it should be thorough; a daily sprinkling is to be avoided; twice a week, well done, in average hot weather is better. Pinch out tomato shoots and, if in flower, shake blossom twice a week to aid pollination.

July.—Sow violas and pansies for next year, and a few more wallflowers and some columbine to give a show for the spring. Layer carnations, pinning in with twigs, and do not allow to get dry. Particular attention must be given to pests both in flower borders and among the vegetables, destroying without mercy, or not only will this year's work be marred but the insects, etc., will increase beyond bounds next year. In the allotment there is plenty to do. Peas should be gathered as soon as the pods are full, else they toughen; picking also means a lengthening of the supply by allowing the late forming pods to mature. Plant out winter greens and sow for spring brassica. Celery and leeks should be planted out. Lift early potatoes. Make another sowing of perpetual spinach (spinach beet) for next year. Pick beans—runner and French—as they become big enough, and so assure more from the same plants. All root crops need attention for loosening earth, watering, hoeing weeds and digging out weeds that are deep rooted; burn these latter.

August.—Chrysanthemums should now be budded and side shoots rubbed out. If red spider appears in the flower bed, syringe thoroughly. The earliest bulbs for next year, snowdrops and so on, should be planted during this month; the larger bulbs can also be put in pots and kept in a warm corner in the open, otherwise keep in cool house. Cuttings of hydrangea can now be taken, heels, and firmly potted in sand till roots start, when re-pot into good but not rich soil. Rose cuttings and evergreen shrub cuttings will root readily in the open if sand is mixed in and watering not neglected. Cover cauliflower heads with leaves to hasten whitening, bend over onions, earth up celery and leeks. Make preparations on allotment or vegetable plot for next year, clear and dig where peas and beans are over, and remember your rotation plan in deciding what will go there for next year.

September.—Next year begins to loom large; the results of this season must be harvested, and make-ready the watchword for conditioning the plots for winter's sweetening. Beet, carrots, potatoes can be lifted and stored; the carrot and beet in boxes of sand or under mounds of earth in the open, the potatoes in clamps. Parsnips are better left in, the frost improves, and they can be pulled as required for the pot. Cauliflowers should have a leaf put over each head for protection, and, if not done earlier, onions bent over from close to the heads. Seedlings of spring cabbage can be planted into growing quarters. Young cauliflower can go into the frame (in pots) for safety during winter, and those still outside dusted around with soot. Cut back fruited raspberry canes to 1 ft. above the ground. Plant the new strawberry bed. Keep the ground loose by hoeing; turn over any ground cropped, watching out for insects and their eggs; burn rubbish as it accumulates. In the flower garden plant out what bulbs will flower in the early spring. Any transplanting of shrubs is done now. Prune rambler roses of old wood and tie up new runners. Take cuttings generally and have a second go at layering carnations if first lot have not provided enough new stock; roses can also be multiplied now by taking cuttings with a heel and thrusting deep into stiffish soil, ramblers and climbers take well but slowly, ordinary bush roses, etc., are difficult to strike.

October.—Those shrubs which are decidous—leaf-losing in winter—can be planted or shifted to other quarters: new roses can also be planted, making ground very firm. Put in pots another lot of bulbs to provide succession. Lift fuchsias and other summer bedding plants such as lobelia, ivy-leaf geraniums, verbena. Take cuttings of shrubs, inserting them deeply, with sand well mixed in. They can go in open; do not disturb next year, they will make better root. Replanting and division of herbaceous perennials can now go ahead. Give the lawn a final mowing before winter sets in. Planting and cutting down is best done now, as also any lifting, such as dahlias, to keep during winter. Lift and store the rest of the root crops.

Do some digging and manuring in the vegetable plots, turn over any already dug up. Any couch grass got out should be burned, and what potato haulms may be dry enough for the bonfire; decayed matter left about breeds disease and harbours pests.

November.—Lime-dress any dug plots, but clean of weeds first. Any leeks or celery still unearthed up should be so treated at once. Cut down artichokes and asparagus, cover rhubarb, gather green tomatoes for chutneying, cover seakale, heel over broccoli, plant horse-radish, blanch endive. Get ahead with more rough digging for frosts to break and purify; lime where sourness is suspected in lower spit, but liming must be done again in early spring for surface. Dress lawn with sand. Gather leaves for composting, particularly beech. Early flowering plants, such as wallflower, polyanthus, myosotis, daisies, if not already bedded out, should be put in at once and protected, till established, from frost. Plant fruit trees. Put in late-flowering bulbs.

December.—If the privet hedge is gappy take cuttings below a joint and somewhere between 8 in. and 1 ft. in length; insert deeply in stirred earth and let alone till wanted. Finish fruit and shrub pruning; prepare for next year by digging and turning; look over catalogues for interesting new floral adventures; burn rubbish, make out the rotation plan for vegetables; cut a good lot of wooden labels—18 in. high saves a lot of bending; clean and repair tools and, finally, remember there's always plenty of right-down useful work to be done this month, which, though not so interesting as in other months, is every bit as vital to success.

Note.—It will be observed that certain instructions are repeated in order to allow for the time differences of succession plantings and also as a last minute reminder.

MORAEA. H.H.P.; 2 ft.; yellow, white; May.

They are of the Iris habit and should be grown in sandy loam, keeping them in the greenhouse. A brown and yellow variety is *bicolor*, 2 ft., and *edulia*, 4 ft., is violet. Increase by division.

MORAINE BED FOR ALPINES. *See* ALPINES.

MORINA. H.P.; 2 ft.; vari-coloured; June.

A suitable subject for a warm place in rockery; they bear pink, white and crimson flowers on long spikes above handsome foliage. The variety *longifolia* has purple blossom. Sow seed in gentle heat in greenhouse in early spring and gradually harden before bedding out.

MOTHER OF THOUSANDS. See AARON'S BEARD.

MOUNTAIN ASH (Pyrus Aucuparia).

If there is room in the garden for the compact spread of the Rowan, it is an added attraction with its graceful foliage and clusters of red berries in the autumn. A sturdy specimen can be purchased already grown to 8 ft. for planting in the late autumn, end of October till end of November, and though a stout specimen it must be firmly staked to withstand the sway of the wind, which, otherwise, would loosen the earth round the stem, letting in too much water, which would sour, and also allow frost to get at the roots. The Rowan or Mountain Ash in hardy, and once established in average soil, with a mixture of chalk, will give no trouble. In digging to put it in, excavate enough to assure full root depth, without side crowding, as in diagram under FRUIT TREES.

MOUNTAIN SWEET. See CEANOTHUS.

MULBERRY.

When in good vigour it yields an abundance of berried fruit, which has a distinctive flavour, more popular in earlier days than now, perhaps because the tree itself matures very slowly. When planting, preferably in autumn, do not root-prune. Once established it needs little attention and less pruning, merely thin out crowded growths, on occasion. The best fruiting kind is *morus nigra*.

MULCHING.

This means covering over the plot with a layer of compost or grass cuttings in order to save evaporation. It is merely laid on, not dug in, its purpose being to prevent the sun drying up the surface soil too rapidly. If left on it also gradually manures the soil. The difference between mulching and top-dressing, is that, while the former is chiefly to conserve moisture, with soil nourishment as an after effect, the object of top-dressing is to manure by laying compost or humus on the surface for a couple of inches depth and leaving the weather and watering to carry the nourishment down to the roots. When top-dressing pot plants, take off an inch of the old soil and then add the dressing, leaving enough room on top to take water. It should be done in spring-time, or, for later maturing plants, in the autumn. Old hotbed material is good for top-dressing. Leaves and material from the compost heap will serve for the shrubbery and the herbaceous border if manure is not available. Hop manure is very useful, but it needs to be covered with a little soil, or in windy weather it will be blown about.

MULLEIN. *See* VERBASCUM.

MUSCARI (Grape Hyacinth). H.P.; 9 in.; blue; March–April.

Very effective planted in autumn in spaced groups, in loam or a good average soil; they can then be left for some years without dividing. They do well, also, in pots in the greenhouse. They have been improved of recent years, good varieties being *botryoides*, blue; *botryoides alba*, white; *heldreichi*, light blue; *neglectum*, black blue; *Heavenly Blue*, bright blue; and one, *azureum freynianum*, blue, which blooms in February.

MUSHROOMS.

Best results are obtained by growing under cover, say in a shed where semi-darkness is normal, and where it is possible to fit hot-water pipes to supply a moist heat. Mushrooms can be grown in the open—but it is rather asking for much work giving inadequate result. Mushrooms grow on prepared manure beds and these beds can only be used for one growth, not a second supply. The mushrooms develop from fungoid growths known as mycelium, popularly called spawn and supplied in prepared slabs. The manure must be absolutely free from impurities and it must be fresh straw manure, stacked not less than 4 ft. high, to ferment, and any dry patches kept moist by sprinkling. After a fortnight thoroughly turn the heap, noting temperature, which should be 150° F. Give another forking a week later, and four days later, when it should not smell acrid, be brown and warm, the heap should be lifted by fork into the shed, turning it all in the moving. A temperature of 70° is right for spawning. If the bed remains too hot, pierce into the body here and there to reduce heat; a dibber thrust in about a foot will do.

Flat Bed.—For starters, a flat growing bed is better than a conical one. Make it a foot high all over, as long as convenient, and 3 ft. 6 in. across. Keep thermometer handy and take tests. When temperature drops to 70° F. put in the spawn (mycelium). Break off pieces, often marked but if not, the size of a plum, of the brick and at 9-in. intervals in criss-cross fashion thrust a piece into prepared holes about 2 in. deep and then filled up, pressing the manure firmly round the spawn in closing hole, to exclude air. After a fortnight the whole bed must be cased with a couple of inches of sterilized soil, top and all sides, pressed down firmly everywhere. The soil must be friable.

The spawn should now do the rest, but draughts must be excluded, temperature kept even, light dim, and in a couple of months the cropping can start. If during the maturing period a white, thready mildew appears on the heap take a brush and remove it.

Ridge Bed.—Make manure into a 2 ft. 6 in. cone with a 3 ft. 6 in. base (or 4 ft. with 6 ft. base if space allows), add soil layer of same thick-

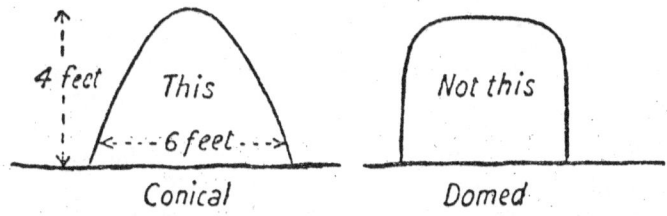

Mushroom Ridge Bed must be conical not domed.

ness and at same time as for the flat bed, but also cover the lot with straw to about 3 in. all over, to hold soil in position, a proceeding unnecessary with a flat bed. Some find it more convenient for attention to put flat beds round sides of shed and conicals in centre.

Mushrooms can certainly be grown in the open, and in lawns or pasture land, but, as stated, for an amateur the preparation necessary and the uncertainty of even fair results make it hardly worth the time and labour. If, however, mushrooms appear spontaneously on such land, a few pieces of spawn pocketed below the surface will develop a satisfactory crop.

MUSK. Trailing pot plant; yellow; June.

Raise from seed in warmth and put into 5-inch pots (or border) in rich soil, with generous moisture, in March for flowering from June to August.

MUSK MALLOW. *See* MALVA MOSCHATA.

MUSTARD AND CRESS.

Sow the seed thickly; merely sprinkle on the soil, or cover lightly in March or April in a sunny spot. Cover with brown paper till germination begins; about four days in warm weather. The cress should be sown three days earlier than the mustard. Sow for succession at intervals of a fortnight until September in the open, and for winter use from October to March in boxes under glass. Many prefer to grow in boxes in summer also, as being cleaner and handier to crop. Gather by cutting with scissors, thus avoiding clinging earth.

MYOSOTIS. *See* **FORGET-ME-NOT.**

N

NARCISSUS.

These should be treated in the same way as hyacinths and daffodils, but plant in a well-worked moist loam. Daffodils, which are classified among the narcissi, are sufficiently numerous to be given under their own alphabetic order. The Jonquil class has small flowers in groups on slender stalks from a central stem. Apart from these the principal narcissi varieties are: *Star*, white, yellow centre; *chalice*, another name for *star; barri*, white, strongly-marked centres; *eucharis* or *leedsii*, white, yellow cup; *angel's tears*, white, of jonquil character; *polyanthus*, a scented variety having small bunched florets; *poeticus*, white, coloured centre, of which there is also a double variety. Other varieties are added frequently.

NASTURTIUM. H.A.; dwarf; crimson, yellows and variegated; July.

Prefer sunny situation but do well in poor ground and shallow depth. The dwarfs are from 6 in. to 1 ft. high. The climbing and trailing varieties have similarly modest requirements; run to 10 ft. in many colours and can be sown in April to May in open, ½ in. deep. They belong to the Tropaeolum class. A modern dwarf variety is *Golden Gleam*, and also the crimson, *Flame* nasturtium.

NEMESIA. H.H.A.; 1 ft.; various; July.

Of South African origin, these free-flowering annuals must be raised in heat and do best in a cool greenhouse. They do well in the open, however, if in a sunny position away from cold winds. Plant the short, shrubby sorts about 3 in. apart; the tall-growing, about 6 in., for full effect in broad borders or large patches. The flower stems rise from tufts of leafage. Flowers are in a bewildering variety of shades and colours and go on for several weeks, indeed by successional sowings in warmth, flowering can be sustained in the greenhouse practically all the year. For spring outside bedding, sow in February, transplant early in May; for summer bedding, sow end of March; sow in July or August for winter greenhouse display, and for spring in the greenhouse sow mid-September.

NEMOPHILA. H.A.; 6 in.; blues; summer.

One of the hardiest of annuals and of much value for edgings or small beds by reason of its compact growth. Seed may be sown either in August, for spring flowering, or in April, for summer flowers, and in the place where the plants are intended to bloom, though they will bear transplanting if it be carefully done. A light soil is desirable in order that the seed may germinate freely and the plants be restricted from rank growth. Put in dry spot and in sun. *Insignis* is an excellent species with sky-blue flowers and varieties of white, purple and striped; *atomaria*, 4 in., has white flowers touched with blue, and has varieties of sky-blue and black, and white and black; *discoidalis* has flowers of dark purple and of dark red, both edged with white; while *maculata* has particularly large flowers of both white and mauve.

NEPAL LABURNUM (Piptanthus Nepalensis). F.S.; 8 ft.; pale yellow; May-June.

Its flowers do not droop like its English namesake, and soon fade. It is best grown against a wall where its silvery foliage is seen to advantage. It requires a sheltered position and light, well-drained loam, and can be raised with ease from seed or cuttings in a frame.

NEPENTHEA. Hothouse; green, purple or red, with distinctive spottings.

This is the curious Pitcher Plant, it having hollow jug-like receptacles, with lids complete, in which is a liquid. Not a subject for general cultivation, and they require a mixture of sphagnum moss, sandy peat, sand, charcoal and fibrous peat to succeed in pots, or preferably baskets, to have a hot, moist atmosphere and a daily syringing.

NEPETA (Catmint). H.P.; 9 in.; blue; June onwards.

A striking plant for the border; it spreads so rapidly that it should have at least 1 ft. all round. A more compact and erect variety, darker blue in flowering and perhaps less graceful is *mussini*, which is 2 ft. high. It is not particular as to soil or treatment and is increased by division, which should be drastic every year.

NEPHRODIUM.

The name for a very considerable genus of ferns, some hardy, others greenhouse and hothouse specimens, increased by spore striking and by division, and grown in rich loam, leaf-mould and some addition of sand and cow manure.

NERINE. Bulbs; varying shades of red; late summer.

The best-known variety, the *Guernsey lily*, first blooms and then matures. It suits either greenhouse or border, needing a rich compost with cow manure, loam and sand. The bulbs do not develop in the early summer, but in autumn flower attractively in colours with a brilliance. They dislike being disturbed. In the open, choose a sunny spot and discriminate in watering.

NEW ZEALAND GLORY PEA. See CLIANTHUS.

NICOTIANA. H.H.A.; 3 ft.; white, magenta; late summer.

This is the tobacco plant and a good mid-border plant, flowering freely but not profusely. Sow in spring under a cloche or in the greenhouse, and as the seed is tiny, barely cover it with soil, and transplant as soon as able to be handled into boxes to harden gradually, after which plant out in the open in rich deep soil in May. A magenta variety is *sanderae*. The white variety is *sylvestris*, which in good soil may grow over 5 ft. Another attractive variety is *affinis*. With their lovely heads of flowers they are among the finest border plants. They are best grouped in threes at the back of a border, the plants spaced 15 in. apart. Although strong growers they do not succeed if crowded with other plants.

NICOTINE INSECTICIDE.

An effective wash or spray for the majority of troubles is a nicotine emulsion compounded of ½ oz. of nicotine extract, ¼ lb. of soft soap, boiled in enough water to keep liquid while being thoroughly mixed, and for use at rate of one part to ten or twelve of water.

NIEREMBERGIA COERULEA. H.H.A.; 6 in.; white; lavender; summer.

The variety *hippomanica* profusely flowers in lavender with a yellow eye, while *gracilis*, 9 in., is white with purple streaks. Both are really perennials, but much better grown as half-hardies, given sandy loam, plenty of water, and kept in the greenhouse. A hardier variety, *rivularis*, is suitable for the open in the rockery, best in moist and sunny situation. It is a creeper.

NIGELLA. See LOVE-IN-A-MIST.

NIGHT-SCENTED STOCK (Matthiola Bicornis). H.A.; 1 ft.; lilac; summer.

The chief claim of these straggly-looking lilac flowers is the perfume exuded freely at night. It will flower in sun or shade, is not particular as to soil, and blooms all the summer and autumn. Sow thinly.

NOLANA GRANDIFLORA. H.A.; 9 in.; lavender bells; June.

Sow in spring in a sunny situation in well-drained average soil in border or rockery. It is of trailing habit, and the lavender colours have white and primrose markings.

NORTHOCLAENA.

These are the gold and silver maidenhairs, increased by spore starting, are hothouse specimens, and require limestone mixed with fibrous loam. Place where there is plenty of light and give good drainage.

NOVEMBER GARDENING. See MONTH BY MONTH IN GARDEN AND ALLOTMENT.

NYCTERINIA. H.H.A.; dwarf; blue and white; summer.

This small free-flowering plant gives off perfume at night. Grows in average soil and no special treatment beyond that for H.H.A.'s is needed. The blue and white variety, 6 in., is *capensis* and *selaginoides*, 9 in., is white.

NYMPHAEA.

The name for Water Lilies, the cultivation of which is by soil around roots in sunk baskets filled with loam within a casing of moss. There are many varieties. See WATER GARDEN.

O

OCTOBER GARDENING. See MONTH BY MONTH IN GARDEN AND ALLOTMENT.

OENOTHERA.

The Evening Primrose (*which see*) is the best-known member of this group, but a beautiful white dwarf variety of trailing habit, *taraxacifolia alba*, is treated as a half-hardy annual, the seed being sown in late spring in warm plot, for July flowering. Another trailer, yellow, is *Missouriensis*, perennial treated as annual.

OLEANDER. F.S.; pink; late summer.

A beautiful double-flowering member of the Nerium family which it should be mentioned is poisonous. A mixture of loam and peat with a proportion of sand suits it best, and though it presents no difficulty in culture it is liable to become infested with aphides and must be regularly fumigated. Slightly prune flowering shoots when blossom has faded. It is largely grown in tubs in the greenhouse and should be kept well watered. The plant will not bear cutting owing to its great tendency to bleed. Propagate by root-suckers, or by slips pulled from the stem and struck in a bottle of water, or in a light soil kept continually wet.

OLEARIUS (Daisy Bush). F.S.; 4 ft.; white; August.

These are welcome because of late summer flowering, and the grey-green foliage making a contrast in the border. A variety having large flowers is *stellulata*, but *Haastii* is the true daisy tree, being quite hardy; *macrodonta* and *myrsinoides* flower earlier but less hardy; *nummularifolia* has yellow foliage; *erubescens* is a distinctive variety; and *insignis*, which revels in dry places, is a rich and profuse bloomer. Plant in autumn in light loamy peat free from lime. Prune early spring. Take ripe cuttings in September in cold frame.

OMPHALODES (Venus' Navelwort). H.A.; 9 in.; white; June.

The particular variety of this class taking the name of Navelwort is *Linifolia*, and it has silver foliage with flowers not unlike myosotis, but white. Blue varieties are *verna* (flowering March), *cappadocica* and *lucillae* (4 in., flowering June). Sow in spring in open in average soil and thin out. A biennial variety, blue, grows to 2 ft.

ONIONS.

One of the secrets of growing good onions is that the soil must be made very firm for sowing, and for transplanting also, if the latter is done. But before then the soil has to be prepared, for though the onion itself matures on the surface, the fibrous roots go deep and consequently well-drained soil is required, deeply trenched and well manured the previous autumn, putting in a layer of matured compost where humus is scarce, and after filling in the upper spits work up into ridges and then leave it to the frost and weather. As soon in the New Year as the ground is dry, mostly in February, level out the ridges and get a fine tilth by raking and apply a dusting of soot. Any favourable time in late February till end of March do the sowing, only covering the soil and thoroughly firming, the drills to be 1 ft. apart. By sowing under glass (*see* INTENSIVE CULTURE) earlier results are obtained. For winter sowing the best time is first week in September, to plant out, March, otherwise the procedure is the

Bending-over Onions.

same as for spring. The spring sowing will be sufficiently forward by mid-April to plant out 6 in. apart, or thin out to the same distance, allowing roots to go down their length, not spread out, and putting the bottom of the young bulb only $\frac{1}{4}$ in. below the surface. The thinning out should be when the onions are a couple of inches in height, and another when double that height, which should leave the 6 in. between. During August the top-grass of the onions must be bent over, so that it touches the ground and remains so, in order to allow better maturing of the bulb, and if good weather gives plenty of sun lift in a fortnight. A rather easier Gloucestershire alternative to bending over is to run the hoe along each row 2 in. below ground to break the roots; this hastens ripening without the trouble of bending over. But in any case lift within three weeks, putting the onions to be sun-dried on sacks or boards, the roots facing the sun. When dried, they can be strung in ropes for storage till wanted. Should any of the onions start for seed, pinch off the seed shoot; the bulb will then continue to grow. Onions are ready for lifting at the end of August or early in September.

For spring onions make a sowing of *Lisbon* in August and protect from frost. The ordinary thinnings from general sowings are also quite tasty as spring onions. For pickling onions, sow any time up to June.

Useful Hints.—To prevent damage by onion fly commonly use sawdust impregnated with paraffin, scattering this alongside the rows of seedling plants. If sown sparsely enough to make thinning unnecessary, the onion fly trouble will be greatly reduced. If onions do not bulb up sufficiently, rake soil from around bulb and it will soon regain its rotundity. If a sowing is amde in mid-August for a winter crop, it is seldom troubled with maggot; nor is a January sowing under glass. It is recommended by an expert of national reputation to plant onions thickly and so get good medium bulbs which keep better than very large ones.

ONONIS. H.P.; 2 ft.; rose; June.

A suitable subject for a made-up bank which is apt to get dry, for while thriving in ordinary soil it does better when the ground is not moist. Raise in spring from seed and subsequently increase by division or cuttings. The seed is sown in open where needed and well thinned as the plant is of shrubby habit. Rose-coloured varieties are *hircuna, rotundifolia* and *splendens*. The variety *fruticosa* is purple and *arvenis* has rose and white blossom.

ONOSMA. H.; 1 ft.; citron; May.

A suitable dwarf for the rockery, where its unusual colour stands out distinctively. Plant in light soil of sandy texture, and, if possible, on limestone sub-strata. The citron coloured variety is *tauricum*, a white variety, *helviticum;* and a rose and white, *albo-roseum*, this last being better treated as an annual. Increase by seed in spring.

OPHRYS. *See* ORCHIS.

ORCHIDS.

This handsome flower has a great number of varieties requiring many different methods of culture which need special study. They, however, are not beyond the capacity of the amateur with hot and cool greenhouses, and for successful rearing special books on the subject should be consulted.

Here, some general remarks may be of guidance. Only few orchids take kindly to sharing a greenhouse with other plants or, rather, other plants cannot thrive as they should under conditions which suit orchids. Consequently it is usual to house them on their own

in either a cool or a warm greenhouse according to species and needs.
In addition to the ordinary ventilators, one or two should be pierced
in the lower structure on the sliding door plan to keep out marauders
and to regulate the volume of incoming air. These ventilators should
be placed in such a position that the current passes over the heating
pipes and so becomes less frigid. In cold weather, by using these,
the top ventilators in the glass sides need not be opened. Those
orchids which do well in a cool house require a temperature ranging
between 45–60°; those requiring a warmer temperature should be
housed separately in an average heat during daytime of 80°, with
a night temperature never lower than 60°, but preferably maintained
at 65°. Variations in temperature should be adjusted gradually.

Greenhouses, whether cool or warm, must have blinds to shade
from extremes of light; the cool house requiring shade as soon as
the sun is on the house and till no sunshine is on the house. The
measure of sunlight depends on the class of orchid, but this is an
observed rule. In the winter all natural light is needed.

The art of ventilation can only be learned by experience and the
needs of individual species, but always use the ventilators in the
apex with reserve. Their use is to keep the air pure.

Suitable potting soils vary with each class and is best ascertained
when buying specimens, but a rich compost in which sphagnum
moss is an ingredient is a common basic factor.

New stock should always be given new pots, for re-potting this
is not so necessary, but each pot must be scrubbed in warm water
and sun or fire-dried before use. The hanging sorts need wire-hooked
wooden baskets, preferably of teak, in which rough fibre forms the
drainage foundation. For pot drainage the crocks should fill at least
a fifth of the pot, and must be washed before being used.

Re-potting work is when new growth shows rooting at base, which
usually is soon after the main plant has flowered. Give extra shade
to re-potted orchids.

Always use rain-water for watering, very slightly warm during
winter, and pour it on carefully to avoid sprinkling the young growth.
Only water when needed, but amply when given. Do not water
through the rose.

The orchid is happily not prone to disease; spot is both prevented and cured by judicious ventilation, atmospheric moisture
and scrupulous adherence to a correct temperature in the house.
Slugs and woodlice have to be guarded against.

A hardy, open-air genus is the ORCHIS (*which see*).

ORCHIS. H.; average 1 ft.; various; spring and summer.

This is the hardy species of orchid and may be grown out of doors. Two other kinds, *Ophrys* and *Spiranthes*, may be included as they conform to the same general treatment; a sandy loam, enriched and with a chalk undersoil, a moist situation and a sunny position in rockery and border. They are increased by off-sets in autumn. *Orchis* is purple and red, flowering in summer; *ophrys*, rose, green, brown and yellow, spring; *spiranthes*, white, yellow and scarlet, spring and summer. Certain kinds of *cypripedium* are also hardy, treated as above, but add sphagnum moss to soil, and give some shade. Their flowers are mostly green, blooming in winter.

ORIENTAL POPPY. H.H.P.; 30 in.; reds; June.

The very minute seed requires no more than a film of sandy soil, sown thinly in a box in the frame or greenhouse in July, carefully brought on and put into position in autumn for flowering next season. Good varieties are *Beauty of Livermore*, large crimson flowers; *Jenny Mawson*, salmon; *Royal Scarlet*; *Mahony*, black-purple; *Perry's White*, blotched purple; and *Peter Pan*, a dwarf.

ORNITHOGALUM (Star of Bethlehem). H.; bulb; dwarf and 2 ft.; white; spring and summer.

They like a warm, fertile garden soil and are increased by off-sets. The smallest is 6 in., *umbellatum*, the Star of Bethlehem. The taller varieties are *nutans* and *pyramidale*, both 2 ft., and flowering in April. Plant at distances of 3 in., from September to October, but thin out rigorously each year. Give protection against frost.

OSTROWSKIA. H.P.; 4 ft.; pale blue; summer.

Once established in a warm position in light, rich, deep soil, not in full sunshine, and somewhat sheltered from wind, these will flower freely. Give plenty of water in dry weather, and in bleak districts lift and winter them in the greenhouse. They can be increased by division; but there are always plenty of self-sown seedlings.

OXALIS. H.A. and H.P.; 6 in.; various; August–October.

A large class mostly useful in rockeries or hanging baskets, and popularly named the Wood Sorrels. A yellow variety, *corniculata*, is 4 in. and free flowering; *cernua*, also yellow, is best for baskets; *corniculata rubra*, yellow, has purple foliage; *deppei* is red; *flori-*

bunda, rose, is a greenhouse denizen; and *enneaphylla* is white. Ordinary soil bolstered with a little sand and leaf-mould suits all, including those which have tuberous roots.

P

PAEONY. H.P.; 3 ft. upwards; various; May–June.

There are two divisions, the herbaceous kind, very much more general, and the tree class. In both categories new varieties are constantly being introduced.

The herbaceous kinds require a well-manured soil and plenty of water during the summer, and being of slow growth do not flower fully until the third year, when they produce bushy flowers of pink, red or white. September and October are the best months for planting. Increase by cuttings; by slips of the root, or by layers half cut through behind each bud. Prepare the ground by deep digging, adding loam if not present; a clay subsoil suits, and once established do not disturb. Choose a shady spot. The tree species also require the same soil character and preparation; it averages 6 ft., and the variety *moutan* has imposing flowers, single and double. A white is *snowflake;* maroon, *Henry Irving;* rose, *James Kelway.* Take the cuttings with a heel in summer and strike under a cloche. Where basal shoots appear, cut them out.

PAINTED LADY. H.A.; 10 ft.; climber; scarlet and white; July.

The foliage is particularly profuse, showing off the blossom. Sow in mid-May in required situation and thin out drastically. Average soil and near a wall or arch.

PALMS.

Propagate by division in April, by sucker in September or by seed. These should be potted in a compost of silver sand and fibrous loam or of grit and fibrous peat during spring or early summer. Take care not to injure the roots. Give plenty of water during winter and summer, and sponge the leaves with warm soft water. In hot weather place in a shady spot and give a little cow manure and soot well diluted (1 in 20), in liquid form. A good variety for the garden is *chamaerops humilis*, which plant during warm weather.

PANSY. H.P.; 6 in.; many colours; June–October.

Pansies require a light, rich soil, well drained but not too dry, and do well in cool but not shady spots. Even if in bud and flower they suffer very little check from being bedded-out, and may be used massed, in beds and borders of selected types and colours. Do not plant pansies that are drooping, but immerse roots in soft water till they stiffen; then water in well when planting and always water freely in dry spells to get good blossom. Snipping off seed pods ensures

True-to-type Pansies
Cut off old & flowering shoots at / leaving central young growth to develop

a continuance of flowering. To ensure the continuance of a good strain trim long shoots and flowered stems, as diagram, leaving central young growth to develop and make fresh root. The pansy may readily be raised from seed in open in South or elsewhere under a cloche or by cuttings taken early in summer and kept under glass in a shady border until well rooted. Transplant in September to bloom early the following year. Take cuttings from the ends of the shoots, slipping them off just below a joint. Propagation is also by root division. Violas take the same treatment.

PAPAVER. H.H.P.; 12 in.; mixed; summer.

The class includes the Iceland Poppy, *nudicaule*, mostly more dwarf than the usual run of poppies, and so, good and graceful for the rockery, the blossom being borne on long stems. It survives the winter with difficulty and therefore is better grown as a biennial. The colour range includes yellow, orange and white.

PAROCHETUS. Dwarf; creeper; blue; August.

This is the Shamrock Pea and does well in a mixture of loam, leaf-mould and sand if given a sheltered position in the rockery. Increase by division in spring.

PARROTIA. H.H.; 15 ft.; scarlet; spring.

A tree which grows better near a wall, or in sheltered position. Give it friable soil, and plant in the autumn. Its foliage colours handsomely in the autumn. Increase by layering, or cuttings struck under a cloche in spring.

PARSLEY.

Sow thickly in a rich soil, from March to April, $\frac{1}{2}$ in. deep in rows. They are slow in starting. To assist its coming up quicker, soak the seed a few hours in warm water. Thin out to 6 in. apart, when large enough, and then leave to mature. For winter use, sow in July and protect in a frame.

PARSNIPS.

Prepare ground well in autumn; if same crop do not manure again, leave rough and get to tilth by end of January. Sow in a rich and somewhat sandy loam, in drills 15 in. apart. Put the seed in successions, February to April; push a dibber well down, fill the hole with loose earth; press a couple of seeds in to about 1 in. and water. This takes time but results in good tapering parsnips without forked roots. When big enough, gradually thin out if needed to 9 in. apart but do no transplanting. Remove all weeds by frequent hoeing. Parsnips are much sweeter if left in till frosted.

PASSIFLORA (Passion Flower). H.H.P.; climber; blue, white; April–July.

Grown in sandy loam and peat in well-drained place against a sunny wall, a splendid show may be expected of this picturesque, free-flowering plant, particularly if by putting crocks around the roots their run is restricted. They do equally well in the greenhouse. In the open plant out March, and water well in hot weather. Each winter prune back to three or four buds of the old wood, and in spring snip off frail shoots. Increase by cuttings taken during the summer,

Paths

of young shoots, and struck under glass or cloche. The blue variety is *caerulea*, and *Constance Elliott* is white.

PATHS.

A path need not be ambitious, but of whatever medium it is constructed should be not less than 2 ft. in width; where space admits it could be double that width. All paths, also, should be thoroughly foundationed with clinker, stone and rubble, a foot below the surface and a layer at least 6 in. thick rammed well in. Over this earth and ash beaten in, and then the surfacing. Crazy paving is usually laid

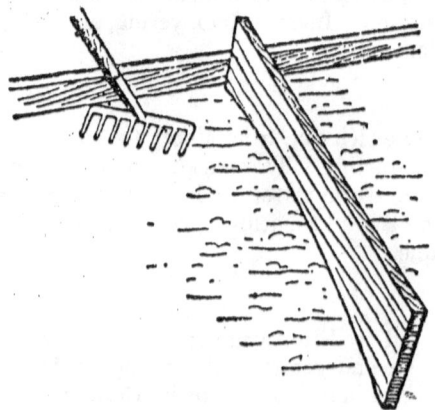

Raking to get camber curve.

Cambering new path.

level, as too is cement and concrete, but beaten earth or gravel paths are cambered (sloped toward each side) to allow water to run off instead of soaking in. To secure the camber, a board is cut the width of the path and the curve of the decided camber (*see* diagram). The underlay of earth between foundation and surface is raked to heap up along the middle and then beaten to conform to the camber, the board being moved along as the work proceeds. It is then much easier to get a good cambering on the surface, rather than attempting to do all the cambering operation on the surfacing material. For eradicating weeds from paths, *see* WEEDS.

PEACH.
To obtain luscious fruit it is necessary to be particular in first planting the tree, mostly against a sunny wall. Excavate 30 in. deep and 5 ft. wide, make drainage by broken shards, which cover with inverted turves, and then fill with soil, of heavy texture and containing chalk, mixed with chopped-up rooted turves and a few old broken bones. Do this filling by first throwing in a few inches on which to bed the roots, well spread out and then do more filling, tread down, put in another layer and firm it, and so on till filled, seeing that the tree branches are 6 in. away from the wall itself. This done, and given netting protection from frosts, and later from birds, the tree should develop sturdily. Pruning is necessary; do it in autumn before leaves fall, and note not to cut away the growth made during the summer, on which comes next year's fruit. This being remembered, pruning is simple and keeps growth open to air and sun by doing away with old wood or weak crowding shoots. Preserve the vitality of the tree by keeping only three or four new shoots on any branch, rubbing the others out as soon as started. The young shoots will bear a crop next year and, in wall peach trees, should be tied in loosely alongside the fruiting branches they will replace in autumn. Of the new shoots, on each branch of last year's growth leave one at the top, another near the base, and possibly one near the middle.

Peach and other fruit trees on walls must be watered freely and often in hot, dry weather. If the leaves are damaged by peach-leaf blister, the affected parts should be cut off and burnt.

PEARS.
The pear, especially when grown as a wall-trained tree, requires root pruning more frequently than any other fruit tree, or it becomes unfruitful. Summer nipping is imperative in pruning the pear, as if all the wood-buds be allowed to remain they will so drain the strength of the tree that fruit-buds will not form—excessive wood growth being characteristic of the pear. For general cultural work that given for FRUIT TREES and for APPLES will apply, noting that the cordon system is often successfully used for the finer kinds of dessert fruit. Ordinary fruit-tree pruning is general but latterly the Lorette system is coming into vogue, for which *see* FRUIT TREES.

Suitable pears for the open garden are Williams' Bon Chretien, Conference, Louise Bonne, Durondeau and Emile d'Heyst.

The pear is not immune from troubles, the worst being scale, for which spray with a mixture compounded of soft soap, 5 lb.; paraffin, 1 gallon to every 25 gallons of water. For other pests *see* APPLE and PESTS.

To store pears they may either be hung by their stalks or placed separately on shelves. They ripen best in a rather higher temperature than apples, as in a room indoors.

PEAS.

Prepare ground in autumn by deep digging and manuring. Sow in double rows 6-8 in. apart, the rows 2 ft. apart. In heavy soil put seed 3 in. deep; in light soil 2 in. deep. Peas mature earliest in light, rich soil; for general crop, a rich deep loam or one inclining to clay is the best. Sow the extra early varieties in February or March and every fortnight for succession until May or June as required. The plants should be kept clean and earthed up twice during growth. The wrinkled varieties are the nicest flavour but are not so hardy as the round sorts, and if planted early should have a dry soil. The dwarf varieties are best suited for small gardens or for forcing, planted in rows 1 ft. apart. The taller kind should be well supported by branched twigs high enough to take full height. Keep the hoe going between rows. Some take the risk of a November sowing to secure an early crop, but frost and birds often combine to defeat the effort. If wanted to store peas, examine and remove all bad ones. Place in the sun until dry, shell and then put in dry jars till needed.

PEAT.

As a component of mixed soil, peat has many uses. It is grand for helping the rooting of seedlings and to foster root growth generally. For lilies put some just below soil after putting in bulbs. It preserves from frost plants such as fuchsias, which are dormant in wintertime, or early spring flowers which are planted in autumn; place it on surface round the stems.

Peat is most effective in granulated form, is excellent for lightening heavy soils, and when black and decomposed is just right for manuring purposes. Fork it into the surface three weeks before transplanting seedlings. Peat moss is a more readily usable form. Note, however, that peat contains only a small percentage of nitrates.

PELARGONIUM. H.H.P.; 2 ft.; reds and white; summer.

Although considered a bit old-fashioned, these free-flowering and attractive perennials make a grand pot display or in the border, if put out after the frosts are over. As bedders they will flower out of doors from early May till autumn if seeding heads are carefully removed.

There are double as well as single flowered sorts, and variegated, dark-leaved, ivy-leaved, zonal and other handsomely foliaged sorts. As a rule, however, the best, bearing fine trusses of bloom, have quite ordinary green foliage. Knock out of pots carefully and plant firmly in loose soil in the position they are to occupy for the season, in light soil and sunny position. They have a bold effect, and when all of one variety and colour are grouped together, they are seen at their best. Take cuttings late July and strike in frame or greenhouse, taking care when they are rooted to protect from frost. Of the ivy varieties, *leopard* is lilac-pink blotched crimson, and *alliance* a bluish white. Among the scenteds, *fragrans*, white with red veins, is desirable, and of the other sorts the classes and varieties are varied enough for any taste.

PENTSTEMON. H.P.; 2 ft.; reds; June–August.

Both for the border and the rock garden the pentstemon, in one or other of its many varieties, is admirable; a tall and handsome plant with spikes of bell-like flowers. They thrive best in a warm soil with some protection during winter. For the rock garden there are various dwarf varieties. Pentstemons may be grown either from cuttings or seed, but they are a little tricky in culture and need a good friable soil, well-drained. A scarlet variety is *barbatus*, and *gentianoides* tends to violet; *azureus*, 1 ft., is blue, as also is *glaber*, 18 in. A good dwarf variety is *menziesii*, 6 in., reds and purples and mauves, this last being *scouleri*. If sown in warmth in February, flowers may be had in the autumn. Cuttings readily take root under a cloche.

PENZANCE BRIAR. F.S.; 6 ft.; pink; June.

The sweet briar of Shakespeare and the eglantine of the early poets. It has been cultivated to increase size, beauty and colour of its original, and is often seen a mass of glorious colour, exhaling fragrant perfume. As a hedge the briar is effective as well as being picturesque. The *Lady Penzance* variety has bronze flowers. Given sunshine and plenty of air they will flourish in any ordinary soil.

Propagation is by cuttings—about 8 in., thrust diagonally into soil.

PERENNIALS.

These, once planted, grow on, yearly renewing themselves by spreading, by offsets, or new growth from base, the outer ones of which have most vitality. Some are increased by division, others develop separate little plants which can be teased out of the clump easier by washing out the ball of soil. It is wise to get new stock in either of these ways every three years, throwing away the old plants. A herbaceous border is mostly composed of perennials so situated that the taller specimens are at the back of the border and due discretion used to group or harmonize colours, and to consider flowering periods (*see* FLOWERING CALENDAR) so as to get a succession of bloom.

PERIWINKLE. *See* VINCA.

PERNETTYA MUCRONATA. F.S.; 3–6 ft.; white; June.

Belongs to the heath family and has attractive berries, varying in colour but mostly translucent rose-pink, in the autumn. Grows best in lime-free soil, preferably peat. Difficult to establish, but quite hardy, in good sun and moist conditions at root.

PERPETUAL SPINACH. *See* SPINACH BEET.

PERUVIAN LILY. *See* ALSTROMERIA.

PESTS ON PLANTS.

For destroying pests among flowers or vegetables, a good all-round medium is Derris, either dusted on young plants or through a syringe with a fine spray. For particular species, special treatments are applied, among which are the following, as recommended by the Ministry of Agriculture.

Black Fly on Beans.—Pinch out the growing points and burn them. In bad attacks, plants should be treated with nicotine dusts or preparations sold for the control of green-fly and used as directed on the packet.

Cabbage Caterpillars.—Cabbages and related vegetables are regularly attacked by the caterpillars. Hand pick the young caterpillars and crush the egg clusters, which are yellow. Derris dust is satisfactory.

Flea Beetle.—Attacks radishes, turnips and green crops both above and below ground. Dust the young seedlings with Derris. In bad attacks the treatment may have to be repeated at intervals of three or four days. If the seedlings are kept growing with plenty of moisture, less damage occurs.

Potato Blight.—To prevent blight, spray the foliage with Burgundy or Bordeaux mixture in mid-July and again at intervals. There are also on the market proprietary copper fungicides which are similar in their effects.

Slugs and Snails.—For slugs a mixture of bran and *meta* powder is effective, but rain and wind causes loss of its properties. To avoid this, place a couple of cigarette tins on their sides sufficiently far apart to allow a third tin with three sides flattened out to be used as a cover, thus protecting the mixture from deterioration. Fresh lime, dusted on the ground, is a common remedy, but not in rainy weather. Bonfire ash, if kept dry and mixed with a little soot and coal ash, is invaluable for dusting over seedlings and young vegetable crops to ward off the attacks of slugs and also enrich the soil. This method is also a protection from the ravages of snails. A good plan to prevent snails crawling up a wall is to daub the bottom of the wall with a paste compounded of oil and soot, over which they will not pass.

Green-fly and Caterpillars are instantly killed by immersion in water heated to 113° F., while beetles perish in water of 125° F.

Fly.—An excellent insecticide for black-fly, green-fly, hop aphis, red spider and woolly aphis:

Steep $\frac{1}{4}$ lb. quassia chips in $\frac{1}{2}$ gal. water for 12 hours and add $\frac{1}{4}$ lb. melted soft soap. Make up with water to 4 gal. and use after showers in warm weather. Or a thin mixture of oil of turpentine and soap may be applied to the stems and branches. For Red Spider, petroleum emulsion is effective.

In addition to the above advice the long experience of an expert agriculturalist on his own extensive acres may be given in brief:

If a run of dry weather checks vegetable growth among young plants, green-fly and other sap-sucking pests get to work. The same happens from lack of hoeing or neglect of cultural attention. For *carrots* use naphthalene powder to guard against fly. For *celery* do the same. For *onion* fly $1\frac{1}{2}$ oz. soft soap to 1 gal. water, sprayed on finely. For *turnip* flea use steamed bone-flour, this also having the advantage of being a fertilizer at the same time. For *raspberry* beetle use Derris powder. For *loganberry* do the same.

When dusting on any anti-pest powder do it particularly as first flowers open and twice before they wither.

For wholesale slugging a long-tried and successful method is salted water; and a pair of tongs is most convenient for picking off the slugs.

PETASITES. H.P.; 6 in.; white; spring and winter.

The variety *fragrans* is the winter heliotrope, and this flowers in mid-winter. The spring flowering variety is tall, 3 ft., and is *officinalis*, better grown in moist soil; a good pond-side plant. Two rockery varieties are *albus*, 1 ft., and *palmatus*, 6 in., both white.

PETUNIA. H.H.A.; 15 in.; various; June–September.

A showy plant with large, rich blossoms, embracing a great variety in shades of colour, marking and form. The single-flowered kind are useful for borders, producing a charming effect when properly massed, and may be raised from seed sown in heat in February or March. They are not now so widely grown as the stems are fragile. The double-flowering sorts need protection in greenhouse for winter and are increased by cuttings taken in August and struck in sand under a cloche. If grown in open they need loam, sand and leaf-mould, well-drained, and after being started, gradually hardened. They do not like manure, but the pot-grown greenhouse kinds may have some in the same soil mixture. The carmine variety is *Countess of Elsmore* and the double purple is *Purple King*.

PHACELIA. H.A.; dwarf; blue, white; May–July.

A compact free-flowering specimen suited to border as well as rockery. The variety *campanularia* averages 9 in., will grow in average soil if put in semi-shade. A taller variety, *tanacetifolia*, is 18 in. and much sought after by bees. Sow in position in spring and thin out.

PHEASANT'S EYE. *See* **ADONIS.**

PHILADELPHUS (Mock Orange). F.S.; 6–10 ft.; white; July.

Well-known hardy perennial often referred to, but wrongly, as *syringa*. It prefers a sunny position and needs only good average soil, with room to spread. Best planted in November, thinned out after flowering to the young lateral growth which springs from the base of the plant. The ordinary sort, *coronarius*, is fragrant and profuse in flowering. The variety *virginale* bears double flowers;

grandiflorus has larger but less fragrant blossom. A greenhouse variety, *lemoninei*, flowers in March.

PHLOX. H.P.; 3 ft.; salmon, white, reds; July–August.

Grow from seed sown not earlier than May. The seed germinates very slowly and the following April will not be too late to plant to bloom from July to August in all shades of red, from palest pink to deep carmine, lilacs, lavenders and whites, many showing an "eye" of deeper tint. Phlox are excellent plants for the herbaceous border, being tall and requiring little attention after planting beyond watering in dry seasons. A light, friable garden soil, a sunny position and moist ground are most congenial. They can be grown as half-hardy annuals, started in heat in winter. Increase by root division.

PHLOX DRUMMONDI. H.H.A.; 3 ft.; various; spring and July–September.

Will grow to full sturdy habit and fine floral clusters, and may be sown in boxes of fine compost indoors, in a sunny frame in March or April, bedding out the seedlings early in May. They will flower profusely most of the summer. Sown outdoors in May the plants may be in flower by July. Keep slugs at bay. Flowers are now in a variety of colours and shades, usually with a dark centre. They like a sunny position and a fairly rich light soil. It is advisable to plant half a dozen young roots, a little apart each way, to form a clump, but take care that they are of one colour and variety. They make striking greenhouse plants.

PHYSALIS (Winter Cherry). H.P.; 2 ft.; scarlet; winter.

Grown for the scarlet pods, which hang gracefully, keep their colour when dried and average 2 in. in circumference. They flower in November and are dried for interior winter decoration. Grow in sunny position in light rich soil, away from strong winds. Sow seed as annuals, or increase by division. A grand variety is *franchettii*.

PICOTEES. H.P.; 1 ft.; white or yellow, marked; summer.

An attractive member of the carnation family and requiring the same treatment. Its characteristic is that the white or yellow flowers have bands of chocolate, pink, crimson, and some are spotted in these colours; there are doubles as well as singles. Strike by cuttings or shoots pulled with a heel in July.

PIN CUSHION. See SCABIOUS.

PINKS. H.P.; 1 ft.; red, pink, white; summer.

Of the carnation family on the dianthus side, and grown under same conditions in the border, though requiring less cosseting. They are largely singles, and self colours without markings. The favourite *Mrs. Sinkins*, is double white and fragrant, and the Pheasant Eye, *munstead*, has pretty blossom. Shoots pulled with a heel in July readily strike. Once established they do not like being shifted.

PITCHER PLANT. See NEPENTHEA.

PITTOSPORUM. F.S.; 6–10 ft.; greenish white; summer.

Its evergreen foliage is dark and shining, and the shrub has a genuine fragrance. In the south it can be grown against a wall or as a picturesque hedge. This variety is *eugenivides*, but *tenuifolium*, has chocolate-purple flowers, *tobira*, cream blossom, and *undulatum*, white flowers having fragrance.

PLANT GROWTH, NEW METHODS. See HORTOMONE, *also* HYDROPONICS.

PLANT LICE, APHIDES.

Make a solution of tobacco or lime-water and repeatedly syringe the leaves and stems of the plants. Ladybirds destroy aphides. *See also* PESTS.

PLANTAIN LILY. See FUNKIA.

PLATYCODON. H.P.; 1 ft.; blue; May–July.

A plant of many names, known as campanula grandiflora, as Wahlenbergia, Edraianthus and lastly the Balloon Flower. A favourite variety is *Mariesii*, which flowers blue, and some white. It has large shiny blooms not unlike the Campanula; should have the sun, grows best in a friable soil and is increased by division. The dwarf Wahlenbergias average only 3 in.; *dalmatica* being violet; *graminifolia*, pale blue; *pumilio*, rose.

PLATYSTEMON CALIFORNICAS. H.A.; 1 ft.; striking lemon tint; June–July.

Give treatment as for annuals, with good average soil. Looks well in rockery.

PLUM.
The plum (of which the greengage is, perhaps, the most delicious variety) does not do well on a cold or clay subsoil, nor in a moist-laden climate. A poor soil really suits it best so long as it has good drainage, for it has a tendency to make a superabundance of wood if the soil be at all rich. As a consequence, frequent root-pruning is generally necessary, and it should not be planted deep—a covering of 6 in. of soil is sufficient. The side-shoots of trained plum trees are shortened by about half in summer, but shoots likely to be useful for replacing old worn-out branches should be left uncut. *See* FRUIT TREES for general culture. The varieties are numerous, their flourishing depending upon selecting them to suit the district, and prevailing soil and meteorological conditions, from dessert plums—Early Transparent Gage, Denniston's Superb and Cambridge Gage; and cooking plums—Early Orleans, Victoria, Pershore, Czar.

PLUMBAGO (Leadwort). H.P. and greenhouse; blue, white; summer.

A graceful perennial of value for the greenhouse and the rock garden respectively. The former, with its delicate blue blossoms, makes a charming training plant for the greenhouse, while the latter is perfectly hardy and forms dense tufts of wiry stems, some 6 in. high, bearing trusses of deep-blue flowers early in September, which last until the frost cuts them off. It is easily propagated by division in spring. The variety *capensis* flowers blue in summer, has a climbing habit and does best under glass. Prune after flowering. The white variety is *alba*, *superba* is rose and a warm greenhouse specimen, flowering in winter. Open-air varieties are *larpenta*, blue; *micrantha*, white, and do not mind average soil. The greenhouse types need peat and loam, half and half, with some added sand.

PLUME POPPY (Bocconia). P.; 4 ft.; yellow; spring.

The *japonica* variety is mostly grown as it also has feathery plumes which are cream coloured. Give it a sunny position, keep it moist, grow in clayey soil of some good depth as it is of vigorous habit. A cream-flowering variety is *cordata*. Increase by division in spring.

POINSETTIA. Hothouse; 3 ft.; carmine; autumn.

These well-known hothouse plants have scarlet or carmine heads showing in vivid contrast above the light green leaves. For soil give it three parts loam and one part a mixture of sand, manure and leaf-mould; it should be potted on as needed. Do not water in winter. Second year flowering is much more attractive. Cut down in March, put in propagating case, and when resulting shoots are 3 in. long, detach and plant in sand, still in propagating case, till rooted.

POLEMONIUM (Jacob's Ladder). H.P.; 2 ft.; blue; July.

Easily grown in sandy loam and increased by division in spring. The tall variety is *caeruleum*, blue; *flavum* and *pauciflorum* are both yellow and both 18 in. A dwarf variety is *confertum*, 6 in., blue, and a 9-in. variety *reptans* flowers blue in May.

POLIANTHES (Tuberose). Bulb; white; spring.

In the south they may do well in the open in sunny, sheltered position, but they find the greenhouse more congenial. They require a rich soil of sandy loam, leaf-mould and humus, and for the open should be planted in November or March, 3 in. deep and 9 in. apart, and left till growth starts, when they may be watered. They can also be started in a frame. November is the popular time for planting the bulbs as they are then available. Increase by offsets started in warmth. The bulb itself only flowers one year, the blossom being on spikes and having fragrance.

POLYANTHUS. H.P.; 1 ft.; various; spring.

The strain has lately been greatly improved in variety and beauty of colours, many blossoms being in pastel shades. Its cultivation is perfectly simple, for it will thrive in any garden soil, though it prefers one which is rich and moist, and flourishes best in a sheltered and somewhat shady situation. It can easily be raised from seed sown in the open during the summer months, and being perennial may be increased by division in autumn or early spring. Division is mostly adopted as giving greater certainty of preserving strains. Lift clumps, immerse in a pail of water, thus silting out the earth, when the rooted offsets can be seen, and the plants divided, to suit requirement, into single offsets, or a few together.

Dividing Polyanthus.

Primulas and primroses are of the same family but are given separate entries.

POLYGALA. H.P.; dwarf; purple; spring.

They like a cool, sheltered position, in loam, leaf-mould and grit, hence are good for the rockery. The shrubby varieties are increased by cuttings in spring struck in heat. It is also a good plant for the greenhouse, where firm potting is necessary. The cream and white varieties flower in summer.

POLYGONATUM. H.P.; 3 ft.; greenish white; June.

This is the well-known Solomon's Seal and grows best in shade in any soil. A pink variety is *roseum*. It should be remembered that its autumn berries are poisonous.

POLYGONUM. H.P.; climber; white; summer.

Useful, because of its rapid growth, for covering fences, or hiding sheds, but it increases so rampantly that care must be taken to keep it in check by rigorous pruning. The flowers are in small racemes.

POPPY (Shirley). H.A.; 2 ft.; delicate colours; July.

Among the annual poppies the Shirley takes foremost place by reason of its variety of delicate colours and profusion of blossom, while the taller *Mikado* varieties, which grow to 2 ft. and are larger and more decided in their colours, are also a favourite in the border. They are not particular as to soil if sown not too early, say in May, and as they dislike transplanting should be thinned out to 1 ft. apart. The French ranunculus annual species is also in many colours. *Perennial Poppies:* the Oriental (*which see*) has orange, pink and scarlet flowers; the Iceland is only 1 ft. high: both flower profusely in their second year, but make a good show in their first season. The perennial varieties have the same cultural rules as the annuals. Poppy seed is very tiny: mix with fine earth and sand and spread this thinly on seed bed and cover slightly. Iceland Poppies belong to the *papavers* (*which see*).

POPULAR NAMES OF FLOWERS. *See cross references.*

PORTABLE LIGHT.

One that can be moved about to start seed, or to protect or bring on young stuff in any part of the plot, and is very handy. That described weighs less than 2 lb., and the size of it adjusted to take exactly a half-yard of unbreakable glass substitute.

The diagrams give the idea. A shows ends 16 in. wide, 5 in. high, rising to 6 in. at centre to allow for top slope, and 1 in. levelled to take top stay, which runs the length of the light (C) and joins up to the other end, so providing the top support, being screwed inside each end flush with top of ends: it can be of 1 in. squared wood.

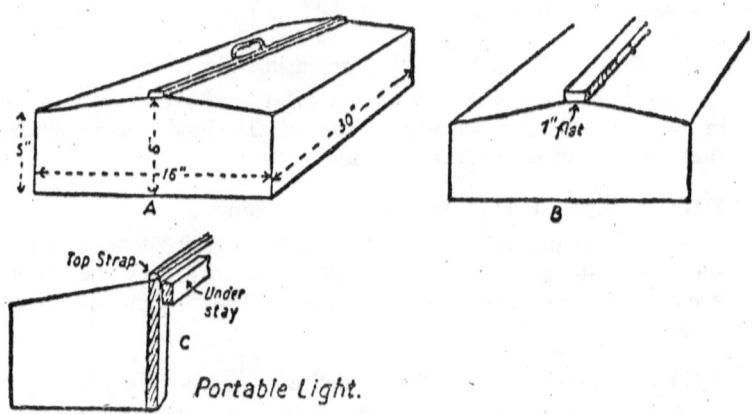

Portable Light.

The sides will be 30 in. long by 5 in. deep. When these are screwed together the "glass" will go over, with a nice margin for securing by gimp tacks nailed through thin 3-ply quarter-inch straps. To keep secure along top, nail a half-inch strap of 3 ply over the window-lite (B) and nail securely to the understay (C). To lift the light an old saucepan-lid handle was screwed on the top strap.

PORTULACA. H.H.A.; 6 in.; various; June.

Grow from seed in warm spot in April or preferably beginning of May. Sow in tiny drills in rockery and it will quickly produce a multi-coloured carpet.

POTATOES.

A few early potatoes can be grown on an exhausted hotbed. A covering of light soil must be given before putting a frame over them, and they must be carefully protected from frost. If started in the middle of January, the potatoes will be ready for use well ahead of the usual time (*see* INTENSIVE CULTURE). Potatoes grown for usual crops require rather deep, light sandy soil, well-drained and of a dry nature. It is best to plant them in ground that has been double dug and well-manured or used for a green crop the previous year. They are a good first crop, too, on virgin soil. Where ground has had a root crop the previous season it is well to apply some fertilizer, a beneficial mixture is quarter potash sulphate, quarter ammonia sulphate and half superphosphate, used at the rate of 6 lb. to the square rod. Seed potatoes are medium tubers that have been placed in shallow wooden trays (*see* diagram) under cover for about a month before they are to be planted. Exposure to light, at the temperature of 60° F., causes the " eyes " to sprout, and if the tuber is planted so as to avoid damage to these tender green shoots, leaving the tip of it just level with the surface soil, the young potato plant will

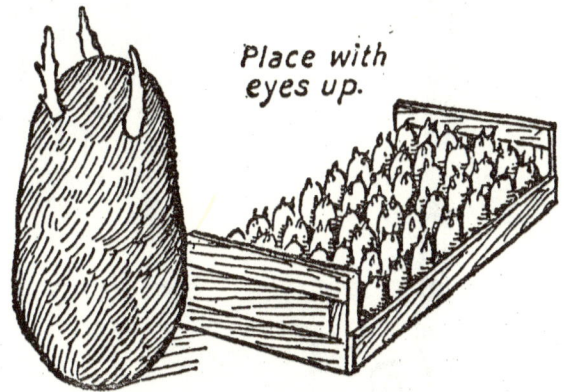

Storing seed potatoes.

start into growth almost at once and much time be saved. Some growers cut the tuber into two vertically so that each piece of the potato has one or two eyes, and plant them for main crop in March or April in rows of 2 ft. apart, 12–15 in. distant in the row and 3 or 4 in. deep. Make further plantings till June. Local conditions decide what sorts to sow. As the leaves grow upwards, and the haulm begins to show, place short, twiggy pea-sticks along both sides of the row, to keep in position some clean, dry straw loosely twisted around each plant. Earth up as soon as the leaves are well above ground. Not only does it help on the growth in the early stages, but when the tubers begin to swell, and those on the top rise through the soil, prevents them becoming greened and spoilt in flavour. See that earthing up has been properly attended to. Often several earthings are necessary between the first and when the plant begins to flower. The best way of earthing is to draw it up around the leaves with a hoe or spade, not higher than 6 in. If the soil is in a heavy, sticky condition, mix up a light compost with silver sand, and use two or three handfuls of this around each young plant, forming a little mound to protect them from the frost. Do not leave

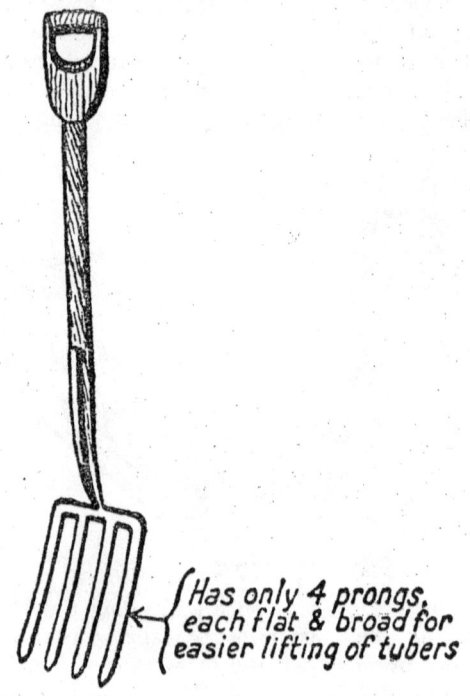

Potato Fork.

a little furrow at top of ridge, it will harbour harmful larva and insects. The main crop matures October or November.

To keep potatoes, first let them dry for an hour or so in the sun. Then they are piled on the ground and covered with earth and straw. The clamp, as this is called, is made by piling potatoes pyramid fashion on a layer of straw and covering with a 6-inch layer of straw over which is a similar layer of earth. Straws are placed vertically from the heap through coverings to allow the tubers to sweat off and left in to provide ventilation. The clamp should have a trench all round for drainage, and whenever opened it should be at the same end, and closed after supplies are taken. A clamp can be any length. Where no facilities exist for making a clamp, it is best to keep potatoes in a dark place, preferably in a cellar, heaped up and covered with straw.

Potatoes are lifted with a special fork (*see* illustration) having only four prongs, which are flat and broad on the surface and grooved on the under side.

An Oxfordshire farmer tells from long experience that unblemished potatoes free from scab can be obtained by putting grass cuttings into the drills when planting the setts. The bacteria, he says, then feeds on these cuttings—vegetable refuse will do if grass is not available—instead of the young potatoes.

Another tip is where setts are cut. Instead of dressing the cuts with lime, cover them with sacks for an hour or two.

It is also maintained that larger tubers come from cut setts, and greater numbers from whole setts, while younger potatoes produce heavier crops than those ripened before being lifted.

POTENTILLA. H.P.; 6 in.; salmon; July–September.

An attractive rockery plant with leaves like those of the strawberry and the salmon colour of the blossom has a tinge of copper. Good average rockery soil, with some grit, and where they get some sun. Sow in spring in light soil, and increase by division, March or October. Dwarf varieties include *nitida*, rose; *ambigua*, yellow; *veitchii*, white. Taller varieties, from 18 in. to 3 ft., are *fruticosa*, yellow; *vilmoriniana*, pale yellow; *mandschurica*, white; *nepalensis*, pink.

POTERIUM. H.P.; 3 ft.; white, purple; July.

Of the herb family, with feathery foliage, doing well in any soil if it has lime and given a sunny position. The white variety is *canadense*, and *sanguisorba* of purple tinge, 18 in. high. Increase by division.

POTTING.

It sounds simple enough and, indeed, is so, if a few cardinal points are always observed:

Keep pots clean; wash them inside and out when putting away after use.

Also wash the crocks and do not stint them when potting up.

Do not use large pots for seedlings and small plants, but just large enough to give root room, with an inch of soil to spare all round. *See* FLOWER POTS for sizes of pots.

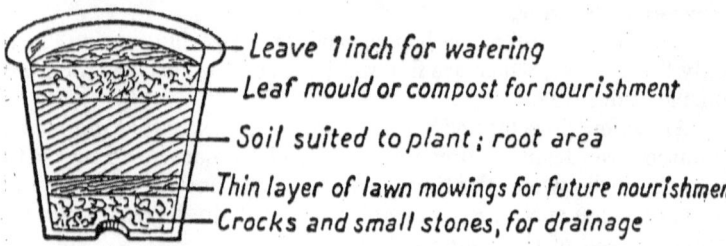

Good average filling for pot plants.

As a rule do not pot seedlings in rich soil; that can be done when they are established.

Soil mixtures should be suited to species: a little study and observation will make wise, but a good all-round mixture would be one part each sand and well-rotted manure; two parts leaf-mould (preferably beech) and four parts of fibrous loam. When potting, the soil should be moist enough to cling together when a handful is squeezed. Soak pots for a few moments, and then let drain before potting. It is a good plan to sterilize soil for potting seedlings of choice sorts, the method is explained under SEED BED.

Do not break up soil of smaller pot; transfer without disturbing roots.

Potting on.

Related to potting is the watering of seedlings. This is best done by placing the pots in a tray or zinc bath containing an inch of water (with the chill off) and let the moisture soak up through the pot-hole. Don't fill soil to top; leave an inch for watering and, when seedlings established, for filling up with richer soil as needed to nourish the roots and support the growing stem.

When roots show through bottom of pot it is time to re-pot into a larger size. This is called potting-on. Potting-off, by the way, is transferring seedlings from boxes to pots, and the process of doing so is pricking out.

In re-potting, tap side of pot to loosen earth, then with a finger at each side of the stem, invert the pot, and press out the root and ball of earth by pushing a twig through the pot-hole. Keep the earth round the root, and, having first crocked the larger pot, and given a layer of soil at bottom, put the transferred plant and its ball in, gradually filling in all round, pressing in as it is done so as to avoid unfilled spaces. Do not re-pot when soil is dry.

PRIMROSES. H.P.; 6 in.; cream; spring.

Primroses require a light, and rather leaf-soil, compost, that is moist, well-drained, but not too sandy or having lime in texture. They like semi-shade, but die in cold positions. The leaves are compact, the flower stem rising clear. Growth is rapid after flowering, requiring to be split up into new plants by midsummer or autumn to assure a show of flowers the next season. Many primroses will flower again in autumn and winter in favourable situations.

PRIMULAS. H.P.; 1 ft.; various; spring.

These are of the same family as primroses (*which see*) and thrive under the same cultural treatment, for the hardy outdoor kinds. Of late years they have been greatly improved in flowering, now comprising many different colours and shades and make a grand show in the fronts of borders or the rockery. Primulas of hardy species: the tall *florindae* (The Giant Himalayan Cowslip), 3 ft. high; *microdonta*, with violet flowers, 18 in. high, and *beesiana*, violet-purple with golden eye—and their cultivated varieties are among the new sorts. The variety *obconica* flowers in the winter. Sow seed in heat in February. There is a greenhouse strain which also has delicate varieties of colour and which can be raised from spring-sown seed. Care in handling is advised as the leaves bring out a rash on hands if contact is made, though not all varieties do this, nor are all persons susceptible: bear this in mind when increasing by division as given under POLYANTHUS.

PRIVET. F.S.; 6 ft.

As a rule these densely-foliated shrubs are rigorously clipped, being much used for garden divisions, but the Chinese privet (*Ligustrum sinense*), if left to flower and grow as a shrub in the garden, is a picture in July, of creamy white spikes as profuse though not so big as lilac cluters. They like sun, infrequent watering and any ordinary soil. Cuttings, after flowering, make root readily. Root prune every three years; it is easily done, sharply slice the spade vertically into the earth 6 in. from the stem.

PRUNING.

The pruning of shrubs, roses and fruit or other trees is a necessary operation and one which the less experienced usually do insufficiently. Pruning strengthens, improves appearance and results in freer flowering. Old branches which will no longer bear flowers, weak shoots which will only yield poor blossoms, and where the growth is rampant, a percentage of good growth can be pruned away with benefit to future flowering.

Roses should be pruned in March or early April, cutting down the growth severely to leave only a couple of shoots on each branch, and cutting out branches which turn inward. This applies to bush roses or standards. Climbers and ramblers need less drastic treatment, but all weak shoots, whether long or not, should be cut right down and only three or four sturdy runners left. This is best done in autumn after flowering. *See also* ROSES.

With shrubs, the pruning is to keep shapely and to save weakening by too rank growth. Old wood should also be pruned away as it harbours insects. Spring-flowering shrubs are best pruned in May or June, or, if later in flowering, in July. Summer-flowering shrubs, prune from March to June, or immediately after flowering. Autumn flowering, mostly prune in March or April, but some are better pruned in autumn after flowering. Winter-flowering shrubs are best pruned in late April or May. Details for particular shrubs are given under SHRUBS AND TREES and individual species.

Trees are pruned occasionally, both the branches and, less frequently, the roots. It is wiser to ask expert advice as individual root treatment is necessary, particularly in regard to fruit trees, but to those who feel competent the following will be useful.

Root pruning of fruit trees is essential to a good crop of fruit. Root pruning may be effected by digging away the soil from the roots until the strong feeders are disclosed, when they may be either severed with a sharp chisel or with a fine-toothed saw, leaving the less sturdy roots untouched.

In cutting away the branches of wall-trained, espalier or cordon fruit trees, care should be taken to use a thin, sharp knife, sufficiently keen to make a clean cut. If the cut be left with a rough, fractured edge, the branch is liable to split, with disastrous results.

For cutting thick branches, the fine-toothed pruning saw should be used, afterwards smoothing the saw-cut with the pruning knife and smearing it over with grafting paste, so as to prevent decay. This paste may be made by melting, over a slow fire, equal quantities

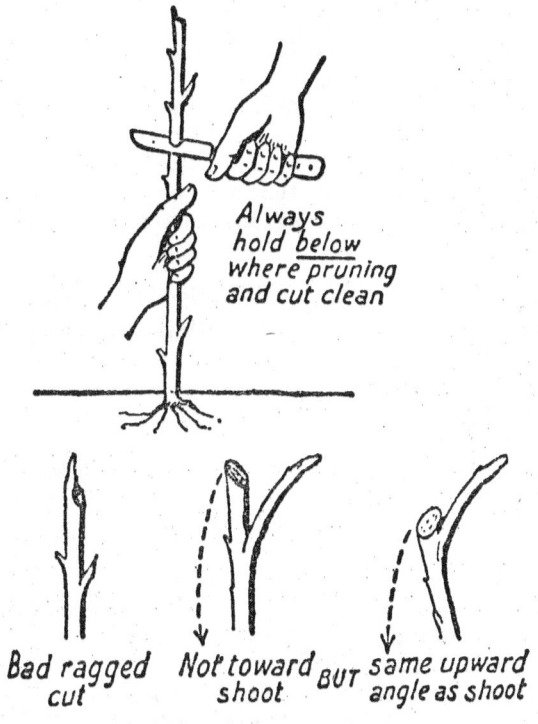

How to Prune.

of mutton fat and beeswax, with about four times the quantity of pitch. It should be applied warm, while it is sufficiently liquid to be spread with a brush. When it becomes necessary to cut off a substantial bough from a fruit or other tree, always start by sawing from the under side of the bough upward for a quarter of the way, and then complete the severance by sawing from the top. The reason for the under cut is to save splintering the bough and tearing the bark by a sudden break as would be the case if sawn from the top at the start; it is seldom practicable to support the portion to be severed. If there is exudation of sap, known as bleeding, the grafting paste mentioned above should be applied, a good coating being given. *See also* FRUIT TREES, APPLE TREES, SHRUBS and TREES.

PRUNUS. Tree; 10–12 ft.; pink, white; spring.

The class to which belong the cherry, peach, almond, etc. The ornamental flowering cherries and the coral blossom of the almond are among the most beautiful medium-height trees. Plant in deeply-dug, well-manured soil and increase by budding. *Amygdalus* is an early flowering and charming almond; *padus* (*watereri*), white, is a fine choice for the cherry, and the beautiful and free-flowering Japanese cherries, *serrulata*, are either pink, rose or white.

PUSCHKINIA. Bulb; 6 in.; white striped blue; spring.

Grow in the same way as Scilla, which they resemble, in well-drained situation and increase by off-sets. They grace the rockery and also make attractive pot plants.

PYCNOSTACHYS. H.H.P.; 3 ft.; light blue.

A warm-house plant of herb habit, growing erectly in loam, leaf-mould and sand, the brilliant cornflower blue flowers coming both in summer and winter. Increase by division.

PYRACANTHA. F.S.; white.

Mostly grown against a wall, in espalier fashion, spreading 10 ft. each way and upward. Its beauty lies in its profusion of red berries in autumn and it has long, sharp thorns, hence its popular name Fire Thorn for the variety *crenulata yunnanensis*. The variety *Rogersiana* has orange berries. Grows in any soil if in sunny position. Increase by short cuttings put in frame, or, less certain, from seed. The pyracantha is among the *crategus* family.

PYRETHRUM. H.P.; 2 ft.; various; June.

A fairly light soil suits most varieties, which are free flowering on long spikes, in various colours, and easy to cultivate. Start in seed pans in spring or summer, plant out when able to handle, for next year's flowering, or sow in heat, earlier, for autumn blooming.

They are increased by breaking up the clumps. There are fine double varieties: *Queen Mary*, pink; *Aphrodite*, white; *Desdemona*, maroon; *Lord Rosebery*, scarlet. Of the singles, good sorts are: *Princess Irene*, white; *Agnes Kelway*, rose; *Jubilee*, crimson; and *Tasso*, vermilion.

PYRUS. Tree; 15 ft.; pinkish; spring.

In this class are the apple, pear and crab. The last is a splendid garden tree, of medium height, by reason of its foliage and its fruit, the latter in shades of red. The Japanese crab is the most vividly coloured. Keep them away from stiff soil and damp situations and plant in well-drained loam. The Mountain Ash (Rowan) and the Quince (*which see*) belong to the group.

Q

QUAMASH. Bulb; 3 ft.; blue; May-July.

They flower handsomely, stellate blossom on spikes, if planted in moist situation in average soil. Plant the bulbs in autumn 2 in. below the surface and 1 ft. apart. Increase by offsets after leaves have withered. Varieties: *Fraseri*, 18 in., flowering July; *cusicki*, 3 ft.; *esculenta*, 2 ft., both blue and May flowering; and a white variety, *leichtlini*, which is 3 ft., flowering July. It is often named *Camassia* in gardening catalogues.

QUARRY.

This is the term for ground which has only a superficial covering of earth, often only a foot in depth, over a sub-stratum of flat porous stone, as in Cotswolds. The only remedy is the gradual and laborious removal of the "quarry" and building up with earth and compost, or only growing shallow-rooting crops and plants.

QUINCE. F.S.

In size more a minor tree, but, given the room it is a gem in any garden, every branch bearing delicate pink, orange, crimson and white blossom. The *Cydonia vulgaris*, which is the common quince, has a shrub-like habit of wide spreading and is in flower almost as soon as the leaves unfold in mid-May. In the autumn the rosy-tinged fruit present an attractive spectacle. The Japanese Quince,

Cydonia Japonica, begins to blossom in January, showing a more decided rose-scarlet than *vulgaris*, and continues till June, the fruit showing in September. A Japanese variety, *alba*, has white flowers. *Cydonia Maulei* is the Pyrus, more slender and smaller in size, but is even more profuse in floriation, becoming a riot of orange-scarlet blossom in April, and as free a display of fruit in the autumn. All quinces are quite hardy, grow in any soil, but flourish in loam and a sunny position. Propagate either by cuttings or seed.

R

RADISH.

Sow for early use in hotbeds during the winter and early spring, or later on in sheltered borders, in well-manured, deeply-dug and finely-raked soil to promote quick growth. Sow thinly 1 in. deep, broadcast or in drills, 10 in apart, and thin to 2 in. in the rows. Protect from birds. Sow at intervals of two or three weeks, March to May for a succession. Sow winter varieties in August (if hot, delay a week or so, to prevent bolting), but lift before severe frost, and store in a cool cellar in sand or a pit. Do not let radishes get dry at any stage of growth.

RAMONDIA. H.P.; dwarf; blue; May.

An alpine which prefers to be placed against the rockery so that its leaves are not horizontal and so do not get damaged in wintry weather. Peat, loam and some grit is their most suitable soil mixture and they are increased by division of robust specimens. The variety *pyrenaica* has purple-blue blossom; *serbica*, pale violet; and *alba*, white. They average 6 in.

RANUNCULUS. Bulb; 6 in.–2 ft.; white, yellow; spring.

Among the cultivated species the Alpine buttercup makes a good plant for the rock garden if set in a moist, sandy and porous soil. Plant bulbs in the latter half of February, claw downwards, about 2 in. deep, and as soon as the leaves fade, after flowering, lift and store till following year. There are tall varieties responding to the same treatment: *lyalli*, white, 30 in.; *aconitifolius*, white, 2 ft., and a double white, *plenus*, 18 in. Good rockery specimens, 6–9 in., are *montanus*, yellow; *amplexicaulis*, white; and *anemonoides*, which is pink and white. The old time ranunculus, *asiaticus*, is more formal in habit than the newer varieties.

RAPHIOLEPIS. H.H.P.; 30 in.; white; May.

This is the Indian hawthorn, having white flowers, *japonica ovata*, possessing some sweetness. Only successful in the South or mild regions with shelter and a soil mixture of loam and peat. Plant in spring and should have branches shortened in March. Increase in spring by cuttings in sand and loam under a cloche.

RASPBERRY.

The soil for raspberry canes should be in a moist situation and be light, of sandy substance, while a yearly dressing of manure is necessary to induce vigorous growth. The best fertilizer is pig manure, either mulched or dug in. Every autumn before manuring is done the stray suckers should be removed and the pruning of the canes attended to. Cut down close to the ground all but four canes, but should they be weak leave only three, two or even one. No cane should exceed 5 ft. in height; if so, cut off. Pruning is required each year, as canes which have borne fruit never do so a second time. Do not crowd; free access of sun and air is vital. Allow 3 or 4 ft. between each plant. The best time for planting is November, and in March cut off sappy tops of new well-developed canes. The roots can be divided in October. Liberal watering and weekly doses of liquid manure are wise in hot weather. Give support by stakes at ends of each row, with wires between to which tie the canes. For medium soils *profusion* and *superlative* are good; for heavy, *Norwich wonder;* for light, *prolific*. Autumn varieties, *Yellow Antwerp* and *October Red*. A fine red variety, *Lloyd George*, fruits in summer and autumn; another favoured variety is *Norfolk giant*.

RED HOT POKER. *See* KNIPHOFIA.

REED MACE. *See* TYPHA.

REHMANNIA. H.H.P.; 2 ft.; purple, white; spring.

A specimen for the cool greenhouse, started from seed sown in warmth and increased by cuttings in spring under cover. The purple variety is *angulata*, of which *Pink Perfection* is the best selection. A dwarf variety, *briscoei*, is 6 in., flowering cream and pink.

RHODANTHE. H.H.A.; 1 ft.; rose; summer.

One of the brightest of the Everlastings for winter home decoration. *Manglesii* has rose-coloured blossoms with yellow centres, while *maculata* may be had with either white or carmine flowers. *Atrosanguinea* is more branched, of dwarfer growth, and bears flowers of bright magenta. Sown in heat in February or March. Seedlings do not transplant successfully except when quite small. *See also* EVERLASTINGS.

RHODODENDRON. F.S.; 4–10 ft. and over; wide range of colours; May–June.

The three dozen varieties allow any taste in colour or size to be gratified. All of them bush-out, so allow plenty of room for growth and ascertain ultimate height of any specimen acquired. A popular variety is *Britannia*, scarlet. *Countess of Athlone* is mauve; *Lady Eleanor Cathcart*, rose blotched chocolate; *Sappho*, white, chocolate markings; *Loders*, white, while *calostrotum* is a rose-coloured dwarf for the rock garden, and *praecox* is a very early flowering mauve, growing slowly to a height of 4 ft. For the rock garden also are the allied yellow *azaleodendrons*, *Broughtonii* and *Smithii*. Grow in heath-mould and peat, but no lime, make a good bottom drainage, and keep in a damp atmosphere as drought kills them. They may be multiplied by grafting and layering, but the best plants are grown from seed, sown in May in a pan of fine heath-mould and gently pressed down. Stand this pan in another with water and cover with glass until the seedlings sprout. Prick out in the second year, and in the fourth year move farther apart, where they should remain till strong enough to be transplanted to the permanent position. In transplanting, take a good ball of earth with the root.

RHODORA CANADENSIS. F.S.; 4 ft.; reddish-purple; spring.

This flowers early and is rather like the honeysuckle. Give it a rich moist soil and plant where it gets some (but not complete) shade.

RHUBARB.

In February or March divide part of the rhubarb bed into plants having one eye apiece, and re-plant a yard apart in good soil. These new plants should be left until next season before gathering sticks, and at the end of the first season after, a good dressing of well-rotted manure should be dug in about the roots in November or December, or a moderate amount of sulphate of ammonia applied to make fresh plantations. It is a good plan to lift one or two roots in December and place them under the staging of the greenhouse, very lightly covered with soil and very occasionally watered. These will give tender stalks earlier in the year than usual. If the roots in the plot are covered with boxes in January and surrounded with leaves and fresh humus, rhubarb will be ready to follow the greenhouse crop. Rhubarb may also be forced in a pit, cellar or a shed if the light is excluded and the plants are protected from rain. Lift the stools with the surrounding soil and pack them closely together in the place prepared. It is not essential to have rhubarb pots.

RHUS. *See* SUMACH.

RIBES. *See* CURRANT, FLOWERING.

RICHARDIA: The Arum Lily, *see* LILIES.

ROBINIA (Acacia).
The handsome foliage and graceful bunching of its flowers give attraction to the Locust tree, as this is popularly named. The trees rise to 20 ft. and more with blossom of a rose colour in autumn. The variety *hispida* or Rose Acacia is of better size for the normal garden, averaging 6 ft. in height, flowering in spring. A yet more handsome variety, *inermis*, averages the same height.

ROCK CISTUS (Helianthemum). P.; trailer; mixed; May–June.
Makes a bright patch of many colours in the rockery. Grow in light soil, with a sand mixture, and start in a sunny situation. Increase by cuttings in the frame or under a cloche in July. The yellow variety, *vulgare*, is mostly grown, but other colours are increasingly offered by seedsmen.

ROCKERY.
To be a success a rockery needs to have adequate drainage. Dig out the site to a couple of feet and fill with rubble, small stones and rough earth. On this build gradually, layer by layer, with good earth having a percentage of sand and loam and grit worked in, so as not to leave spaces. Gradually reduce width and breadth of layers so as to get a good angle of slope, and arrange all surface rocks so that the pockets have an outward upward angle for the rain to get into the soil-filling instead of draining down the surface (*see* diagram).

Do the job thoroughly, for if rocks are piled anyhow and soil not well packed in, the weathering will silt the earth down so that the roots will come across cavities without earth. Granite is the best material, but sandstone and limestone are easier to obtain and do quite well, though not so lasting. Vary size of pockets and also of

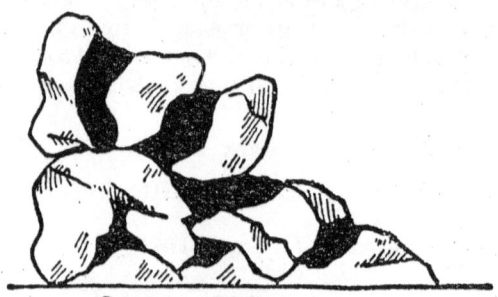

Rockery Pockets.
Incline inwards so that rain moistens but does not wash out soil.

the rocky chunks. There are many dwarf border plants that are suitable, such as the aubretia, saxifrages, alyssum, heuchera, London pride, dianthus, arabis, campanula and ageratum. The more ambitious should consult a florist for the rarer suitable rockery plants, including Alpine (*which see*). Always plant firmly and make sure pockets are filled at base.

ROCKET. *See* HESPERIS.

ROCK JASMINE. *See* ANDROSACE.

ROCK LYCHNIS. *See* VISCARIA.

ROCK ROSE. *See* CISTUS.

ROMNEYA COULTERI. F.S.; 5 ft.; white; summer.

Only grow if in warm Southern district away from bleak winds. Its flowers are large and the shrub is striking. Grow in light, rich loam, well-drained, and shelter in greenhouse during winter. Increase by seeds started in heat in spring, being careful about hardening the seedlings.

ROSARY PEA. *See* ABRUS.

ROSE CAMPION. *See* AGROSTEMMA.

ROSEMARY. F.S.; 3 ft.; lilac; April.

The spiny leaves of this historic shrub are distinctive for shape and dark green coloration, while its delicate perfume is grateful. The leaves do not fall in winter, and the blossom starts early, coming to perfection late in April. A white variety is *Rosemarinus officinalis albus*. Any garden soil suits if not heavy, provided in a sunny position. Multiply by cuttings in a cold frame.

ROSES.

When planting a rose-bed avoid the proximity of trees, and do not expect flourishing plants if this advice is ignored; if an existing bed is under trees do not make sure of failure by putting others there. They grow well, however, against a wall, or can give a satisfactory show in a capacious tub. If roses have come from a distance via carrier, before planting soak the roots for twenty-four hours and shelter from wind.

Making Ready.—Plant very firmly, treading tightly round the roots, and see that in filling the hole the soil is firmly packed everywhere. One secret of success is firm planting, trodden in with the boots so that the plants are rigid from the start, with the "collar" at soil level. This can be made more certain by trying the depth, and if the collar is 1½ in. below the level of the excavation made for planting the rose, when filled and the ground settled down, it will be nicely at the desired level.

Time to Plant.—Any time between November and mid-April; it makes little difference when, though perhaps November to December is favoured, but do not do so when the ground is soaking wet or during a ground frost. If such conditions prevail when they arrive from the grower, dig a trench, put them in, loosely but well covering with earth till a favourable planting time. They will be all right thus for a month. In planting, put Hybrid Teas 18 in. apart; give strong growers a few inches more; for those that are slow in bushing say only 15 in. Give roots a good spread; water in liberally, and tread in soil very firmly after planting.

Pruning as a useful rule should be every spring, but different kinds have their little habits, which must be kept in mind. A slow grower can be pruned hard back; a vigorous grower, bearing smaller roses, can have a moderate pruning. Chinas and Polyanthas need only slight pruning to remove weak or dead growth, cutting enough

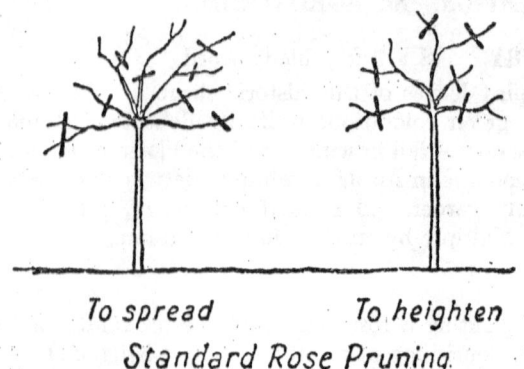

To spread   To heighten
Standard Rose Pruning.

to foster shoots from the base. In pruning, remember that the lower the shoot the better the bloom. A first-year rose should be hard

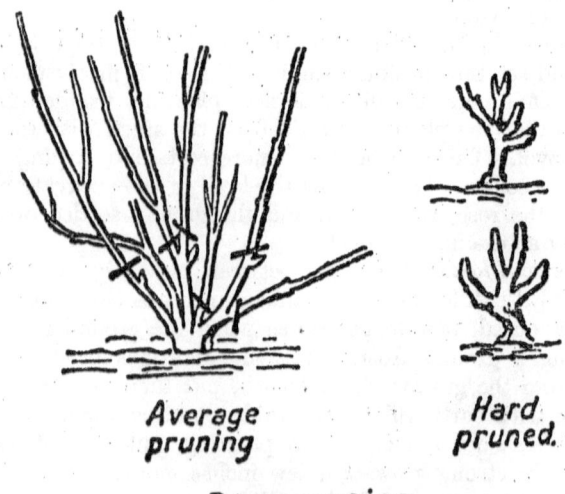

Average pruning   Hard pruned.

Rose pruning

pruned, to three or four strong eyes only. Singles need pruning as well: there is a fallacy that they do not, or only very slightly. Pernetianas need only slight pruning. Prune off suckers from below the collar, but any that are above it are good new growth and should not be touched. In general, rose pruning divides into: Ramblers—when new cut back to half a dozen eyes and eliminate altogether any weak shoots. Later, when some strong shoots are established, pruning need only be slight and according to space to be covered. Always autumn prune also the flowered shoots to within two buds of base. Climbing Hybrid Teas should be pruned at end of March, cutting back strongest shoots by pruning off two-thirds of their length and removing altogether the weak shoots. To encourage lateral growth, and free blooming, cut laterals to within a couple of

Planting Rose cuttings.

buds of the main stem. If pruning has been neglected for a season or so, prune tips only in November; cut back harder in March, and the following month give a further tip-pruning.

Budding is dealt with in its alphabetic order.

Climbing roses should be wound round supports rather than tied.

General Treatment.—Don't plant roses *in* manure, put it a few inches lower than roots, so that when making growth they reach the required stimulant. In spring give a mulch of manure.

Any good soil will be found satisfactory for roses, though a rich, leafy loam with a clay subsoil is best. Cleanliness, sunshine, plenty of air and keeping clear of greenfly and blight are essential. Autumn is the best season for planting, which should be done in mild, moist weather. To obtain fine roses it is usually necessary to pick some, or all, of the side buds of a cluster.

Do not use strong crude fertilizers, specially suitable ones are on sale. Keep the soil loose 5 or 6 in. from the surface, using a small, thin-pronged fork for the purpose. Give plenty of soft water in June if May happens to be very dry. Examine daily for greenfly and caterpillars.

Cuttings can be taken in August of climbers and ramblers and struck in sand; but bush roses seldom strike from cuttings. Take long cuttings about 10 in. with a heel (A) and side-shoots trimmed off, then place in trench; at 6 in. deep with sand at bottom, filling in and firming. Water well, then leave alone till spring.

Blight.—To clear from blight, sprinkle the trees when still damp with the morning dew with a mixture of equal quantities of sulphur and tobacco dust. After a few days the insects will disappear and the trees should then be syringed with decoction of elder leaves. A dusting of Derris is an effective precaution or sometimes a spraying of liquid Derris is to be preferred.

There are hundreds of different varieties of roses which can be selected from Nursery catalogues to suit requirement and suitability to district, soil and weather conditions.

One interesting variety noted in a leading seedsman's catalogue, is an annual rose, raised from seed, growing to 15 in.

ROTATION.

In vegetable gardening, the system of rotation of crops materially assists production. Simply explained it means that the same crop is not grown year after year on the same plot, as that would exhaust from the soil the chemicals that particular crop needs and yet for crops of another sort the soil would be good. Therefore an allotment, or part, is divided into three sections and what is grown on No. 1 the first year (*see* CROPPING PLAN) is grown on the second section next year, and on the remaining section for the third year. On the first section for the second year another kind of crop is grown, moving to the second and third sections on succeeding years. A third variety fills the first section for the third year, and passes to the other two in due course. Then the whole process is repeated, as the soil has renewed the chemical quality required. As indicated in a later paragraph, some variation to suit needs and likings can be made on rotation crops, so long as their chemical needs are the same.

The following table will act as a guide in carrying out a system of rotation, and also in applying artificial manures to particular plots in order to supplement dung:

Group 1.—Crops requiring chiefly phosphates and potash: potatoes, peas and beans.

Group 2.—Crops requiring chiefly nitrogen and phosphates: cabbage, cauliflower, sprouts, broccoli, etc.

Group 3.—Crops requiring nitrogen and potash: beet, carrot, parsnip, radish.

Certain crops requiring the three elements in more equal proportions: onions, leeks, turnips, celery and fruits do not benefit by rotation. They need ground that is manured every season.

The plot should be divided into three sections, A, B, C, for rotation, in accordance with the plan below, which shows how the crops are changed over during the three years:

1st Year	2nd Year	3rd Year
A	C	B
B	A	C
C	B	A

If the plan is followed, as each crop matures the land will become free in time for the digging and planting or seeding of the following crop.

Interpreting the diagram given above, the combined recommendations of the Royal Horticultural Society and the Ministry of Agriculture on the allotment being divided into a three-year rotation suggest the following spread of crops for each year, in each of the three sections into which the plot should be divided:

First Year.—*Section A:* Beans, Leeks, Onions, Peas, Tomatoes, with Beet, Carrots and Celery as succession crops. *Section B:* Beet, Carrots, Parsnips, Potatoes, with Lettuce, Onions and Spinach in succession. *Section C:* Broccoli, Brussels Sprouts, Cabbage, Cauliflower, Kale, Spinach Beet.

Second Year.—*Section C:* Beet, Carrots, Parsnips, Potatoes, with Lettuce, Onions and Spinach as succession. *Section A:* Broccoli, Brussels Sprouts, Cabbage, Cauliflower, Kale, Spinach Beet. *Section B:* Beans, Leeks, Onions, Peas, Tomatoes, with Beet, Carrots and Celery in succession.

Third Year.—Section B: Broccoli, Brussels Sprouts, Cabbage, Cauliflower, Kale, Spinach Beet. *Section C:* Beans, Leeks, Onions, Peas, with succession crops, Beet, Carrots, Celery. *Section A:* Beet, Carrots, Parsnips, Potatoes, Swedes, with Lettuce, Onions and Spinach in succession. *See also* ALLOTMENT, CROPPING PLAN, FERTILIZERS, HUMUS, MANURING.

ROWAN. *See* MOUNTAIN ASH.

RUDBECKIA. H.A. and H.P.; 18 in.; Gold marked claret; late August.

They thrive in ordinary soil, if well-drained, in sunny situation and staked early for the taller varieties which include *grandiflora*, 3 ft.; *laciniata*, 4 ft., with yellow greenish blooms; *purpurea*, 4 ft., red-purple. These taller sorts are all perennial, but grown as annuals they are more vigorous; otherwise increase by division. The annuals average 18 in.; *Golden Sunset* has chestnut markings, while *Autumn Glow* has golden yellow ray florets with a maroon disc.

S

SAGE.

This fragrant herb grows best on chalky soil, but will thrive in any of average fertility. It seeds freely and young robust plants result, or they can be propagated from heeled cuttings taken in spring. *See also* SALVIA and HERBS.

ST. JOHN'S WORT. *See* HYPERICUM.

SALPIGLOSSIS. H.H.A.; 3 ft.; various; August.

Sow under glass April or May, preferably with some heat, when can be handled prick out, 3 in. apart in boxes, and gradually harden for planting into a warm spot in May or June in well-manured, well-drained soil. The flowers are particularly beautiful in many warm colours delicately veined, particularly *sinuata*, a variety always sought after. A perennial variety, *linearis*, is only 1 ft., purple, flowering in August.

SALSIFY.

An edible root, cream coloured, like a parsnip in shape and of pleasant flavour. Their treatment is the same as for parsnips, except that at maturity they are lifted and stored.

SALVIA (Sage). H.H.A.; 18 in.; red, blue; summer and winter.

This family includes *splendens*, clear green foliage and brilliant scarlet flowers; *patens*, flowers of intense blue. *Roemeriana*, deep crimson, is of compact dwarf growth. All these may be treated as half-hardy annuals. Other varieties are *azurea*, a perennial which will thrive in the open in mild districts, with fine 3-in. spikes of pale blue flowers in autumn and, in the greenhouse, in winter, and *cacalioefolia*, also perennial in warm situations, with grey-green downy foliage and erect stems bearing flowers of deep blue. *Heeri* is scarlet, blooming in winter under cover. A dwarf variety, *argentea*, is only 6 in. and has silvery foliage. All thrive in loam, sand and manure, and seed should be sown in heat in December or January for summer flowering.

SAND VERBENA. See ABRONIA.

SANGUINARIA. H.P.; 6 in.; white; spring.

Plant in sandy peat and leaf-mould, preferably in clumps. *Canadensis* is a good variety; *major* has larger flowers. They flower before the leaves break. Increase by division in autumn.

SANTOLINA. H.H.P.; dwarf; yellow; July.

A carpet plant for rockery or edging, doing well in light soil in dry situation. A favourite variety is *chamaecyparissus* and it should be planted in autumn. Increase by cuttings either in spring or autumn.

SANVITALIA PROCUMBENS. H.A.; 6 in.; yellow; July.

There are singles and doubles; admirable in rockeries and a pretty edging. Sow under glass early April, prick out, harden and plant in position in May.

SAPONARIA. H.A.; pink, white; July.

There is a tall variety, *vaccaria*, 2 ft., free flowering and a dwarf, *calabria*, 6 in., with pink stellate blossom in spring if sown in September; also *alba*, white. Perennial varieties are *ocymoides*, purple rose of trailing habit; *officinalis*, 3 ft., pink; and *flore pleno* a good double variety. The red annual variety is *viccaria*. All do well in average soil.

SAVORY.

An aromatic herb for culinary use as flavouring. Sow in spring in open as annual in average soil. Old plants can be cut back. The leaves and stems are cut, dried and stored in autumn.

SAVOY.

Sow during May, ¾ in deep, on a seed bed prepared in advance (*which see*) and transplant end of July, 2 ft. apart each way, to autumn dug and manured quarters, hoeing in a little superphosphate and sulphate of potash (two parts phosphate to one of potash) before putting in the young plants, also firming over the ground before planting. General culture as for cabbage.

SAXIFRAGE. H.P.; 3–8 in.; rose, white, crimson; spring.

They comprise many varieties, all good for the rockery or Alpine garden, easy to cultivate and spreading rapidly. They do not all take the same soil, and cultural discrimination is needed in regard to the different classes. For instance, the encrusted or silver saxifrage, which is classified as *euanizoonias*, with foliage of greyish silver, prefers a limestone subsoil. It carries the blossom on short spikes, except *cotyledon* and *longifolia*, which have tall spikes and fine flowers, the latter variety being only increased from seed. The large leaf saxifrage, with pink flower spikes, is *megasea cordifolia*. Blooms in April.

The Mossy saxifrages belong to the *dactyloides* variety, and grow closely, in cushions of foliage from which the spikes rise in free flowering mostly white and pinkish. These require a cool position and are about the easiest to bring along successfully. When the foliage browns off it is time to divide for fresh stock.

Another favourite variety is *diptera* for growing in hanging baskets or large pots in the greenhouse. The species *sarmentosa* is popularly known as Mother of Thousands, and quite hardy. The only outdoor *diptera* variety is *fortunei* for rockeries in warm situation and with light soil.

The *kabschia* group has many attractive specimens and may be counted as a popular class; they include the tufted Rockfoils, their foliage being beautifully marked grey and green, of silvery appearance, and their floriation in various delicate colours. These like lime being mixed with loam, leaf-mould and grit, revel in the sun, and are increased by division.

A small but distinctive class is *peltiphyllum* of which *peltata* is the best and suitable for bordering a pond, the pink, and white flowers contrasting with the large tinted leaves. It needs moisture and is increased by division.

Another small division is *porphyrion*, which has some beautiful specimens, though difficult to cultivate and reluctant to flower unless in poor soil in a cool position, having some sunshine and being kept well watered. They are a rockery carpet variety with red and purple blossom.

London Pride is a saxifrage of the *Robertsonia* class. There are many other varieties of less importance.

SCABIOUS (Pin Cushion). H.A.; 3 ft.; various; August.

By habit biennials, they are nearly always grown as annuals by starting in the frame or greenhouse in the winter, kept from frost and planted in the border in June for late July and August flowering. They show to advantage if grown in clumps of each colour: pink, white, claret, salmon. A good average soil is suitable, preferably of light texture. The dark crimson is *atropurpurea*, which also is fragrant. The Caucasian Scabious is perennial and varying from rich dark blue to the lighter azure, with also some whites. In this variety is also a dwarf, *graminifolia*, 1 ft., and blue.

SCARBOROUGH LILY. *See* VALLOTA PURPUREA.

SCARLET RUNNERS. *See* BEANS.

SCHIZANTHUS. H.H.A.; 18–30 in.; various; autumn.

Sow in the spring, if possible on gentle heat, and plant out in beds as the seedlings progress to make a display in the autumn; or sow in September, pot off separately, winter under glass, giving as much air and as little water as possible. The seedlings should be thinned well, and in open given a good compost. If the tops are pinched while in winter quarters a profusion of bloom will result. A beautiful variety, *papilionaceus*, is purple spotted; *grahami* is lilac; *albus*, white; *retusus*, rose and orange, and inclining to dwarf height. A hardy variety, *pinnatus*, 18 in., flowers purple and yellow in summer. Cut foliage as well as blossom for decoration indoors.

SCHIZOPETALON. H.A.; 9 in.; white; summer.

Grown in average soil from seed sown in April where wanted, and thinned. The flowers are attractively fringed and have perfume. The variety *wisetonensis* is the butterfly flower, though more strictly this is the *Schizanthus*, and to promote bushiness the tips of shoots should be pinched off. It flowers in a range of delicate colours. *Walkeri*, the white variety, flowers during July and August.

SCHIZOSTYLIS. H.P.; 15 in.; scarlet; early winter.

Gives a bright splash of late colour. It is a gladiolus in miniature, hence its popular name, "Winter Gladiolus." The strongest variety is *coccinea*; other varieties, also hardy, being *Mrs. Hegarty*, pink; and *Viscountess Byng*, rose. The Kaffir Lily belongs to this genus, a pot plant, liking loam, leaf-mould and sand, and the shelter of the cool house during the winter.

SCILLA. H.P.; bulb; 1 ft.; blue; spring.

These beautiful spring flowers demand only the simplest culture. The bulbs are planted 2 in. deep in early autumn, will bloom from February to May, according to kind, and need no attention for years beyond a yearly top-dressing of manure. There are numerous varieties, the best of which are: *festalis* (bluebell) *hispanica*, each 1 ft., blue, rose and white and flowering in April. The varieties which are 6 in. and flower in February are *bifolia*, *sibrica*, blue and white. A 6-in. variety, *italica*, blue and white, flowers in April. As well as a rockery and border plant, they look well and do well in pots.

SEAKALE BEET.

Sow in April in good soil 1 in. deep in drills 18 in. apart. As soon as large enough to handle, thin out to 4 in. apart, and in a couple of weeks to 8 in. apart. Hoe well and keep watered. It is also called Swiss Chard and Silver Beet.

SEDUMS.

A considerable class known as Stonecrop, thriving under dry conditions, any soil of almost no depth, and on walls and in rockeries. They vary in height and colours: *spectabilis* is the tallest, 18 in., and pink; *sieboldi*, also pink, is 1 ft.; the *acre* varieties include white, 6 in.; yellow, 3 in. A 4 in. variety, *cereuleum*, has blue flowers in summer. Increase by division.

SEED.

The Seed Bed.—It is good to prepare this in advance, of sufficient capacity to start plants, whether for vegetables or the garden. Having settled on how much is needed, choose it in a part of the garden or allotment which does not hold water above average moisture, and which gets enough sun to warm the earth. Then give it a one spit digging, and before returning the soil put in some stones for drainage, lime to sweeten, and see that all weeds are eradicated, then reduce to a fine tilth of medium texture allowing an easy root run. It does not need manuring. It is better to start seed on ground of average fertility, and when transplanting assure that the plot has its share of compost or fertilizer. Some find it pays to sterilize the soil for the seed bed.

Sterilized Soil.—The ideal seed bed, as outlined by the Horticulture Institute, Merton, is built up with sterilized soil. To sterilize is a simple affair. First make up the soil to a suitable fineness, then dry in the sun. Boil up $\frac{1}{2}$ an inch of water in a saucepan, and into it put the dried soil, and continue the heat for a short time; the escaping steam thoroughly sterilizes the soil. Larger quantities can be done in a copper or metal drum, using 2 in. of water, and putting the soil into a sack, which suspend in the copper to steam for half an hour. When cool, mix with it by bulk one part of sand and one of granulated moss or peat to every two parts of soil. This makes an excellent sowing compost; then thoroughly mix with every bushel, $1\frac{1}{2}$ oz. (6 teaspoonfuls) of superphosphate and $\frac{3}{4}$ oz. (4 teaspoonfuls) of chalk. A rough and ready measure is that a bushel equals four fillings of the average pail. If the seed bed is not being used at once, delay putting in the phosphate and chalk till just before sowing. The actual bed can occupy a corner of the greenhouse staging or be laid in the open with a wood or stones surround to distinguish it. Another way of sterilizing soil is to water with formaldehyde, using a $\frac{1}{2}$ lb. well mixed into 2 gal. water. Where sterilization is not resorted to, trouble can be minimized by mixing silver sand with the seed when sowing, thus securing more effectual evaporation during the seedling period.

Seed Sowing.—The terse advice in this direction is "use common sense." A tiny seed only requires a film of soil; some are microscopic and these should have sand added, and thoroughly shaken with them, then sown with only a film covering. Larger seed can take greater depth—delphinium not more than a half-inch; lupins an inch, and so on, adjusting to size of seed. Water a few hours before sowing; firm the surface very gently after sowing any but the minute seeds, taking care not to pick up soil and seed with whatever is used for the firming, as a boot-sole sometimes does. Do not water them, but protect from sun, and next day water (with the chill taken off) through a fine spray. Transplant in good time. Do not discard all weaklings but thin out their neighbours, the less robust seedlings sometimes develop into the best plants. *See* hints on "Transplanting."

Seed Saving.—Keep an eye on the sturdiest plants, not of necessity the largest, but those growing robustly, free from disease or insect attack, and in flowers producing the finest blossom. Tie one or more spike or truss with white tape for later recognition, and when the seed forms pick some so that the rest can develop fully. When mature pick off, shake into an envelope or dry in sun till ready for shaking. Store in shallow cardboard boxes, or matchboxes, and complete the drying under cover, but where sun penetrates, such as on a greenhouse shelf, or in a room by the window. Before storing, but when quite dry, shake to and fro in folded newspaper to polish and remove dust. The amateur will generally find it easier to buy his requirements: it needs skill to recognize fully ripe seed, and some experience in drying, but the seed of a favourite plant could well be experimented with.

Vitality of Seed.—Their vitality varies. Some will still grow well in the third year from buying; others will do no good a year after purchase. The cost of new seed each season is little and the disappointment of old seed failing is as great as the wasted labour. When purchasing seed make sure it is of the current year; packets have the year when put up stamped thereon.

SEMPERVIVUM (House Leek). H.P.; 1 ft.; red; June.

Very much the same habit as the Sedum (*which see*) in its ability to grow anywhere under any conditions. The 1-ft. class is the one usually grown, *tectorum*, flowering red in summer. The *arachnoideum*, red, 4 in., flowers earlier; *arenarium*, 6 in., is yellow. Both these and the sedums do well where there is lime. Increase by offsets.

SENECIO.

A wide genus, including *Doronicum* (*which see*) and *Jacobaea* (*which see*). A hardy specimen is *pulcher*, a perennial, 1 ft., flowering purple in autumn; *macrophyllus*, perennial, is hardy but prefers a sheltered position, and has yellow flowers; *clivorum*, 3 ft., with orange blossom, while not hardy will thrive in a sunny position sheltered from the wind. The Cape Ivy is in this family, for which see *Macroglossus*, and there are various evergreen varieties, such as *rotundifolius* and *grayi*; the latter has grey foliage, is dwarf, grows in any position and likes chalk. On the average a good ordinary soil suits all.

SENSITIVE PLANT. *See* MIMOSA PUDICA.

SEPTEMBER GARDENING. *See* MONTH BY MONTH IN GARDEN AND ALLOTMENT.

SHADE-LOVING FLOWERS.

These include periwinkle, anemone, spiraea, wood hyacinths, violets, lily-of-the-valley, hellebore, daffodils, primroses, veronicas, Solomon's seal, forget-me-not, plantain lilies and many others.

SHALLOTS.

Plant the separate offsets February or early in spring in rows a foot apart. They should be 2 in. deep (*i.e.* the depth of the bulb, with point only just below the surface) and 6 to 8 in. apart. Gather in July or August. If dried, hung in strings and stored, they will keep till next year. Cultivate in well-matured, deep-dug ground; cow and horse dung below the roots is admirable.

SHASTA DAISY. H.P.; 2 ft.; white; July.

The characterstic is the fringing of the white petals, which is attractive. There is no difficulty in culture as it will thrive in any average soil, but it is well to stake to support the long stalks of the flowers, otherwise they bend. A good variety is *William Robinson*; *King Edward* flowers profusely and *Mrs. Lothian Bell* flowers earlier than the others. Give plenty of room, plant in October and prevent rampant growth.

SHEPHERDIA. F.S.; 8 ft.; yellow; spring.

Hardy specimens of the variety *argentea* have silvery leaves and in the late summer scarlet berries. They should be planted in spring in sandy loam with some well-rotted beech leaves at base, well firmed in and staked. Increase by detaching rooted suckers in autumn.

SHORTIA. H.P.; dwarf; white and rose; spring.

Pretty in rockery or Alpine garden, being 4 in. high and double coloured. A shady position in sandy peat is best. Increase by offsets. A white variety, *Galafolia*, has a pink sort, *rosea*. *Uniflora*, flesh colour, is only 4 in. A 9-in. annual variety, *californica*, is more of the *baeria* genus, but often called a *Shortia*. It flowers in June with an abundance of golden stellate florets. The perennials are increased by offsets, but only from the more vigorous plants.

SHRUBS AND TREES.

Obviously the first step is planting, and in each case the hole, *see* diagram, FRUIT TREES, should be dug of sufficient width to take the spread of the roots and about 2 ft. depth, or more, depending on the length of the main root, the bottom of which should rest on soil below which is rubble for drainage, then compost or manure for future sustenance when the shrub or tree is established and making new growth.

Planting Points.—In planting do not put in too deeply; this is a common fault. Plant just low enough for the old ring showing previous ground level to be at the surface. If lower, the bark at that part rots by the rains, makes a harbour for insects, and future growth is spoiled. After the drainage, and the manure or compost, put in a layer of the appropriate soil mixture, firm it and rest the roots on that. Then put in a substantial stake not less high than three parts the length of the shrub, and hammer it in a foot deep, staying with some stones if the soil is very friable. Then put in the shrub and fasten to stake *not* by a direct tie, but encircle the stake, make fast with a sailor's knot, wrap a couple of inches of hessian or sacking round the main stem of the shrub and continue the tying from stake around this protecting wrapping, using enough string to withstand the strain of gales. Then complete filling in soil, treading in firmly and watering copiously. If the shrub is put on a lawn skim off the turf for a couple of feet all round. It is usual to thin out the branches of newly-planted shrubs so that the rest may make stronger growth.

When to Plant.—In planting, be guided by the nature of the shrubs. If it is evergreen, do the planting in September or early May; if it loses its leaves in winter (deciduous), plant in October. In any case it is considered best to do all planting or re-planting between late September and March. By doing so before Christmas a season is saved, for if planted in the January to March period shrubs or trees will establish all right but will not have the advantage of the longer period for development and may miss a flowering.

Pruning.—Details of needed pruning are given in the entries of named shrubs and trees; others are particularized below, but it may be taken as a universal guide that where flowers grow on year-old shoots, prune away older and decayed wood and any growth which impedes light. If in current year's growth, prune off more freely wood that has had its day at flower bearing. Although ornamental trees do not need such systematic pruning as fruit trees, it is wise to prevent overcrowding and to secure a symmetrical branch system.

The comeliness of many trees is spoilt because more than one leading shoot is allowed to grow. The shoot that extends the main stem should be kept clear of subsidiaries. Some of the flowering trees, crab and laburnum for example, branch out naturally and possess no definite leader; they are improved by thinning out shoots which crowd the centre of the tree.

Suckers from the graft-stock and shoots on the stems of standard trees should be cut away.

Shrubs which bear their flowers on the fresh shoots that have still to grow may be pruned in January. Chief of these are ceanothus

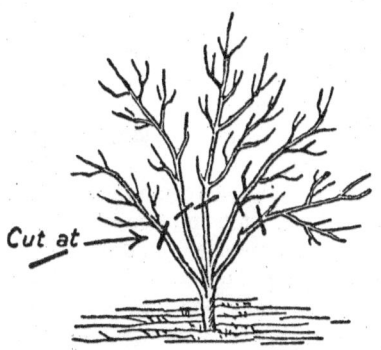

Hard pruning for such shrubs as Buddleia & Deutzia.

Gloire de Versailles and other varieties of that type; spiraea japonica and its varieties; clematis of the Jackmanii and viticella types; hypericum calycium; and buddleia variabilis. Golden elder and the purple-leaved sumach, whose charms lie in their richly-coloured leaves, also need to be pruned hard.

Some of the shrubs which bloom in June and early July are pruned as soon as the flowers are over by cutting out the old branches or parts of them, to force the growth of fresh shoots for next year's blossoming. These include Philadelphus or mock orange, buddleia alternifolia, deutzia and weigela. Lilac bushes should be thinned out and broom (cytisus) cut to prevent the seed developing and so lessening next year's robustness.

There is much pruning to be done during January among ornamental trees and shrubs. The flowering crabs, for example, become overcrowded with small shoots if pruning is neglected for a few years, and a good deal of thinning out is required. Extra vigorous branches which spoil the shape of the trees should be shortened to restore the balance of growth.

Lilac bushes often fail to flower well because shoots and branches are crowded. January is the time to thin them out. Any suckers should also be cut out, to save the main bush reverting. The same applies to shrubs in general.

Certain shrubs that bloom in late summer are pruned by cutting back the shoots early in the year, say January. Some are given in an early paragraph; others are hydrangea paniculata and spiraea Douglasii. Summer-flowering heathers should be cut over with sheras to remove the old blooms.

A Useful Selection.—A good selection of flowering shrubs would be: hamamelis mollis, spiraea arguta, forsythia spectabilis, berberis stenophylla, lilac, rhododendron, deutzia crenata, philadelphus Virginal, weigela florida, escallonia langleyensis, viburnum plicatum and hydrangea paniculata.

For shrubs that are grown for the sake of their coloured berries a brilliant display of scarlet or orange-scarlet berries is given by the firethorns; these shrubs are often planted against house walls, though they are happy in the open and even more attractive there. Cotoneaster, guelder rose, berberis, some of the roses (rubrifilia, Moyesii, rugosa, and pomifera) and the crabs are among the finest of the shrubs having autumn berries.

Such matters as situation in relation to the general amenities of the garden and the harmonious blending of its flower-colours with its neighbours will naturally be taken into consideration.

The "All Shrub" Border.—Those who have a border entirely devoted to shrubs can claim certain advantages over the herbaceous border. By its very nature a shrub border never presents a desolate appearance in winter, and for the interested gardener there is always something doing. In addition to all this, shrubs are economical of upkeep. A considerable number, indeed, show a decided preference for being left alone. They all ask, however, for careful planting, an operation on which their future success very largely depends.

Where it is decided to have an all shrub border, it is of advantage to its beauty so to dispose shrubs of differing flowering periods that there is a show all the year in every part of the border rather than the patchy effect of grouping. To this end the following table will be useful: *Early Flowering:* Ribes, hamamelis, magnolia, almond, prunus, forsythia, spiraea, rhododendron, daphne, etc. *Late Spring and Summer Flowering:* Kerria, broom, laburnum, azaleas, pyrus, lilac, ceanothus, buddleia, cydonia Japonica, roses. *Autumn Flowering:* Clematis, ericas, veronica, hibiscus. *Winter Flowering:* Viburnum, prunus, chimonanthus, jasmine, lonicera, rhododendron.

SHRUBS, FLOWERING. See FLOWERING SHRUBS and individual specimens indicated under their names by the letters F.S.

SIDALCEA. H.P.; 2 and 3 ft.; pink, crimson; June–September.

This is the Greek Mallow which will grow robustly in average soil, but prefers a moist loam and is increased by division. A white variety is *candida*, 2 ft., flowering in June; *listeri*, 3 ft., flowers pink in September.

SILENE (Catchfly). H.A.; dwarf; pink, white; June–July.

An effective early summer display from seed sown in autumn in light dry soil. The tallest, *Armeria*, is 18 in., with good foliage and fine heads of white or pink flowers of aromatic scent; *pendula*, in its many forms and colours, is valuable as a bedding plant; *Alpestris* is a hardy perennial, a compact Alpine plant which may be grown from seed sown in autumn. Quite early in summer it is covered with glistening white flowers and may be freely used in the rock garden. *Acaulis*, 3 in., is another Alpine, growing in firm tufts of beautiful light green in which appear masses of pink or crimson flowers. *Schafta* is a useful variety for late summer flowering—a hardy perennial spreading into tufts 5 or 6 in. high and bearing from July to September large flowers of reddish purple.

SISYRINCHIUM. H.P.; 1 ft.; purple; May.

A member of the Iris family which, though hardy, prefers a warm sheltered position in rockery. Plant in October in peat, leaf-mould and sand, either in pots for greenhouse decoration or for planting in the open. The purple variety is *grandiflorum* and *Bermudianum*, blue, 9 in. A taller variety, 2 ft., is *striatum*, yellow. Increase by offsets.

SKIMMIA. F.S.; 4 ft.; white-green; fragrant; spring.

An evergreen of which the hardiest variety to plant is *Fortunei* as the other kinds are not bisexual and require pollination. The male shrubs do not bear the red berries which give an autumn beauty to *Fortunei*. Increase from seed started in heat. Plant in spring or autumn where some sun and also shade, in good loam.

SMILAX. See ASPARAGUS PLUMOSA.

SNAKE'S HEAD. See FRITILLARY.

SNAPDRAGON. See ANTIRRHINUM.

SNOW ON THE MOUNTAIN. See EUPHORBIA MARGINATA.

SNOWDROP. H.P.; 6 in.; white; spring.

A few bulbs to start with, put 2 in. deep and 6 in. apart, will soon increase to fine clumps. Plant offsets in a moist, shady place, September, at a depth of about 3 in. Take up once every three or four years after the leaves have withered. Good varieties are *elwesii, plicatus, allenii*. The common variety, *galanthus nivalis*, singles and doubles, are as good as any in their simple beauty.

SNOWDROP TREE. See HALESIA.

SNOWFLAKE. See LEUCOJUM.

SNOWY MESPILUS. See AMELANCHIER.

SOIL.

The nature of the soil is ruled by what is underneath the surface soil; rock, gravel, sand, or clay, or a mixture of two or more of these. After that it will be found that the condition of the soil, where friable and light, or heavy and sodden, is the result of its exposure, or not, to the sun and whether or not it has been already dug over, and cultivated at some time or other.

Varieties of Soil.—A heavy soil is unsuited to the majority of quick-flowering plants; the first thing to be done as a rule is to dig it all over, leaving it exposed to the action of sun and weather all the winter. Where the soil is naturally light and friable digging it over thus once or twice will bring it into a suitable state to be planted. A medium or sticky soil needs digging and breaking with fork until it can be raked into quite fine texture, or tilth as it is called.

Small stones, being useful for drainage, need not all be removed, though where in quantity the majority should be collected.

Soil Mixtures.—It is usual to mix soils for the purpose of lightening clayey ground or giving binding to sandy or very friable (loose) soil. This is done by adding coarse sand to clay, with humus (stable manure), lime to break up heavy clods, and compost (vegetable refuse, rotted). For soil which is light add rotted turves (loam) and well pulverized clay in smaller proportion. Peat is also good to be added to any class of soil; it is vegetable matter that has not decomposed but contains useful acid foods. It is sold by all seedsmen.

Drainage.—Where soil, on being dug out, has water collecting in the lower spits, drainage in the form of clinker or broken brick should be put at the bottom, or, if the expense can be incurred, drainage pipes laid.

The various soils suitable for plants are given in this work in the entry of each particular plant, and under digging, seed and other like general operations further advice may be noted.

Fertilizers are chemical compounds added to foster growth.

Insects, etc.—Where soil is infested with wireworm or insect it is well to fumigate with gas lime, using 1 lb. per sq. yd. For surface pests, fumigation can be dispensed with by the use of salt or fresh soot, each in the ratio of 14 oz. per sq. yd. Soot is less useful in a fresh condition; use it as directed under SOOT. *See also* DIGGING and SEED.

SOLANUM. H.P.; 15 in.; red berries; winter.

A wide class, including the Winter Cherry (*see* PHYSALIS), the Egg Plant (*see* AUBERGINE) and the *capsicastrum*, which has bright red berries in winter, following inconspicuous white-pink clusters of florets during the summer. It is freely called "Winter Cherry." Late in spring, after only keeping slightly damp in greenhouse, cut hard back, give water, and when new shoots appear, detach and persuade to root in warmth in sand, and when fully struck pot up in loam, sand and good fertile peat. The variety *crispum* has yellow berries. The variety *jasminoides* is a climber with a profusion of white blossom from July to September, in the greenhouse.

SOLDANELLA. H.P.; dwarf; blues; April.

Equally suited to the Alpine garden or rockery, being only 3 in. high. The best varieties are *alpina* and *pusilla*. A lilac variety, *minima*, and a white, *alba*, are only 2 in. They like a rich soil mixed with sand and an autumn top-dressing of leaf-mould. Start by seed in frame and increase by division. Plant in cool situation where there is moisture, and protect them in winter from water-drips.

SOLIDAGO VIRGAUREA. *See* GOLDEN ROD.

SOLOMON'S SEAL. *See* POLYGONATUM.

SOOT.

A perplexing substance to many because, although a fertilizer of value because of the potash, soda and ammonia it contains, if it is thrown on the soil its goodness is wasted. It should be put into a bag and that hung in a tub of water, wholly immersed, for more than a week and the resulting liquid watered into the crops. The main use of dry soot is to protect seedlings from insects and slugs, but the soot should have been weathered in the open for some time before being laid round the young plants.

SOUTHERNWOOD. *See* ARTEMISIA.

SOWING. *See* SEED.

SPARAXIS. H.H.P.; 1 ft.; various; summer.

A pretty bulb grown in the same way as the Ixia, which it resembles. Plant in September. They grow well in pots, half a dozen in a 5-in. size. A tall variety, *pulcherrima*, grows 3 ft. or more and is hardy.

SPARTIUM. H.P.; 10 ft.; yellow; July.

Practically a shrub by habit, it will grow in even poor soil so long as there is some sand. It flowers profusely and is useful as an effective background. A good variety is *junceum*, popularly known as Spanish broom. Increase in early autumn by cuttings struck in sandy mixture under a cloche.

SPECULUM (Venus' Looking Glass). H.A.; 8 in.; purple; June.

Easily grown from seed sown in April in the open in average soil. The bell-like flowers range from purple to deep violet with a white base, making a fine show by its unusual colouring. The white variety, *album*, should be sown a fortnight later, choosing a sunny spot.

SPEEDWELL. *See* VERONICA.

SPHENOGYNE. H.A.; 1 ft.; yellow, purple marked; June.

Of comparatively recent introduction, and if sown outdoors in April will freely bloom in June and continue giving marguerite-like flowers, yellow with dark, glistening spots around the central disc. The wiry stems are a foot or so above the fern-like foliage. Plant about 6 in. apart when transplanting. It likes a good, light compost of loam and peat and plenty of sunshine. Sow thinly in boxes of fine soil under glass for earlier flowering. Strictly speaking, this annual is the *anethoides* variety of *Ursinia*.

SPINACH.

For spring and summer use, sow thinly either broadcast or in drills, 1 ft. apart and 1 in. deep, as early as the ground can be worked, and every two weeks for a succession. Thin out to 6 in. and use the thinned-out plants for the pot. For winter and early spring use sow Prickly Spinach in September, in well-manured ground; cover with straw on the approach of severe cold weather. The richer the ground the more delicate and succulent will be the leaves, and these can be stripped constantly, every ten days, and more will come. For Perpetual Spinach, *see below*.

SPINACH BEET (Perpetual Spinach).

Sow broadcast an inch deep in an open sunny spot from February to May, well watering in. Thin out to intervals of about a foot, hoeing between the plants. Sow at three fortnightly intervals to assure continuous supply of these succulent leaves. If sown in drills, thin to 18 in. apart. Pull coarse leaves to increase young growth.

SPINDLE (Eunonymus). F.S.; 8 ft.; white; May.

The blossom of the spindle is inconspicuous, but the beauty of the shrub or tree—for height ranges from 4–8 ft. and more—is in the exquisite colour and formation of its coral pink seed pods, each in triple clusters and much of it. A variety, *aldenhamensis*, has pods of deeper colour, but the usual variety is *Europaeus*. Two newer varieties are *planipes* and *yedoensis*, which are very picturesque in autumn. A good rich soil is best, and not too sunny a position. Increase by cuttings in autumn taken from ripe wood.

SPIRAEA. F.S.; 4 ft.; white and red; spring.

A beautiful shrub with graceful fern-like free foliage topped by spikes of tiny florets which are over by June, but in autumn the foliage turns crimson, giving colour at a dull season. Of the dozen and more varieties the best whites are the hybrid *arguta* with double flowers; *ariefolia*, spraying habit; *prunifolia*, beautiful autumn foliage;

flore pleno, 5 ft., and double; *Henryi*, of bushy habit, and the August flowering *Lindleyana*. Of the pink and red varieties, *japonica callosa* is best. *Douglasi* flowers in July and is 5 ft. high, and *salicifolia*, a pink.

All must be given moist situation in rich loam and plenty of watering. Only thin early flowering varieties, others cut well back in spring. Propagate by division.

The larger species of *Spiraea* are notorious for throwing out suckers, which should always be detached. Some have such wandering roots that they are a nuisance anywhere near a flower border. *Spiraea* (*Sorbaria*) *arborea* is an irresistible invader. It is a glorious sight when in flower, but those who cannot give its roots ample room should pass it by. *Spiraea canescens* is as bad, and needs a place to itself or in the shrub border.

SPIRANTHES. *See* ORCHIS.

SPLEENWORT (Asplenium).

A free-growing fern of deep green colour, well suited for growing in copse or on banks where it can have some shade from the sun. The smaller kinds are useful for the wall garden. The Lady Fern is the true spleenwort. A good fern for decoration in a room is *bulbiferum; flaccidum* is graceful in a hanging basket. The Maidenhair spleenwort is *trichomanes* and can be grown in the open. The Bird's nest fern, *nidus*, is a specimen for the hothouse. The shield ferns are classed as *aspidium* which like coolness and moisture and a soil mostly composed of leaf-mould and peat.

SPRAYING.

A stirrup-pump is excellent for spraying on insecticide, liquid Derris and so on, but take care to pump through clean water after each use in order to keep the valves free from grit or sediment.

SPRING MEADOW SAFFRON. *See* BULBOCODIUM.

SPRUCE FIR (Abies).

Among the varieties of Spruce Firs, the *abies* is that also known modernly as *albertiana, douglasi*, etc., the original name being kept for *pectina* (Silver Fir), *balsamea* and so on, and characterized by flat leaves, soft in texture, and their cones vertical instead of drooping. They grow to considerable height and are only possible for large spaces as their expanse takes sunlight from borders and their root area nourishment from plants in the vicinity. If grown, plant in autumn in deep, fertile soil reinforced with plenty of decayed turves.

STAGGER BUSH. See KALMIA.

STAPHYLEA COLCHICA. F.S.; 4 ft.; creamy white; spring.

The bladder nut, as is its popular name, is light and attractive in appearance and its bunches of blossom stellate in formation. Likes shade, moisture, loam, and is increased by cuttings or layering. It is classed as tender. Job's Tears, the rural name for the *pinnata* variety, is hardier but not so full in blossom.

STAR OF BETHLEHEM. See ORNITHOGALUM.

STAR OF THE VELDT. See DIMORPHOTHECA.

STATICE. H.A.; 12-18 in.; rose, puce; in spikes; July.

Sow in spring in open where wanted and thin as needed. They flower freely. *Sinuata* (purple); *suworowi* (lilac-pink); *bonduelli* (yellow) are the annuals. Perennial varieties are *gmelini* (dark blue); *incana nana* (pink), 9 in. *Profusa*, blue, is a greenhouse subject. Give good friable soil with loam and cow dung.

STEPHANANDRA. H.P.; 6 ft.; white; July.

Plant either in autumn or spring in average soil. The variety *flexuosa* is artistic in its graceful arching bracts relieving the small white blossom. A variety with larger flowers, *tanakae*, has leaves which take on a brilliant autumnal tint. Increase from root suckers.

STEPHANOTIS. Hothouse climber; white; all summer.

They flower with delicious fragrance and the blossom continues in generous clusters, which can be cut for weeks. Grow in turfy loam and sand, with leaf-mould; pay careful attention to watering and syringing and see that there is good drainage. Thin out old wood in winter. The usual variety grown is *floribunda*, but *elvaston* has made headway of late. Take side-shoots to increase by bottom heat, in pots, or in a propagation case.

STERILIZING SOIL FOR SEED BEDS. See SEED.

STERNBERGIA. See AMARYLLIS.

STOCKS.

The difficulty about stocks is that all seed contains a percentage of singles and a certain number do not survive transplanting. In consequence sow thickly and plant closer than needed so that the singles—which are straggly—can be thinned out before blooming. *The Ten Week* (H.H.A.) should be sown under glass in early spring and planted out in April and May to flower in July to September. Or they may be sown in the open from late April onwards to flower in early summer. The taller *Bromptons* (biennial) if sown in July and planted in sheltered positions will flower next autumn till the frosts. If sown in April they flower same year. The *Intermediates* (biennial) also bloom outdoors during or near winter. A rich moist, sandy loam, containing lime, suits them, and they thrive best in a sunny position, growing neat and compact, to a height of from 9–24 in. with laden flower-spikes of charming colours, including rose, scarlet, lavender, mauve, white and yellow. The doubles may usually be recognized by their long concave, pale green leaves; the single ones have a deeper green foliage which is convex and firmer. The night-scented stock is *Matthiola Bicornis* (*which see*). There are also the *Queen* stocks and the *Emperor* stocks which are treated in the same way as the Intermediates. The French stocks, particularly the variety *Beauty of Nice*, which is salmon for spring flowering is sown the previous July. A perennial variety, *All the Year Round*, is hardy. All kinds grow best in fertile soil and loam. The range of colours in all sorts is large. Virginian stock is treated under its own name.

STOKESIA. H.P.; 18 in.; blue; August.

They look well in rockery as well as the border, and thrive in a friable soil containing loam. The species *cyanea* is mostly grown, of which the purple variety is *purpurea*, *alba*, the white and *praecox*, earlier flowering. All like a sunny position.

STRAWBERRY.

So long as adequate preparation of the bed is made there is no difficulty about getting a good crop. One point which growers discuss interminably is the age plants should be allowed to attain—there are the one-year, two-year and three-year " schools," but perhaps the majority get new plants after a fruiting for two years. Certainly the third crop, though usually abundant, is not so good in size and flavour, unless much attention has been given; and to put in fresh stock annually, when a second year crop can be relied on to be robust and abundant, is so much waste of labour and expense, besides the ground required to carry out the one-year method. Having secured young plants, put them in in September, 9 in. from each other, with 18 in. between each row. In the second year, to allow for increase in size, every alternate plant is taken up, which leaves 18 in. all round.

The ground needs preparation well ahead, say in June, by deeply digging and amply manuring a sunny spot, putting in some loam, but not making the ground too friable. Strawberries do not care for light, loose soil. Put the manure in the second spit and mix well with the soil. Keep the plot open and weed-free by hoeing, and when planting see the ground is moist and firmed. Put the young plants in up to crown, which keep uncovered, and as they become well established protect from frosts by litter or straw, and do so also when they are in flower, usually in early May. At this time also an application of an appropriate fertilizer helps matters along, nitrate of soda at 1 oz. per sq. yd., or a three-part mixture of superphosphate to one each of sulphates of ammonia and potash. Do not remove the straw as it prevents the fruit being splashed by soil in rainy weather. This all done a rewarding crop may be expected, which gather at its peak and then clear ground of straw, weeds, take off early runners, fork over the ground between the plants, lift alternates as indicated above, in readiness for an even better fruiting next year. It hardly needs to be explained that the runners make the fresh stock, for leaves of new plants soon appear, and by putting these into pots, round the old plants, i.e. not severing from parent, they will root in about a month or six weeks, and where new stock is to be grown from these, naturally, the runners are not severed till the striking is certain. The young plants are kept in the pots, which can go into a frame till planting time, August. In this way a succession from own first-year stock is secured and will do well provided a careful watch is kept not to pot runners of weak or diseased plants.

There are many new varieties, and old ones continue in favour. *Laxton's Maincrop, King George V, Royal Sovereign, Givon's Late Prolific* are all favourites.

STRELITZIA. Greenhouse; 3 ft.; orange and blue; spring.

An unusually handsome plant, popularly known as the Bird of Paradise Flower. Even if not possessing a warm greenhouse it is worth while trying to bring it to flower in a conservatory, or in the South in a warm, sunny border, well drained, for the brilliance and shape of its blossom. An outstanding variety is *augusta*, having purple and white flowers. Mix pulverized brick with loam and grit as a growing compost. *Kewensis* is a newer hybrid variety. They only grow from seed, sown in warmth.

STREPTOCARPUS. Greenhouse perennial; 9 in.; various; July.

Kept in a warm place on the staging they flower purple, lavender, rose, white in compact trusses rather like a primrose and are at their best in the second year. Sow in heat in spring and prick out into pots, having a mixture of leaf-mould and sand in a majority of loam. Keep well watered. They are best increased from seed.

STUARTIA. F.S.; 8 ft.; creamy white; summer.

Give a position in the sun but sheltered from wind and plant in loam, peat and good compost and freely water in summer. They are very much like the Camellia, the best varieties being *pentagyna*, *virginica* and *pseudo-camellia*. Increase by layering in autumn and plant out in spring.

STYLOPHORUM. H.P.; 1 ft.; yellow; May.

The cultivated form of the Celandine, of poppy-like habit, liking a cool situation. Give it a good friable soil and divide in spring.

SUCCESSION.

This is not quite the same as Rotation, which is growing a different crop on the same ground in each of three or four years. Neither is it successional sowing, which means sowing at intervals of, say, a fortnight over six weeks or a couple of months, the seed of the same flower or vegetable in order to get results following on in succession to maturity. The term " succession " indicates a good following on crop to be put in as soon as the first is lifted, so as to make fullest use of the ground available, without a period of rest or fallow. They are also called " catchcrops." Thus when:

> Turnips are cleared put in cauliflower,
> Onions (spring) are cleared put in cabbage,
> Early Peas are cleared put in leeks,
> Potatoes (July) are cleared put in turnips.

A crop of lettuces and radishes can be grown and gathered before runner beans go in. Other " followings " will suggest themselves to the practical man, as may be expedient, according to soil and climate; North or South; bleak or mild districts, etc. *See also* CROPPING PLAN, ROTATION.

SUCKERS.

Short shrift should be given to suckers which grow from the roots of roses and various classes of shrub. In roses the suckers come from below the graft and are throwbacks to the briar stock from whence they develop; no roses will grow on them, and strength is filched from the main plant: cut them away rigorously. Nor is the shrub family exempt; the spiraea is a notorious offender and needs similar restriction.

SUGAR PEAS.

The pods are cooked and eaten with the peas. Grow in the same way as green peas.

SUMACH (Rhus). H.; 6 ft.; various; spring.

The true sumach is the variety *typhina* with greenish yellow flower; it is not particular as to soil and can be layered in September. The taller 6-ft. variety, *cotinus*, has light purple flowers; its popular name is the Smoke Plant. They like the sun, should be planted in October, and each season the old wood should be cut out.

SUMMER CYPRESS. *See* KOCHIA.

SUNFLOWER. *See* HELIANTHUS.

SUN ROSE. *See* HELIANTHEMUM.

SWAN RIVER DAISY. *See* BRACHYCOME IBERIDIFOLIA.

SWEDES.

They follow the same cultural rules as Turnips (*which see*), are sown in May, ¾ in. deep in drills 16 in. apart, and thinned out to each plant being a foot apart. The fly pest in dry weather is dealt with under TURNIPS.

SWEET ALYSSUM. *See* ALYSSUM.

SWEET PEA. H.A.; 6 ft.; many colours; all summer and autumn.

The culture of the sweet pea requires care but no special knowledge; it seems ever ready to do its best under any circumstances

—even in a prolonged drought. An ordinary garden soil, well and deeply dug in the autumn, and enriched below with a fair amount of manure, an average forking and pulverizing of the ground in the spring, and with some protection against slugs and snails and birds, a bounteous crop may be relied upon; while to maintain a continuance of bloom it is only necessary to cut the flowers day by day and never permit a single seed-pod to be formed. A wide choice of colours is available nowadays. Grow either in groups of three or four plants, each 15 in. from the next, or in rows, and stake rows early with well-branched sticks of good height—say 6–8 ft. For obtaining early bloom, make an autumn sowing, but otherwise sow about mid-

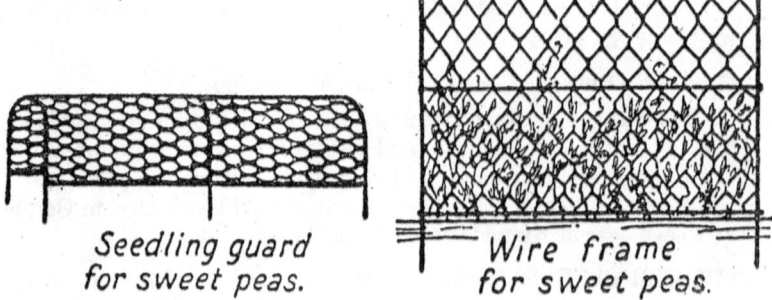

Seedling guard for sweet peas.   Wire frame for sweet peas.

February, gradually hardening the young seedlings and planting them out as early in April as the weather permits. Keep peas well watered at every stage of growth.

If the aim is to produce blossom of exhibition quality, take special steps in preparing the soil: in autumn decide site of next year's plot, dig a trench 3 ft. deep and into it put garden and vegetable refuse, covering each layer with an inch or so of earth. When to within a foot from top, fill up with earth of medium tilth and leave to settle till seedlings are put in from seed sown in a deep seed bed of sterilized soil (*see* SEED).

Do not crowd sweet peas among other plants; they need plenty of air and light, and indeed only show in full beauty if well away from other tall plants.

A pea guard to foil birds and a useful wire frame for support are here shown.

SWEET SULTAN (Centaurea). H.A.; 18 in.; blue and white; July.

Sow late spring where to flower and prolong by cutting the long spikes of bloom periodically. They are fragrant. A dwarf variety, *depressus*, is blue, as is the taller variety, *moschata*. There is also a perennial variety, 2 ft., which should be started in pots, and kept in shade till ready to plant out. A pink variety is *dealbata* which is particularly graceful. All varieties are easy to grow by sowing in a sunny spot in the late spring and growing on in well-drained soil with loam mixed in.

SWEET VERBENA. *See* VERBENA and LIPPIA.

SWEET WILLIAM. H.B.; 24 in.; various; June onwards.

Sow in the open in June or July for flowering in the following summer. The seed should be sown in a shady spot in drills of finely-sifted soil, and covered very lightly, and the seedlings transferred to their final positions as soon as they will bear removal. The colours are white, red, pink, maroon and speckled. The most suitable soil is a sandy loam, with some lime, and an open, sunshiny position is necessary. New varieties include doubles, as also a hybrid class, Sweet Wilvelsfield (*see below*), which flowers freely during the summer months. A characteristic of the Sweet William is that it can be transplanted at any stage of growth with hardly any setback if kept well watered. Increase by cuttings, which readily strike, or by root division.

SWEET WILVELSFIELD. H.A.; 18 in.; pink, crimson; summer.

A new free-flowering species combining the qualities of the pink and the Sweet William. Sow in spring in average soil in sunny position.

SYCOPSIS SINENSIS. F.S.; 10 ft.; red and yellow; February-March.

Hardy and evergreen, the blossom reminding of witch hazel. Plant in autumn in friable soil. Increase by layers in late summer.

SYMPHORICARPUS. H.P.; 6 ft.; rose; July.

As its popular name, Snowberry, indicates, this shrub after flowering has white berries and so carries its attractiveness into autumn.

It grows freely in average soil, and looks and does well at the back of the herbaceous border. Increase by suckers or cuttings, heeled, in autumn.

SYNTHYRIS. H.P.; 6 in.; violet; spring.

A good specimen for growing in semi-shade in average friable soil. The usual variety is *reformis*. Increase by spring division.

SYRINGA. F.S.; 4–6 ft.; white; June–July.

Require good average soil, open sunny situation. Strike cuttings of young wood in frame. Prune old shoots but not fresh ones, which give next year's bloom. *Bouquet blanc* has double flowers; *voie lactée* has very large single flowers; *Manteau de Hermione* is a dwarf double cream and fragrant. Lilac belongs to the syringa family.

T

TACSONIA. Greenhouse climber; crimson.

The various varieties should be grown in loam, sand and a fertile soil with beech leaves and compost in it: thin out growth to prevent leafage at the expense of blossom; cut flowered shoots right back in winter to stimulate new life, and take shoots into propagating case till rooted. Varieties are *van volxemi* (cool house) and *insignis* (warm house). They look better if loosely tied to wires leading to roof of greenhouse.

TAGETES, SIGNATA PUMILA.

These are the African and French marigolds (*see under* MARIGOLDS).

TAMARISK. F.S.; 10 ft.; sandy pink clusters; spring and autumn.

It is seldom a success to try to propagate cuttings from the tips. Take a substantial branch, as thick as the finger, and cut short lengths with nodes, put in sand and strike with some bottom heat. Once established in good soil, with sand or chalky mixture, they need little attention except autumn pruning to keep shapely. Plants should be put in with ample root room in the spring. Hardy varieties are *chinensis, gallica* and *hispida*.

TANAKAEA. H.P.; 6 in.; white; June.

Planted in good soil, not heavily manured, but with a third sand the variety *radicans* of this rockery plant, less known than it deserves, has artistic plumes of blossom. Increased by spring division.

TANSY (Tanacetum). Herb; H.P.; yellow; summer.

May be planted in April and used for its medicinal and herbal qualities. It flowers in yellow balls, and has a parsley-like leaf. Grow apart, as it rapidly increases by underground suckers.

TARRAGON.

A salad herb, perennial and hardy. Put plants in in April. Average soil.

TASSEL FLOWER. *See* CACALIA.

TECOMA. Climber; scarlet; late summer.

Not quite hardy, but in the South they do well under the shelter of a wall or on a trellis where they can get plenty of sun. They twine as they climb, and their tubular flowers, some scarlet and white, are distinctive. They are best planted in spring in the greenhouse, and if the season is bleak keep them there. A good loam, with some sand, is the best soil, and they are increased by root cuttings. The 3-ft. *radicans* is the open-air variety, and *thunbergi* is in bloom September to October. A brilliant flowering variety, *grandiflora*, nearly hardy, is the Trumpet Flower proper. Another variety, *jasminoides*, has red and white flowers.

THALICTRUM. H.P.; 1–4 ft.; yellow; June onwards.

The various kinds take kindly to the same soil mixture of sandy loam and prefer a moist situation. The shorter variety, *adiantifolium*, is a dainty border or rockery plant averaging 10 in. and having foliage not unlike the maidenhair fern. An early spring variety, *anemonoides*, is 3 ft., as also is *aquilegifolium*, purple flowering. The taller variety, *dipterocarpus*, is a newer sort, being 4 ft., and having warm purple blossom with anthers of orange; *album* is the white flowering specimen of this variety. Increase by root division in spring.

THINNING OUT.

The process of reducing the number of seedlings resulting from sowing seed in drills or groups is known as thinning out. This rather wasteful way has long been, mostly in rural districts, of putting in more seed than necessary and then, when seedlings are too close together, pulling up most of them, preferably the weaker, so as to leave one in every 6 in. to grow on. The slower way of putting in just enough seed, spaced to what room plants need to mature properly, is a much greater economy of seed, but seldom adopted, the argument being that, if seed does not fructify, time is lost and there are unsightly gaps. The time element has some value in vegetables, which take long to mature, hence the persistence of the custom. The brassica, that is green vegetables generally—cabbage, cauliflower, broccoli and so on—are allowed to grow to 4 in. in height, then thinned out, and when 6 in. high transplanted to their growing quarters, adequately spaced, as directed in the entries for particular vegetables. Root crops, such as carrot, turnip, parsnip, beet, shallots and such should never have their seedlings transplanted, but must grow where sown, hence more sparse sowing is recommended, with thinning out, to full growing space *which see* under particular entries, or the seed sown to the full spacing for maturing and the risk taken of coming up—onions do not mind transplanting. A list of those which can or cannot be transplanted is given under VEGETABLES. With flowers, the quantity of seed is usually so small as to be of no great concern or expense, hence thinning out is usual. Hardy and half-hardy annuals should be thinned out as soon as in the fourth leaf, thereby giving the plants a chance to develop into fine flowering specimens. When thinning out, particularly vegetables, firm the earth again around those left in.

THRIFT. *See* ARMERIA.

THUYA.

A hardy, dense hedge can be formed by thuya, which is also known as Arbor Vitae, instead of the usual privet or quick hedge. Give a well-drained loam with added manure or compost.

THYME.

As well as the herb, there are neat flowering varieties which add brightness to the border; *albus*, white; *coccineus*, red; *serpyllum*, pink; *atropurpureus*, purple. All are quite hardy, not particular as to soil and, as well as self-sown increase, can be multiplied by division. *See also* HERBS.

TIARELLA. H.P.; 8 in.; white; April.

A charming member of the saxifrage family, with *cordifolia* as favourite, flowering in dainty racemes. Peat is suitable soil, but it will grow satisfactorily in any soil. Increase by division.

TIGER IRIS. *See* TIGRIDIA.

TIGRIDIA (Tiger Iris). H.H.; bulb; various; late summer.

A brilliantly-hued species, the blossom of which is spotted on a red, white, pink or yellow ground. Put in a warm spot, well drained, in spring or autumn and give a sandy, friable soil. Lift in November. The flowers soon fade, but are beautiful while they last.

TITHONIA (Mexican Sunflower). H.H.A.; 5 ft.; orange; July–August.

Grow in a rich soil with a good proportion of loam. The usual variety is *speciosa* which has a reddish tinge to the orange. Sow in February or March under glass and with gentle heat, harden before putting into sunny border in May, or keep for flowering in the greenhouse.

TOBACCO PLANT. *See* NICOTIANA.

TOBACCO WASH.

Boil ½ oz. shag in ½ pint water, putting in cold and bringing slowly just to boil: let cool, and apply with camel-hair brush as needed to remove insects. Syringe plants afterwards with cold water.

TOMATOES.

Tomato seed may be thinly sown in November to get early supplies in May or at the end of January for July tomatoes. Put one seed each in well-drained pots filled with light soil. Cover with glass and keep at an even temperature of not less than 60° till germination starts, then transfer and keep near the glass until well established (*see* " Intensive Methods "). The transferred seedlings should be put singly into 4-inch pots, drain the pots with one " crock," and a little rough soil, and plant the seedlings up to their seed leaves.

Any good loamy soil will be suitable for this operation, but it should be *warmed* before use, placed in a warm position, carefully watered, and shaded from bright sunshine. Keep near the glass, so as to make sturdy plants; when rooted through, transfer the plants to their fruiting quarters. If to be grown in pots, 9½ in. is a suitable size, and in these the plants should be planted deeply so as to admit of subsequent top-dressing. For outdoor cultivation, sow in a hotbed in March, and when the seedlings are a few inches high, pot them singly into 3-inch pots; carefully harden off, and finally plant out at the end of May under a south wall allowing plenty of room. The plants must be plentifully supplied with water during the period of growth. Tomato plants will need the support of sticks when they are in their final position. If grown in beds, plenty of room must be given. The best soil for tomatoes is a fibrous loam mixed with a little sharp sand, leaf-mould and well-decayed manure. Add more soil as the roots grow, and do not use manure which has not fully fermented. Give a pinch or two of nitrate of potash or kainite occasionally, but do not use cow dung as manure. Nip off all side-shoots, allowing only the flower trusses to grow from the main stem, and where robust keep only three trusses.

Tomatoes raised from seeds sown in February in a heated glasshouse will provide plants to be grown in large flower-pots under glass. They will bear fruits in early summer. Yellow tomatoes are well suited to growing under glass, and their fine flavour makes their cultivation worth while.

The seeds are sown in boxes or pans filled with light soil in a temperature of 60–65°. When the seedlings are 2 in. or so high they are placed separately in small pots and subsequently re-potted as becomes necessary. If the greenhouse is still housing wintering plants, tomato seed can be sown in January on a hotbed and transferred to a heated greenhouse when 2 in. and potted on as above.

For greenhouse culture of tomatoes always place pots on sunny side, keep ventilation active, water at roots, avoiding wetting foliage. Get from seedling pots into fruiting pots as soon as good growth is made; or make a bed of good rich earth on the stage of house (sunny side) piled upon slates, with rubble at bottom for drainage. By this method the branches can be trained up near glass, as shown in sketch, by bamboo or wire, both at sides and arch. Keep a temperature of 60° or near, to help early fruiting. In a lean-to, put the pots on the wall side, they then get the sun and also any heat the wall may diffuse.

A recommended method of watering growing tomatoes in the open is to sink a 3-inch pot near the root of each plant and water through that, thus securing more effectual irrigation. The idea is illustrated unter WATERING.

When the fruit is turning red they can be picked and ripened by exposing to sun, or kept wrapped in flannel and in a warm position. For chutneying, any green tomatoes should be picked off before the plants die and stored till needed in a cool, dry, airy place where they will be protected from the frost.

When the skin of ripening tomatoes cracks it means they have not been watered regularly, particularly in times of drought; the

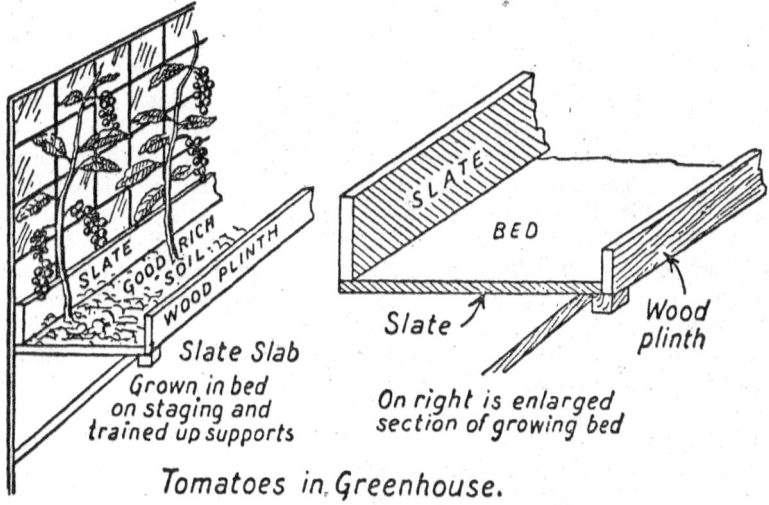

Tomatoes in Greenhouse.

natural watering of succeeding copious rain causes the cracking. Therefore, keep watered regularly at all times either by the can or the rain.

American experts produce seedless tomatoes in abundance by watering the plants with beta naphthoxacetic acid just as flowers are developing. It sets the fruit, but the flowers never open—a point which need not cause alarm, as a good crop will develop. Used as a vapour for greenhouse tomatoes, the result is even more satisfactory.

A recommended strain for growing in the greenhouse is *Potentate*, another good one being *March Beauty*. For general culture out of doors, use *Open Air*, *Lister's Prolific*, *Maincrop*, and for early fruit,

Early Market. The latest usage is to put walls of straw in the soil between each plant, put it 10 in. deep and 2 in. thick. It is claimed to be of benefit to growth and also more easily allowing water to get to the roots.

TOOLS.

The ordinary tools used in gardening need no description. The spade, the fork, the rake, the trowel and so on. The use of the dibber is explained where, as for parsnips, it is best used; the flat-pronged fork is used for potato lifting, and there illustrated; the bulb planter is shown under bulbs; the various hoes and their special uses under hoeing. There are, however, various tools of newer invention which may be described and which are here illustrated.

No. 1 is a Flexible Rake, the prongs of which are of rustless steel and has a transverse bar which can be moved backwards and forwards and screwed into position to bring the prongs closer together, or farther apart to adjust to need in gathering leaves and mowings or in scarifying moss on the lawn, as also to break up tilth in varying grades. The flexible prongs do not bring out roots or injure grass and enable effective use on uneven ground without clogging.

No. 2 is the Cultivator. The shaped teeth and the particular curve enable the dug ground to be fined more rapidly and effectually to a useful depth as well as quickly removing weeds and harrowing between rows.

No. 3 is a Cultivator which goes deeper into the soil, a miniature plough in fact by which clods are cut and broken and the plot prepared with greater speed than in the old way.

No. 4 is an effective Cultivator to which a hoe is attached so that by merely reversing, weeds can be removed without a change of tool as preparation of the soil proceeds.

TOP-DRESSING. *See* MULCHING.

TORENIA. H.H.A.; 1 ft.; blues; summer.

The varieties average 1 ft. in height and are best flowered in hanging baskets or pots in the greenhouse. The blossom ranges from pale mauve to violet-blue. The seed needs heat to start and the seedlings given a more temperate atmosphere, pricked off when quite small and potted singly. The purple variety is *asiatica; flava* and *fournieri* have some yellow among the blue, and *compacta* is less spreading. Grow in loam, peat and sand in equal proportions. They

255

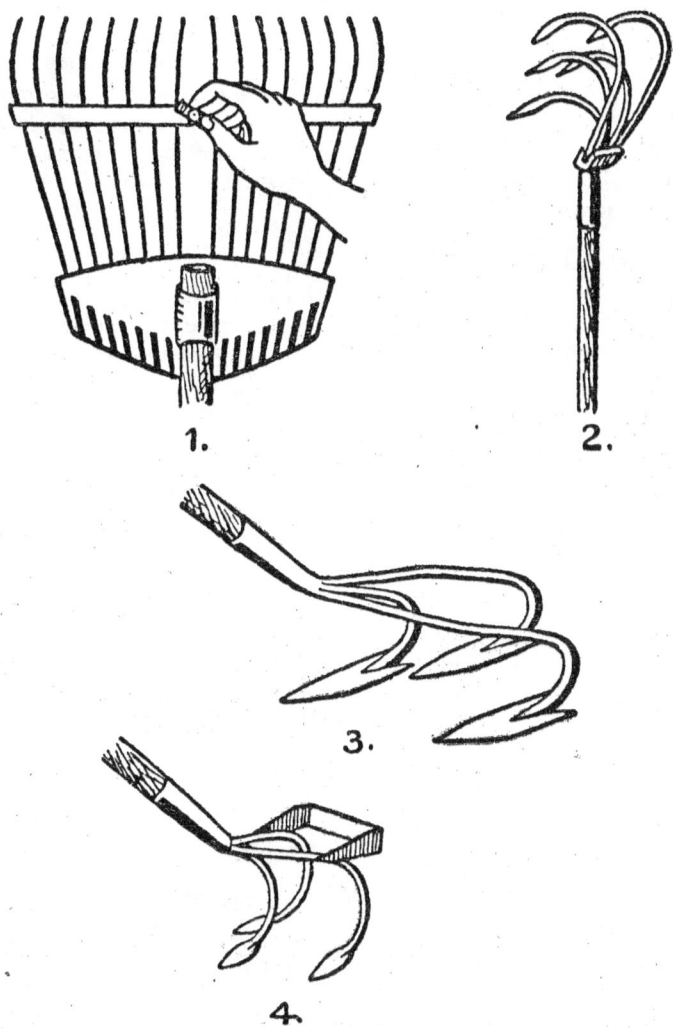

Some modern tools.

are best raised annually, though they are of perennial habit and can be increased by cuttings taken in spring and struck in heat.

TRACHELIUM. P.; 2 ft.; pale blue; July–September.

A greenhouse subject which flowers rather like gypsophila. *Caeruleum* is the preferred variety; grown in loam, leaf-mould and sand, and the plants early top-pinched to induce bushiness. *Album*, the white variety, has the same treatment. Increase by cuttings in frame or gentle heat in spring.

TRADESCANTIA. H.P.; 1 ft.

A foliage plant of drooping habit and suited for hanging baskets in greenhouse, or in border they are effective, particularly *virginica*, which is blue flowering. Average soil suits, and increase by division. Keep well watered.

TRANSPLANTING.

Lift without damaging roots and get out all the roots. Have the hole plenty big enough to spread the roots in its new situation. Water well before putting in, fill soil, press firmly all round, water again,

Right   Wrong
Avoid setting in too deeply.

Planting Seedlings.

put a stake to save loosening in the wind, then let it alone to recover and make good on its own. Coddling is the great fault of the beginner.

When transplanting well-developed plants, to minimize setback sink a 3-inch pot beside each, and water into pots, thus irrigating roots more thoroughly. The same method assures better watering of plants growing on a slope.

When transplanting seedlings water where they are to go with boiling water and put in while soil still warm. This method almost banishes any chance of failure. *See also* THINNING OUT.

TREE HEATH. F.S.; 7 ft.; dense, fragrant white flowers; May.

Botanically the *Erica arborea*. The Mediterranean Heath, 6 ft., has rose-coloured blossom and feathery foliage. Both are spring flowering, are hardy, prefer moist subsoil, in sunshine. Seed and division for increasing.

TREE MALLOW. *See* LAVATERA.

TRICHOMANES.

This interesting class of ferns includes the Killarney Fern (radicans) in its particular varieties. Give usual treatment for ferns—a moist greenhouse, shade, adequate drainage and a soil mostly of fibrous peat, with a little loam for binding.

TRICUSPIDARIA LANCEOLATA. F.S.; 10 ft.; red; February-May.

Of unusual form, flowering like an unopened fuchsia and in profusion. Even when small it flowers well. A white variety is *dependens*. Grow in fibrous peat and increase by layers.

TRICYRTIS. H.P.; 2 ft.; yellow and white; autumn.

The foliage is herbaceous in striking contrast to the blossom, which has purple spottings, the chief variety being *hirta*. It is best suited for the rockery, in which, or in the border, it thrives in a sheltered position if the rhizomes are planted in sandy loam during the spring. Increase by offsets.

TRILLIUM. H.P.; dwarf; white; May.

An admirable plant for a cool corner of the rockery, doing well in a peat mixture kept moist. The usual variety is *grandiflorum*, 9 in., and the bulbs should be planted in October, 2 in. deep, in groups; it is the Wood Lily. A blue-red variety, *erectum*, is 1 ft., and *stylosum*, rose coloured, while *recurvatum* has variegated foliage. When crowded, divide in autumn and fresh groups will flourish.

TRITOMA (Red Hot Poker). *See* KNIPHOFIA.

TRITONIA. H.; bulb; 2 ft.; orange; summer.

The bulbs should be planted in light soil having sand. Put them in 3 in. deep during the autumn and give protection of straw or ash while the frosts are on. The favourite variety is *crocata* which flowers rather like montbretia, but the orange ground has red or brown spottings, doing best in a sunny well-drained situation. They are also a success in pots in the greenhouse.

TROLLIUS. H.P.; 2 ft.; golden yellow; spring.

A free growing plant in almost any soil but preferring a moist, shady situation with a clayey texture. The variety *ledebouri* germinates quickly and flowers a bright yellow, 2 ft. A deep yellow is *asiaticus*, and a paler hue *europaeus*, both 18 in. A dwarf specimen, *pumilus*, is 12 in. Increase by autumn division.

TROPAEOLUM.

The nasturtiums, which belong to this group, are dealt with under their own name, as also is Canary Creeper, also in the group. Other varieties of tropaeolum are here given: *lobbianum* is a fine climber —an annual—with hairy foliage, and flowers in various shades of scarlet, orange and yellow; while *majus* is a similar variety but lacking the hairiness in foliage. *Tuberosum* is another distinct variety, tuberous-rooted and usually confined to the greenhouse, as in the open it flowers so late that it is often spoiled by the frost. It is a graceful trailing plant, producing showy flowers of scarlet and yellow, and in the house the tubers may be started at any time from September to March. In the open the tubers should be planted in spring and lifted in autumn for storage in a dry place. It will flourish in the poorest of soils.

TRUMPET FLOWER. *See* TECOMA.

TUBEROSE. *See* POLIANTHES.

TULIPS. H.; bulb; 12–24 in.; various; all spring.

Tulips thrive in any good soil, though succeeding best in that which is sandy and well drained. Plant bulbs in October or November, about 6 in. apart and 4 or 5 in. deep. Either lift as soon as the stems begin to fade and store for the summer, or, as they multiply freely, leave them in the ground (unless the soil is cold and wet) for two or three years, after which they should be lifted. The tulip is continually being developed both in variety, colour and period of flowering. Results in pot culture are not so fine as in plots, nor is their average height suitable for fibre culture, unless done in large and well-based bowls. For fibre culture *see* BULBS. There are too many kinds to list; a dealer will select those which flower in April or early spring; as, too, give a colour range in the Darwins, which bloom in May; and also recommend the best of the ordinary or cottager's tulips. The general culture directions given for BULBS may be followed.

TUNICA. H.P.; dwarf; pink and white; July.

A dainty saxifrage of only 3 in. height which should be sown where it is to bloom. Sow in spring in a soil of loam and sand. A double white variety, *alba plena*, is also hardy. It is better to make annual sowings.

TURNIPS.

These can be grown for the turnips or for the turnip-tops. A good plan is to use the thinnings for the pot, though the tops of older plants bulk more. Turnips want well-manured ground and a moist situation as they should be grown quickly to be at their best. Sow in late March immediately after good rains for first crops, make later sowings early in August for the winter supply. Sow in rows, ½ in. deep, and thin out to two to the foot. There should be 15 in. between each row. A satisfactory fertilizer is superphosphate dressed at about 2 oz. per sq. yd. Do not let grow big; those about 2 in. across are best for the pot.

Some growers, where space is limited, adopt the old practice of sowing turnips and carrot together; the turnips, growing more quickly, can be pulled in good time to let the carrots grow on without check. Turnip-tops are not everyone's taste, being rather harsh, but health-promoting. They shrink tremendously in the boiling. If growing for tops, sow *Green Top Stone* in September and do very little thinning. To guard against the fly, dust or spray with Derris as soon as the seedlings show fourth leaf. Store turnips in boxes or clamps, as carrots.

TYPHA.

This is the Reed Mace or Bulrush, growing beside or in water; a marsh plant, the dark red heads of which can be gathered in autumn and dried for decorative purposes. Grow beside ponds in moist ground and increase by division.

U

ULEX. *See* GORSE.

ULMUS.
This is the elm tree.

UMBILICUS.
A class of succulents used for bedding, being dwarf and of spreading habit. It is hardy; bears the popular name of navelwort, and is included in the *cotyledon* genus. A sandy loam is a suitable growing medium.

UNGERNIA. H.; bulb; 18 in.; red; summer.
Put the bulbs in loam with a quarter of leaf-mould, sand and manure mixed. Plunge in pots in greenhouse or frame in autumn, and either grow on in larger pots inside, or put out in May in sunny border. Increase by offsets.

UROSPERMUM. H.P.; 12 in.; yellow; July.
An easily-grown herbaceous specimen, which thrives in average soil and is best treated as an annual by sowings in spring.

URSINIA. H.A.; 12 in.; orange; summer.
Best down in position in border and thinned. Choose a sunny situation, and sow in spring in a mixture of loam and peat. The variety *anethoides* has a daisy type flower, the brilliant orange petals having a dark purple zone; *golden bedder* has fine flowers self coloured without zone contrast. As the seedlings are susceptible to late frosts they can be started in frame or cloche in late March. Increase by cuttings under bell cloche.

UVULARIA. H.P.; medium; yellow; May.
These useful herbaceous plants are grown in sandy loam, flower in massed florets not unlike lilac and are increased by division.

V

VACCINIUM. Flowering shrubs with edible fruit.

This family includes the bilberry, cranberry, blueberry, blackberry, whortleberry and huckleberry, all edible and all more or less palatable. For the garden, certain of them have decorative attraction in flower and also fruit and, being hardy, are easy to cultivate if grown in sandy peat and given adequate moisture. The more striking are: *corymbosum*, white blossom, blue-blackberries; *myrtillus*, rose flowering, blueberries; *vitisidaea*, pink flowers, red fruit. The foliage, taking on autumn tints, add to the picture. Increase by suckers or cuttings struck under glass in summer.

VALERIAN. *See* **CENTHRANTHUS.**

VALLOTA PURPUREA (Scarborough Lily). H.H.; bulb; 18 in.; crimson; August–September.

Plant the bulbs in 6-inch pots, double sandy loam to leaf-mould, at end of July, putting them 6 in. deep. Keep them in the greenhouse near the glass during the winter, apply liquid manure as the buds form and then till they flower use water in moderation, but more freely during summer heat. Top-dress annually rather than re-pot.

VANCOUVERIA. H.P.; 15 in.; lilac, white; May.

Grow in a moist sandy peat and give a shady place. The white variety is *sibirica*, and the lilac, *hexandra*, with graceful, fern-like foliage. Increase by division.

VEGETABLE MARROW.

Sow seeds 3 in. apart on a gentle hotbed early in May; when strong enough to handle, pot off singly, carefully harden off and finally plant out 15 in. apart in June or end of May if forward enough and the weather mild. The seed may also be sown in the "open" late in May, and protected with hand-lights (*see* CLOCHES) until frost is past. The plants succeed best in very rich, heavily-manured soil and should be plentifully supplied with water during hot weather. An occasional application of liquid manure will also be beneficial.

Allow lots of room for the long, trailing stems, see the young marrows do not rest in damp grass; a hurdle and some pea sticks for the shoots to rest upon is excellent. When marrows are a foot long, cut for use; the other fruit on the stem can then develop more freely. It results in more and finer marrows if the stems are not allowed a greater length than 6 ft.; it also results in forming fruit setting with greater certainty. The bush sorts are treated in the same way; they are not of trailing habit. It is best to pollinate each kind as the flowers are not bisexual. The male flower has a thin stem, but the female shows a swelling (the marrow-to-be) below the blossom, as illustrated under cucumber. Good sorts are *Custard, Long Green, White Green, Moore's Cream*, and in bush varieties *White Bush*.

VEGETABLES.

The wide range of edible plants, brassicas (the cabbage family), legumins (peas and beans), roots (onions, leeks, potatoes, beet, carrots and so on), creepers (marrow, cucumber), salad varieties, etc., are each treated under their respective names, and the general lines of ground preparation, soils, composts, pests, tools, fertilizing, rotation and the varied associated operations both for allotments, gardens or intensive culture also find guidance under each appropriate heading. Cropping, sowing and maturing schedules are included, such as on facing page, and everything necessary to achieve success.

VEGETABLES, EARLY. See INTENSIVE METHODS; COLD FRAME CROPS; CLOCHE CULTURE.

VEGETABLES, STORAGE OF.

Cabbages and so on are usually eaten as soon as cut, but the root crops can be stored for use during the winter in one or other of the following ways:

Onions should be lifted before the frosts begin, and *shallots* early in August. Store in an airy damp-proof building; tie the tops together and let them hang in bunches.

Carrots, Turnips and Beet should be lifted in October. The tops should be trimmed and the roots packed in boxes between layers of sand or soil. If stored out of doors stack in heaps with sand between and cover with straw or other material. When taking for use, start at one end of the pile and continue thus, not taking out haphazard.

Potatoes after digging should be left six hours in the air to dry

VEGETABLES: WHEN TO PLANT AND WHEN READY FOR USE

The following is compiled from Ministry of Agriculture advices:

Species	Quantity of Seed	When to sow	How to sow: Rows	How to sow: Plants	When available as food. Weeks from sowing in brackets
Beans (Broad)	¼ pint	Feb.–March	1 double row	6 in. by 9 in.	July (18)
Beans (Dwarf)	½ pint				
Beans (Dry Haricot)	¼ pint	Late April–early May	2½ ft.	9 in.	July–August
Beans (Runner)	¼ pint	Late April–early May	2½ ft.	9 in.	Winter
Beet	¼ oz.	Mid-May	–	9 in.	July–Oct. (16)
Broccoli (Sprouting)	1 pkt.	(1) April (2) June	15 in.	6 in. (thin)	July–April
Brussels Sprouts	1 pkt.	Mid-May Plant mid-July	2 ft.	2 ft.	April–May (26–30)
Cabbage (Spring)	1 pkt.	March Plant May-June	2½ ft.	2½ ft.	Nov.–March. (32) (34)
		July–August –early October Plant September	1½ ft.	1½ ft.	April–Jan. (20) (24)
Cabbage (Winter)	1 pkt.	Mid-May Plant mid-July	2 ft.	2 ft.	April–Jan. (20) (24)
Cabbage (Cold Districts)	1 pkt.	April	1½ ft.	1½ ft.	Autumn. (12)
Carrots (Early)	¼ oz.	April	1 ft.	6 in. (thin)	June–May (24)
Carrots (Maincrop)	1 oz.	June–early June	1 ft.	6 in. (thin)	June–May (24)
Cauliflower	1 pkt.	Feb.–March	2 ft.	1½ ft.	June–Sept. (24)
Celery	1 pkt.	May–June	18 in.	10 in.	November. (36)
Kale	1 pkt.	May Plant mid-July	2 ft.	2 ft.	January–April
Leeks	¼ oz	March Plant July	1 ft.	6 in. 9 in.	March–May (32)
Lettuce (summer)	¼ oz	March, and every 14 days	Between other crops	9 in.	May–October. (12)
Lettuce (Winter Hardy)	1 pkt.	September	1 ft.	9 in.	Spring
Marrow	1 pkt.	May	–	3–4 ft.	July–Feb. (24)
Onions	1 oz.	Mid-February	1 ft.	6 in. (thin)	July–June. (24)
Parsley	½ oz.	March–April	–	6 in.	November. (18)
Parsnips	½ oz.	Mid-February–mid-March	15 in.	6 in. (thin)	Nov.–March. (30)
Peas (Early)	½ pint	March and April	2½ ft.	3 in.	June–July (10–12)
Peas (Others)	1 pint	March and April	2½ ft.	3 in.	June–July (10–12)
Potatoes (Early)	14 lb.	March	2 ft.	1 ft.	July–March. (24)
Potatoes (Others)	14 lb.	April	2 ft.	1 ft. 3 in.	July–March. (24)
Radishes	1 oz.	March onwards	1 ft.		May–June (8)
Savoy	1 pkt.	Late May Plant July–Aug.	2 ft.	2 ft.	January–March
Shallots	1½ lb. sets	February	1 ft.	6 in.	January–December
Spinach (Summer)	½ oz.	Mid-April	1 ft.	6 in. (thin)	Summer. (9)
Spinach (Winter)	½ oz.	September	1 ft.	6 in. (thin)	Spring
Spinach Beet, or Seakale Beet	½ oz.	April	–	8 in. (groups)	January–October. (10)
Swedes	½ oz.	End June	15 in.	6 in. (thin)	December–March
Tomatoes	–	Plant end May	–	15 in.	Aug.–Oct. (22–24)
Turnips (Roots)	½ oz.	July	1 ft.	6 in. (thin)	October–March
Turnips (Tops)	½ oz.	August (end)	1 ft.	Sow thinly	April

Note that as a rule dates given for sowing, etc., are mainly for the South. In the North, or in bleak districts, sowing and transplanting should be a week to a fortnight later, and autumn work a corresponding time earlier.

and then stored immediately in boxes in a frost-proof dark shed, if a clamp is not convenient.

Marrows, for keeping, should be harvested when really ripe and dry and hung in nets.

Parsnips, Leeks and Swedes are best used from the ground as required. In early March parsnips should be lifted and stored, and leeks lifted and heeled in. This prevents spoilage.

VEGETABLES, TRANSPLANTING.

Certain vegetables when sown in open can be transplanted without undue interference to growth: others cannot.

Vegetables which can be transplanted: Broccoli, cabbage, calabresse, cauliflower, celery, cucumber, endive, kale, leek, lettuce, onion, savoy, sprouting and purple broccoli, tomato, vegetable marrow.

Vegetables which must not be transplanted: Asparagus, broad beans, beetroot, carrot, dwarf French beans, Jerusalem artichokes, parsnip, peas, potato, radish, scarlet runners, seakale, shallot, spinach, turnip.

VENIDIUM. H.H.A.; 2 ft.; white, yellows; summer.

Of South African origin, these stand out distinctively in the border by the greyish foliage and the brilliant orange blossom, purple zoned, and have the advantage of easy cultivation in average soil, even though the seed, which sow in May, germinates slowly. The variety *calendulaceum* can be sown in open in March in sunny position; *fastuosum* is half-hardy and should be started in the greenhouse. Hybrids include white and varying grades of yellow, all variegated.

VENUS' LOOKING GLASS. *See* SPECULUM.

VENUS' NAVELWORT.

Known to florists alternatively as OMPHALODES *(which see)* and CYNOGLOSSUM LINIFOLIUM.

VERATRUM. H.P.; 3 ft.; various; summer.

Can be successfully grown in any average border where loam and friable clay is present or can be worked in. The popular name is False Hellebore, and the varieties are *album* (white), *album viride* (green) and *nigrum* (dark purple). Increase by spring division.

Verbascum 265 Veronica

VERBASCUM (Mullein). H.P.; 4 ft.; pink; June–August.

The pink variety yields a plant of tall and elegant habit with a stout stem, from which spring many lateral branches covered in June with flatly-opened flowers. The colour is a delightful pink shade with maroon eye. Easily cultivated in any normal garden soil with sunny situation. Grow from seed; existing clumps can be divided in spring. The older yellow-flowered variety, *Thapsus*, is popularly known as Aaron's Rod *(which see)*.

VERBENA.

A half-hardy perennial, brilliant in colour, excellent in habit and of long continuance in bloom. It may be raised from seed sown in the open in March on a well-prepared bed, though probably the more certain method is to sow in boxes (in March) put into a frame, the seedlings potted as soon as large enough, and planted out towards the end of May. A well-manured, well-dug, sweet soil is essential for their welfare. There is no difficulty in obtaining seed which will come true to colour, such as white, purple, violet, rose, pink and scarlet. The lemon-scented variety is *Lippia (which see)*.

VERONICA (Speedwell). F.S.; 3 ft.; blue, white; spring and onwards.

The shrubby veronicas are a prolific family, easy to cultivate in sandy loam, though not particular as to soil, of hardy habit and free flowering on tall spikes above the dark foliage. *Andersoni* is popular, with purple flowers, and more so is *Traversii*, white. A lilac flower is in *augustifolia*. A shorter variety, late flowering violet, is *elliptica*, and a dwarf hardy species, 18 in., is *Haastii*, while rockery varieties are *cupressoides*, violet; *Lyallii* and *Guthriana*, deep blue. A trailing variety is *prostrata*, and one of pyramidal habit in flowering, *spicata*, 1 ft., bright blue. Take cuttings after flowering and strike in cold frame. As well as the shrubs, the genus includes annuals and vigorous perennials. Plant the shrubby variety in April or September; lift and divide every fourth year, re-planting only the younger outer crowns. Trim each year to keep in shape. Propagation is by cuttings of matured wood struck in a frame in August. The annual species should be sown in the open in September and thinned out to distances of 5 in. The perennials are propagated by division in March or October. Blues and whites are more general, but there is a yellow (*aurea*) variety.

VESICARIA (Bladder Pod). H.A.; dwarf; early autumn.

Grown for their coloured seed pods, and thrive in ordinary soil in the border. Increase by division.

VIBURNUM (Guelder Rose). F.S.; 6 ft.; white; spring.

The variety mostly known as the guelder rose is *opulus*, larger flowering varieties being *plicatum* and *macrocephalum*. One profusely flowering, 5 ft. high, branching horizontally is *tomentosum Mariesii*, not so well known but quite hardy. A scented variety is *Carlesii*, which flowers January to February. *Henryi*, growing to 10 ft., has red berries in autumn, *plicatum* is of medium height and *pyrenaica* a purple-flowering dwarf, 1 ft., which blooms in May. A scented variety, *fragrans*, flowers in December to January. Give all plenty of sun and good soils. Increase by cuttings in autumn under a cloche. *Laurustinus* (*which see*) belongs to the same family.

VIGNA. H.H.A.; climber; red, purple, yellow; July.

Easily grown if started in heat in the greenhouse and given a warm spot against wall and in light sandy soil.

VILLANOVA. H.A.; yellow; September.

An easily-grown annual which thrives in average soil.

VIMINARIA. Shrub; 2 ft.; yellow; July.

It is evergreen and a greenhouse specimen growing best in a mixture of fibrous loam and peat, with some sharp sand worked in. Increase in spring from half-ripened wood, taking heeled cuttings and starting under glass in gentle heat.

VINCA (Periwinkle). H.P.; trailer; blue; June–September.

A trailing evergreen, vigorous in growth and indifferent as to soil. As a covering for rough banks or for patches of ground made bare by the shade and drip from the trees it is very useful. The common periwinkle, *major*, 2 ft., has glossy leaves and mauve-blue flowers; while a smaller growth, *minor*, 1 ft., has as well as a blue flower a white flower and variegated foliage.

VINES.

Grapes flourish best under glass, though they will grow in a warm situation, *see* GRAPES. The grape vine belongs to the *vitis* family, a large group which includes the Virginian creeper, entered under its division *amelopsis*. Other vines for trellis or pergola are *himalaya rubrifolia*, which is highly recommended and has purple shoots; *henryana* doing well on a north wall and with red autumn tints and *coignetiae*, large leafed and of rich autumnal colouring.

VIOLA. See PANSY.

VIOLET. H.P.; 4 in.; blue; spring.

Plant in frames in soil made up of calcareous (chalky) earth, leaf-mould and loam to obtain a steady succession of crops. The plants may be increased by root-division. They do not take well to border planting.

The violet is a member of the viola family, *viola odorata*, and prefers a rich soil, in which plant in September. Keep well watered in hot weather, and give a shady situation. By propagating the root runners, planted firmly, groups or beds can be made. A single blue is *La France;* a white double, *comte de Brazza;* the fragrant double, *Parma*, is lavender hued. The Dog's Tooth violet (*which see*) is *erythronium;* the Bog violet, which is found in marshland is *pinguicula*, of which a cultivated variety, *caudata*, suited for greenhouse, bears carmine flowers in the autumn. A water-garden violet is *hottonia*. The Dame's violet is one of the Hesperis group (*which see*), and the African violet, *saintpaulia ionantha*, is only 4 in., a warm house subject grown in a mixture of loam, leaf-mould and sand, flowering a deep blue in August. It is increased by leaf cuttings after flowering. Any violets to flower in pots must have all runners removed on lifting from the bed so as to assure full development of the crowns, and the pots placed near glass till sturdy.

VIOLET GRASS. See IONOPSIDIUM ACAULE.

VIRGILIA CAPENSIS. 4 ft.; rosy purple; July.

For those with a tall greenhouse or conservatory this subject makes a striking addition, flowering richly and growing from 4 ft. upwards according to robustness and favouring circumstances. Give it a tub and set in equal parts of loam, peat and sand. It is of leguminous habit, and attention must be given to careful watering. To increase, take half-ripe shoots and strike in a propagation case.

VIRGINIAN CREEPER. See AMPELOPSIS.

VIRGINIAN STOCK. H.A.; dwarf; pink, white, mauve; June–July.

Will thrive in any soil and by its dwarf habit and free flowering is well adapted for border edgings. Although it may be sown in spring, as other annuals, it flowers more effectively when autumn sown. Pick off blossom as it fades.

VIRGIN'S BOWER. *See* CLEMATIS.

VISCARIA. H.A.; 1 ft.; various colours; summer.

Easily grown, free flowering, not particular as to soil, these make brilliant groups in the border in a range of colours in blues and reds, and some whites. They can be sown for succession from May to September in open, thinning out as needed. There is a 6-inch dwarf variety. They are popularly known as the Rock Lychnis.

VITEX. F.S.; 8 ft.; lilac; August.

Can only be grown successfully in very mild districts. Plant in spring in sandy loam and peat. It has aromatic leaves. Increase by cuttings in greenhouse, or under cloche in spring.

VITIS. Climber; has artistic autumn tints.

The family includes the grape vine and the small-leaved virginian creeper. There are varieties having coloration of leaf and fruit in autumn: *pulchra, armata, labrusea, Henryana, Himalayana, Wilsonii* and others. A hearty fibrous loam suits all, and all are increased by layers or cuttings.

W

WAHLENBERGIA. H.P.; dwarf; blues; June–July.

Growing to only 6 in. on average it suits the rockery, if its somewhat trailing habit is taken into account in spacing. Give it gritty loam and a sunny spot; its bell-like flowers will develop in beauty. The variety *serpyllifolia* yields violet-blue flowers in June; *saxixola*, half-hardy, is lilac, June flowering; *tennifolia*, flowering July, is violet and, like *kitaibelii*, hardy; this last is July flowering, blue. Increase by spring division.

WALLFLOWER. H.P.; 18 in.; Clarets, yellow, browns; spring.

The seed is often sown too late. May or even April, if the weather be favourable, is none too early, and enables the plants to attain a sturdy growth before being transplanted to their places (in limed soil) in July in readiness for blooming in the early spring. Keep the transplanted plants well watered till established. It seeds prolifically, hence select pods not only from the best bloom, but also form the plant of the best form and habit. The wallflower is not merely a border plant but flowers to perfection in the crevices of old walls— dwarfed, it may be, yet compact and full of blossom. Pinch out the centres when young, before transplanting, to make bushy plants, otherwise they get leggy and stalks break off. Extra bushy plants can be grown by putting lusty seedlings into holes made a foot apart with a dibber; put in seedling, fill with water and only then fill in earth, firming down all round as filling proceeds.

There is a dwarf strain reaching only 8 in., and also a beautiful double variety, 18 in., for growing in pots in greenhouse or conservatory. The so-called Siberian wallflower is Cheiranthus (*which see*).

WALL GARDEN.

Little satisfaction attends this if the wall is of brick, but where walls of the Cotswold type exist—flat stones built up without cementing—they can be made effective by packing earth into the intersections, taking care to fill interior cavities. The saxifrages, arabis, aubretia, wallflowers, cerastium, valerian, sedums, alyssum, dianthus, etc., are appropriate subjects.

WANDER PRIMROSES.

These may be described as bright mauve primroses. They do not rise far above the leaves and look like masses of green relieved by a profusion of blue studs. Outside the West Country they are only beginning to be appreciated as they ought, for they flower in the spring and go right on to Christmas, need no attention and thrive in any soil. For a border edging they are admirable. Take up each year, autumn or spring, and divide the many young rooted offsets.

WATER GARDEN.

The water garden can be a modest affair or an elaborate accessory to the sunk garden. Use of overflow water can obviate running a special supply by laying a pipe from collecting runways made below the gutters of house, greenhouse or garage. Concrete the pool area, and provide near the surface a drainage pipe to carry off superfluous water into a soak-away well below the ground some distance beyond, preferably where there is a slope. The edges can be laid Cotswold fashion for at least 18 in. with loose flat stones well packed with ash or earth, in which latter carpet plants can be grown. Water lilies, *nymphaea* (*which see*), including *odorata minor, marliacca, Gladstoniana*, are effective, and such acquatics as *nuphar advene* and *stratiotes aloides*, as well as *typha latifolia* (mace reed), *hottonia paulustris* and various other moisture-loving subjects. If only a shallow depth, *aponogeton distachyon* (winter hawthorn) looks well.

WATERING.

When doing so, do it thoroughly and when the sun is not strong. Little and often causes the roots to come too near the surface and get baked by the sun, or bruised: a good soaking gets right down among the roots and they remain firmly in position. Plants differ in their needs; experience will tell: as a rule, two good soakings a week will suffice in hot weather; once a week during mild spells. Always water seed beds some hours before sowing. Give plenty of water to seedlings an hour before putting in, and also when transplanting generally. One expert says he seldom loses young plants in transplanting because he uses the water boiling and plants before the soil has cooled.

Do not water direct from tap, where it can be avoided. Fill a bath or clean drum, in morning, first placing where sun can warm during day, and use the water from that. It is naturally slower than hose-work, but is more beneficial, or a stirrup-pump connected to a requisite length of hose can be operated from the bath if two persons are available.

When watering seedlings plunge pots or boxes in a little water rather than damage tender shoots by top watering. If seedlings in plot, sink an empty flower-pot in middle of bed when putting in seedlings and water through that. This is also a good plan when putting in plants which require a lot of watering (such as tomatoes). By sinking a 3-inch pot beside each, water can get direct to the roots and the wetting of tender foliage avoided. Never water in heat of day. The value of dew as an irrigant is not so fully obtained as could be, because the Dutch hoe is insufficiently at work between the rows and round about plants to keep the surface broken. The night dews can then enter the soil and keep roots moist. If hoeing is neglected, the sun simply cakes the earth and the reviving value of the dew is lost.

In the heat of summer it is a good plan in the flower garden to syringe as well as water. Signs of the need of water in the open are wilting, flower buds not opening and earth cracking. For a pot, if

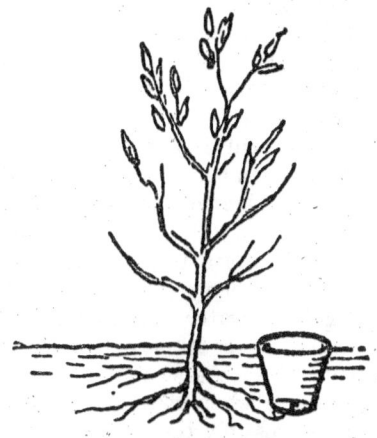

Root Watering through sunk pots.

on tapping it gives a hollow ring, then water. In copious watering, if this is done from the spout without the rose, the violence of the stream is broken by tying a bit of flannel to the spout.

The can is not done for when it leaks. Spread tar over the crack and add a layer of boiling pitch. Allow to harden and the can has a new lease of life.

WATSONIA. Bulb; 1 ft.; white; summer.

These cape bulbs have graceful spikes of white flowers, the best varieties being *ardenel* and *meriana o'Brieni*. Start in pots and either grow on—in larger size—or plant out in early summer in leaf-mould and loam, with a proportion of sand. There are red and orange varieties. Increase by offsets when plants at rest.

WEATHER. *See* BUCHAN'S COLD AND WARM SPELLS.

WEEDS.

As soon as the annual weeds appear, uproot them with the hoe, and with regard to the deep-rooted perennial weeds, such as dandelion, nettle, thistle, dock, etc., all must be dug up and burned. Pulling up and leaving part of the root is no good. Watch flowering weeds and make sure to destroy before the blossom opens, else their prolific seeding will make endless future trouble. Weed-killing mixtures can be purchased: they are used during a fine spell in spring. Lawn weeds are best dug out with a stumpy knife. Rank weeds, such as nettles and bindweed, can be destroyed in a single season by first cutting down to ground and then covering the area with lawn mowings and keeping it so covered till they have gone. Another less used but effective plan, where ground not in cultivation, is to water with a weak solution, enough to give pink colour to the liquid, of permanganate of potash.

To get rid of weeds on gravel paths sprinkle the weeds or moss with salt during damp or dewy (but not rainy) weather. Alternatively, mix into 2 gals. of water 1 lb. each of lime and sulphur, and pour over the infested area. Another trusted procedure is to treat paths with a mixture of creosote (1 pint) to each gallon of hot water; keep the rose on the can when watering and do not forget that the hoe in constant use is possibly the best insurance policy of all.

WEIGELA. F.S.; 6 ft.; rose-purple; June.

It is classified as Diervilla, but earlier was put in the wide and varied family of the honeysuckle, *caprifoliacae*. The attractive foliage unfolds from the brown bud-casing in April, a light, fresh green, and in about four weeks the bell-like flowers follow in full clusters, which deepen in colour. Of the differences in tints, *floribunda* is purple; *grandiflora*, pink; *japonica*, red; *candida* and *Hortensis nivea*, white; *Eva Rathke*, deep crimson. The shrub is free growing and profuse in flowering on long gracefully curving shoots, which prune after flowering. Put in open position in spring or autumn; let it be warm but not dry, in any ordinary soil. Take cuttings end of May and strike under glass.

WHITLAVIA. H.A.; 1 ft.; blue and white; summer.

The variety *gloxinioides* is charming in the border, and the name indicates its character, like a miniature gloxinia with blue lips and white throat. The variety *grandiflora* is purple. Sow outside in spring in a light, rich soil.

WHORTLEBERRY. *See* VACCINIUM.

WIGANDIA. H.H.; 6 ft.; lilac; summer.

Its attractive foliage makes it desirable as much as the blossom, but they are better cultivated in warm Southern gardens, being of sub-tropical habit, and in a richly-manured sandy loam. Seed is sown in heat in March. Two good varieties are *vigieri* and *caracasana*, the latter for preference.

WILD OLIVE (Elaeagnus). F.S.; yellow; May.

The variety gives no difficulty on sandy soil or a percentage mixed into average border. An added attraction is its silvery berries in autumn. An autumn-flowering variety is *macrophylla*, also yellow; *glaba* flowers white in autumn. Increase by cuttings in autumn.

WINDFLOWER. *See* ANEMONE.

WINDOW BOXES.

Less seen in urban districts since the vogue of great blocks of flats in closely-populated districts. The chief points to remember are: have drainage holes; drainage crocks at bottom; a friable soil on the rich side; attention to watering without overdoing it; selecting plants which are not gross growers; and a fresh supply of soil every season. It is not much trouble to sterilize the soil and the benefit is great: how to do so is given under SEED. Remember that it is poor work to block ventilation to any room by overcrowding the window-box with tall specimens.

WINTER ACONITE. *See* ACONITE.

WINTER CHERRY. *See* PHYSALIS.

WINTER JASMINE. *See* JASMINE.

WIREWORM.

Dig in a thick sowing of quicklime (hydrated lime) and allow the ground to remain fallow for a winter. Traps may also be used in the shape of slices of potato, carrot or turnip buried about 1 in. in the earth. Stick a skewer with each piece to show its position and destroy the catch every morning. If it is virgin ground a first crop of potato clears much of the trouble.

WISTARIA. F.S.; 15–20 ft.; celestial blue; June.

Grows to greatest luxuriance against a wall or house, or can be trained as a standard. There are many varieties, the best being *floribunda multijuga*, a decided blue, or *chinensis sinensis*, mauve, and the best climber. There is a white variety, *chinensis alba*, and *flore pleno* is a double. A fine variety is *multijuga*. They must have a sunny position, in well-drained loam, with a sandy texture, and plenty of manure, and should have the side-shoots cut back somewhat in summer, followed by a winter pruning. To increase, layer young shoots, but do not detach for at least a year.

WITCH HAZEL (Hamamelis). F.S.; 6–9 ft.; yellow; winter.

Of these feathery blooming shrubs the most striking is *Mollis*, quite hardy, as also is the less tall *japonica*, with crimson shades on the golden flowers, while *Zuccariniana* flowers a pale yellow, and *vernalis* is red and yellow. All are hardy and will grow sturdily in light, loamy soil. Cut out dead wood after flowering. Propagate by seed or layers.

WOOD FERN.

This will thrive under trees or in shady parts of the garden (even in a town garden) if given plenty of water. The more delicate sort should be grown in well-drained leafy loam.

WOOD LICE.

This garden pest is very destructive where young and tender seedlings are concerned—especially in a frame. In cases where they have infested a frame, they can generally be destroyed by pouring boiling water along the sides of the frame. If this is not effective in ridding the frame of the pest, a sure way of getting rid of them is as follows: In common with earwigs, they love darkness and a dry, snug retreat, so a small-sized flower-pot, with a slice of fresh potato or apple as a bait and filled up with dry moss, will prove an alluring trap. Two or three of these pots should be placed in the frame or bed, and the next morning they will probably each contain a large number of the insects, which can then be destroyed by knocking the whole contents of the pot into a pail of hot water. The earlier in the morning the traps are cleared the better will be the catch and, of course, the traps must be relaid from day to day until the pest has been completely removed.

WOODRUFF. See ASPERULA.

WOOD SORREL. See OXALIS.

WOODWARDIA.

A class of handsome, lusty-growing ferns mostly for greenhouse but in warm sheltered positions do well in the South, the mixture being a mixture of peat, double that of loam and a little sand. The crested variety is *brownii; japonica* has broad fronds, and *radicans* is most useful inside, in large baskets, the arching fronds being very graceful.

WOOLLY APHIS. See AMERICAN BLIGHT.

X

XANTHOCEPHALUM. H.P.; yellow; summer.

Of a shrubby character with varying grades of yellow blossom and doing well in sunny position, grown in a light, sandy loam. It is sometimes treated as an annual and kept in the greenhouse. Increase by cuttings started under glass in sand.

XANTHORHIZA. F.S.; 30 in.; purple; spring.

A welcome denizen of the garden, because the blossom comes before the leaves, which are toothed. Give it a moist place in loam and peat, and plant in autumn. The variety grown is *apifolia*. Increase by layering in autumn, only severing when growth shows a good rooting.

XERANTHEMUM. H.A.; 2 ft.; purple; summer.

This is an everlasting when dried, the chief colour being purple (*annum*) though there are kinds in mixed colours. Sow in average soil in spring. For drying, gather the blossom before fully mature and dry in a cool place where air circulates.

XEROPHYLLUM. H.P.; white; May.

The small flowers cluster as does the lilac. Plant in moist situation in a mixture of peat and loam. Increase by division.

XIPHIOIDES. *See* IRIS (ENGLISH).

XIPHIUM. *See* IRIS (SPANISH).

Y

YARROW. *See* ACHILLEA.

YEAR'S WORK IN GARDEN AND ALLOTMENT. *See* MONTH BY MONTH IN GARDEN AND ALLOTMENT.

YUCCA.

More a curiosity than anything else, because it takes a number of years before it blooms and afterwards does not come yearly into flower. The usual variety is *gloriosa*, white, July, and others are *augustifolia* and *filamentosa*. They attain a height of 8 ft. and the foliage is evergreen, like stiff, thick leek-leaves branching out to considerable length. Grow in friable, rich soil; avoid clay and damp position.

YULAN. *See* MAGNOLIA.

Z

ZACINTHA. H.A.; yellow; summer.

The variety to grow is *Verrucosa*, which will flourish in a light soil of average fertility.

ZAUSCHNERIA. H.H.; shrub; 1 ft.; scarlet; summer.

The flowers being a very bright scarlet makes the plant distinctive in the rockery, or as a wall plant. It needs plenty of sun and well-drained light loam. Increase by cuttings or division.

ZEA. H.H.A.; 3 ft.; grass.

A useful variation for the border by reason of its gracefulness, particularly *gracillima variegata* which has handsome leaves. It thrives in average soil.

ZENOBIA. H.P.; shrub; 4 ft.; white; summer.

The graceful drooping blossom is very attractive, that of *speciosa* particularly so. The variety belongs to the *andromeda* family. It requires a moist situation, preferably on a slope, and regular watering must be given. Grow in sandy peat and increase by layering.

ZEPHYR FLOWER. *See* ZEPHYRANTHES.

ZEPHYRANTHES. Bulb; various; August.

A pretty 6-in. crocus-like specimen, flowering yellow, white, pink and rose, mainly suitable for greenhouse, but in very mild districts the variety *candida* can be grown in dry, sunny border. Plant bulbs 4 in. deep in light, rich well-drained soil in mid-May or June. Increase by offsets. It is known as the Zephyr flower.

ZINNIA. H.H.A.; 18 in.; various; July–September.

A half-hardy annual which has been so improved that it ranks as one of the most effective of our bedding plants, especially the double varieties, which are shorter and more compact than the single. The plant is delicate and needs a sheltered, sunny situation. The seeds should be sown before the first week in April in heat, and hardened before bedding out. Transplant before seedlings have made much growth, somewhere in early June. Transplanting should always be done in showery weather, and if dry days follow, each plant should be covered with a flower-pot till sunset. Transplanting, indeed, involves so much labour that in many parts of the South it is now the practice to sow the seeds in the open in May. Except in cold places this is successful. Among the colours are white, orange, reds, apricot, salmon, mauve, ranging among doubles, singles; cactus dahlia flowered; talls, 2 ft.; dwarfs, 15 and 19 in.

ZIZIPHORA. H.P.; shrub; blue, red; summer.

It grows in average soil, requires no special treatment and can be increased from cuttings. Some amateurs grow the shrub as an annual.

ZONAL GERANIUM. *See* PELARGONIUM.

ZYGADENUS. H.P.; bulb; white, green; summer.

Is best grown in peat and in a moist situation, and when raised in pots must not be allowed to get dry. Increase by division.

ZYGOPETALUM.

One of the strong-rooted orchids, *mackayi* being suitable for the cool house, with increased heat during the colder months. Pot in a mixture of fibrous loam, peat and sphagnum moss. They prefer shade and dislike root disturbance, though on signs of sourness the soil must be renewed. The flowers are in various colours. Increase by division.

www.ingramcontent.com/pod-product-compliance
Lightning Source LLC
Chambersburg PA
CBHW021138230426
43667CB00005B/166